The Yoga of Tibet

THE WISDOM OF TIBET SERIES

The Buddhism of Tibet and The Key to the Middle Way
by Tenzin Gyatso, The Fourteenth Dalai Lama
and The Precious Garland and The Song of the Four Mindfulnesses
by Nāgārjuna and the Seventh Dalai Lama

Tantra in Tibet: The Great Exposition of Secret Mantra 1
by Tsong-ka-pa

The Yoga of Tibet: The Great Exposition of Secret Mantra 2 and 3
by Tsong-ka-pa

A Lamp for the Path and Commentary
by Atīśa. Translated and Annotated by Richard Sherburne, S.J.

THE WISDOM OF TIBET SERIES

THE YOGA OF TIBET

The Great Exposition of Secret Mantra: 2 and 3

TSONG-KA-PA

Introduced by His Holiness Tenzin Gyatso,
the Fourteenth Dalai Lama

Translated and Edited by Jeffrey Hopkins

Associate editors for Tsong-ka-pa's text:
Lati Rimpoche and Denma Lochö Rinbochay

Assistant editor: Elizabeth Napper

UNWIN HYMAN
London Sydney

First published in Great Britain by George Allen & Unwin 1981
Second impression 1987

UNWIN HYMAN LIMITED
Denmark House, 37-39 Queen Elizabeth Street, London SE1 2QB
and
40 Museum Street, London WC1A 1LU

Allen & Unwin Australia Pty Ltd
8 Napier Street, North Sydney, NSW 2060, Australia

Allen & Unwin New Zealand Ltd with the Port Nicholson Press
60 Cambridge Terrace, Wellington, New Zealand

British Library Cataloguing in Publication Data

Tsong-ka-pa
The yoga of Tibet.
1. Yoga (Tantric Buddhism)
I. Title
294.3′4′43 BQ8918.6

ISBN 0–04–294119–9 Pbk

Set in 11 on 13 point Times by Alan Sutton Ltd, Gloucester, England
Printed in the USA

*Published under the aegis of
the Library of Tibetan Works and Archives
with the authority of
His Holiness the Dalai Lama
as revealing oral tradition*

May whatever merit there is in presenting this book on Action and Performance Tantra serve to benefit each and every sentient being throughout space.

Translator's Note

Homage to Vajradhara

This book is a continuation of *Tantra in Tibet*. Centred on the second and third parts of Tsong-ka-pa's *Great Exposition of Secret Mantra,* it presents the profound process of meditation in Action and Performance Tantra. This explanation of the main features of the Action and Performance systems should clear away misconceptions about the tantric path and lay the groundwork for those who wish to cultivate these tantras upon receiving initiation from a qualified lama.

Part I is an introduction by His Holiness the Dalai Lama, whose commentary on Tsong-ka-pa's text was received in 1974 and subsequently translated and edited. His lucid exposition of the meditative rites of deity yoga — the distinctly tantric process in which a yogi cultivates appearance in a Buddha's divine body — affords an accessibility to Part II, Tsong-ka-pa's text itself. Part III is a short supplement primarily on the structure of the path in Action Tantra. It is drawn from Na-wang-bel-den's *Presentation of the Grounds and Paths of Mantra* as well as the oral teachings of Lati Rinbochay and Denma Lochö Rinbochay, both philosophy masters and tantric lamas, the former being abbot of the Shar-dzay College of Gan-den and the latter, abbot of the Tibetan Monastery at Kulu.

Part II was orally retranslated into Tibetan for Lati Rinbochay for the sake of correction and verification, and a complete commentary on the same was received from Denma Lochö Rinbochay. Elizabeth Napper, a doctoral candidate in Buddhist Studies at the University of Virginia, provided crucial help in editing the entire manuscript.

A guide to Tsong-ka-pa's text, following his own mode of division of the contents, is given in tabular form in an appendix. The chapter divisions and their titles in the Dalai Lama's commentary and in Tsong-ka-pa's text were added to facilitate understanding. The transliteration scheme for Sanskrit names and titles is aimed at easy pronunciation, using *sh, sḥ,* and *ch* rather than *ś, ṣ,* and *c.* With the first occurrence of each Indian title, the Sanskrit is given, if available. Often Tsong-ka-pa refers only to the title or the author of a work, whereas both are given in translation to obviate the need for checking back and forth. The full Sanskrit and Tibetan titles are to be found in the bibliography, which is arranged alphabetically according to the English titles of sutras and tantras and according to the authors of other works. The Tibetan originals of key terms have been given in a glossary at the end. Photographs of the thirty-eight seals or hand signs (*mudrā*) are given in the middle of the text; the formation of several of these is speculative since a full-fledged transmission of their practice has not been found among the refugee lamas in India.

JEFFREY HOPKINS
University of Virginia

Contents

Seals or Hand-Signs (*Mudrā*)

The names of the seals are taken either from Tsong-ka-pa's text or from Varabodhi's *Clear Realisation of Susiddhi,* except for those which are bracketed, these being inferred from the context. All but numbers 29 and 37 appear in Varabodhi's text, Tsong-ka-pa's source. Several are similar to those given for the *Susiddhi Tantra* in the Chinese canon (*Taishō daizōkyō, Zuzō* 8, [3164, 3165]: 1 – 58). The photographs are by Mr John Buescher and Professor Harvey Aronson.

I
Heart of Mantra

by

His Holiness

TENZIN GYATSO

The Fourteenth Dalai Lama

Translated and edited by Jeffrey Hopkins

Techniques for Improvement

All of us have attained a human life; we are, in a sense, incomparable among the various types of sentient beings as we are able to think about many topics with a subtler mind and are endowed with vaster capabilities. Dogs, birds, and so forth do communicate, but only humans can settle and ascertain deep topics on the basis of words; it is obvious that there are no other sentient beings capable of as many thoughts and techniques. Nowadays, humans are engaging in many activities that were not even objects of thought a century or two ago. The metaphors of the poets of the past, such as 'the wonderful house of the moon', are becoming actualities.

Still, it is definite that we must die and prior to death must all suffer inadequacies, whether in terms of resources or our own bodies. Our sources of happiness and welfare are essentially our body, companions, and the use of resources — gaining happiness in dependence on good food, clothing, companions, and conversation. These are said to be sources of happiness and comfort, but are in fact sources of suffering.

After our conception a body which is a basis of suffering is formed. When we gather relatives, friends, and companions, we form the basis for the suffering of losing them. We make effort over our whole lifetime, thinking 'May I be happy and comfortable', hoping for the arising of happiness and comfort, and temporarily we achieve a little superficial pleasure. However, in terms of their own inner nature all these means serve as bases of suffering. In essence, we must all spend our lives suffering either physically or mentally. The mass of people suffer in terms of food, shelter, and clothing and even those who have these suffer mentally.

In general, the countries of the East have had less material progress and thus have great suffering from poverty. In the West, though poverty is not severe, there is the suffering of worry and not knowing satisfaction. In both East and West, many persons spend their lives in jealousy and competition; some think only of money, and when they meet with conditions unfavourable to their wish develop a dislike or enmity for these unfavourable circumstances from the very orb of their heart. Within and between countries people are disturbed, not trusting and believing each other, having to spend their lives in continual lies and deceit. Since the most we can live is a hundred years, what point is there in spending our lives in jealousy, deceit, and competition?

People have made great effort right up to this century, thinking to become free from suffering, but we cannot point to even one person in the world, no matter how rich he or she is, who has no worry — except for those who have the inner happiness of renouncing the material way of life. Without internal renunciation it is difficult to achieve happiness and comfort.

Seeing that the people of the world could not achieve happiness solely in terms of food and clothing, many teachers including Buddha — whether they were capable or not of presenting the final mode of existence of phenomena — set forth teachings for the achievement of happiness and comfort in terms of the mind — inner happiness. Among these the best is the doctrine of dependent-arising of Buddha, the King of Subduers, who taught it to others exactly as he knew it, in accordance with their dispositions, interests, and beliefs. Born in the Shakya clan over 2,500 years ago in India, the country of Superiors, he established limitless sentient beings in the path of liberation through the sport of his speech. Among the many religious systems of the world the doctrine that he taught is without parallel.

Although it may seem, when we superficially look at it, that happiness and comfort can be achieved in dependence on external factors, in fact, if one's mind is tamed, there is happiness and comfort even as a householder. If one's mind is not tamed, there is no happiness and comfort even as a monk or a scholar learned in doctrine.

The essence of the 84,000 bundles of doctrine is just to tame this wild mind, not letting it go under the influence of the afflictions — desire, hatred, and ignorance. When the mind is no longer polluted by afflictions or their latent predispositions, then its taming is complete. The aged should engage in a method suited for old age; the young, in one suited for youth; the learned, in a method suited for the learned, and those not so learned, in one suited to their abilities.

Religion does not mean just precepts, a temple, monastery, or other external signs, for these as well as hearing and thinking are subsidiary factors in taming the mind. When the mind becomes the practices, one is a practitioner of religion, and when the mind does not become the practices one is not.

Do we not see among our acquaintances that their happiness is proportionate to the extent to which they have tamed their minds? Also, considering ourselves, is it not the case that as much as we tame our minds, so much do we have happiness and comfort? We have happiness of mind and freedom from anxiety to just the degree that our minds are tamed. To that same degree are unsalutary deeds of body and speech lessened; as much as they are lessened, so much is lessened the accumulation of bad karma. As much as that diminishes, so much does hope of ending cyclic existence arise.

At this time, when we have a physical life-support of a human such that we are capable of many techniques and thoughts, it is very important to engage in religious practice. It is our own choice to have no belief, faith, interest, or wish to practise. Buddha did not forcibly say, 'You must practise'. The great commentators will not bring guns and swords. We must ascertain the need for religion with reasoning. Once we want happiness and do not want suffering, we should engage in the means to achieve happiness and eliminate suffering. Practice is based on reasoning, not force; it is up to oneself.

Indeed, if we think about it, happiness of mind comes with religious practice. No matter how much goes wrong, one reflects that this is the nature of cyclic existence, that these are irreversible effects of actions accumulated in the past, that, even if the Blessed Buddha were here himself, he could not stop the unfolding of these effects. One reflects on the cause and effect of actions and the nature of cyclic existence, and, if capable of more thought, one engages in meditation, giving away whatever happiness one has and assuming the sufferings of other sentient beings, having tnought about the faults of cherishing oneself and the advantages of cherishing others. It is confirmed by our own experience that as much as one can engage in such thoughts, so much is there peace of mind; therefore, methods for taming the mind are extremely valuable.

The time for engaging in these techniques is now. Some feel, 'I did not succeed in this lifetime; I will ask a lama for help in my future life.' To think that we will practise in the future is only a hope. It is foolish to feel that the next life will be as suitable as this. No matter how bad our condition is now, since we have a human brain, we can think; since we have a mouth, we can recite mantra. No matter how old one may be, there is time for practice. However, when we die and are reborn, we are unable even to recite *'oṃ maṇi padme hūṃ.'* Thus, it is important to make all effort possible at this time when we have obtained the precious physical life-support of a human.

Religious activities involve mixing the mind with the practices — causing the mind to become the practices. Among these the lowest is to turn away from the marvels of this lifetime and seek to provide for the next lifetime. One should also turn away from the marvels of future lifetimes and seek to become liberated from cyclic existence entirely, thinking from the depths of the heart, 'How nice it would be if I did not have to take rebirth by the power of contaminated actions and afflictions!' Then one identifies ignorance as the root of cyclic existence and seeks by overcoming ignorance to attain a state of liberation. This is a middling mode of the mind's becoming religious practice; it is very good — the internal motivation is steady and decided.

Then, not just thinking of oneself, one realises that all sentient beings, self and others, equally want happiness and do not want suffering. Oneself is just one; others are as vast as space and, therefore, should be cherished more than oneself. Based on this, one generates a mind wishing to free all sentient beings from suffering and the causes of suffering and, motivated by that aspiration, seeks from the depths of the heart to attain Buddhahood for the sake of all sentient beings. This is the highest mode of the mind's becoming religious practice.

At the least, one must have turned away from this lifetime; there is no way without reversing attachment to this life. Death is definite, but the time of death indefinite. We make many plans for the future, but there is no certainty that we can carry them out. Even monks and nuns plan this and that, to go here or there, to meet acquaintances, and so forth; yet there is no certainty that before carrying out these plans we will not see the time of death.

Since the choice is in our own hands, we should make sure, using our past experience as an example, that the months ahead are not wasted. There is no way to return the years that have already passed. We cannot say, 'I have erred', and exchange those years. Wasted time is gone. If we ourselves do not take care, then, even if someone at our side attempts to force us, he cannot help at all.

We may not wish to engage in religious practice or we may wish to but because of our own fault postpone it, but we are not bereft of a religion to practise. Within Buddhism, the most profound is Mahayana; within Mahayana the most profound is Secret Mantra; and common to all four tantras is deity yoga, which contains within it the important essentials of the entire path. Transmitted from Vajradhara, deity yoga was formulated in India on the basis of much profound thought. Being the simultaneous unification of method and wisdom in one consciousness — the appearance of oneself as a deity, such as Vairochana, coupled with realisation of emptiness — it is the essence of tantra. Merely ascertaining the significance of deity yoga aids the mental continuum, not to speak of the immeasurable improvement that occurs through incorporating it into daily practice.

Purpose of Deity Yoga

In all four tantras — Action, Performance, Yoga, and Highest Yoga — it is established that a practitioner must view his or her body as a divine one. However, some persons are frightened by viewing their body this way. Discriminating their own body as unclean — composed of lumps of flesh, blood, and bone — and themselves as possessing all types of fetters, they feel that it would not be suitable to meditate on themselves as deities. For the same reason they also consider that it would not be right for an actual deity — meditated in front of them — to dissolve into and become undifferentiable in entity from themselves. Unable to fit the higher paths into their minds, they are outside the sphere of such practice.

The Wisdom Vajra Compendium (Jñānavajrasamuchchaya), a Highest Yoga Tantra, says that such trainees abide in Action Tantra. Taken literally, it would seem to be saying that such persons — given that they have the other qualifications of a tantrist — would practise Action Tantra. Thus it seems that according to this text, in Action Tantra there would be no generation of oneself as a deity or consideration of the pledge-being [oneself imagined as a deity] and the wisdom-being [the actual deity] as one undifferentiable entity.

Indeed, many texts of the Action class do not clearly explain meditation on oneself as a deity; rather, they describe a process of imagining a deity in front of oneself and receiving a feat, or capacity for a special activity, from that deity. However, Buddhaguhya and Varabodhi, both great scholars of Action Tantra, point out that it is not that self-generation is not taught in Action Tantra.

For example, the *Concentration Continuation (Dhyān-ottara)* and other Action Tantras describe repetition of mantra after (1) generating oneself as a deity, (2) generating a deity in front of oneself, (3) imagining a moon at the heart of the deity in front, and (4) imagining the letters of the mantra to be repeated around the edge of that moon. These are the four branches — self-base, other-base, mind (the wisdom consciousness realising emptiness appearing as a moon), and sounds, specifically the letters of the mantra. Thus, it is clear that this Action Tantra explicitly teaches self-generation.

When through the force of continued practice a mantrika [tantric practitioner] has naturally the pride of being a deity, he comes to possess the capacity to achieve quickly feats of secret mantra. He meditates until his own body appears as a divine one as if in direct perception, with adornments and so forth swaying. He clearly sees the deity and hears its exalted speech, whereby he is blessed, resulting in a longer lifespan, unusual increase in wisdom, and so forth, all of which promote progress in the path.

Since Action Tantras prescribe such meditation necessarily involving self-generation, it is clear that there is deity meditation in Action Tantra. Thus, the *Wisdom Vajra Compendium* is referring not to all Action Tantra trainees but to those unable to do deity yoga.

The word 'yoga' means in general to join one's mind to an actual fact but here it can also refer to a joining or non-duality of the profound — realisation of emptiness — and the manifest — appearance as a deity. In order to achieve the feats of pacification, increase, and so forth, it is absolutely necessary to have emptiness yoga and deity yoga. Hence it is clear that there is deity meditation in Action Tantra.

There is no doubt about deity yoga in Performance Tantra since the *Vairochanabhisambodhi (Vairochan-*

ābhisaṃbodhi) and *Vajrapani Initiation (Vajrapāṇy-abhiṣheka)* clearly describe it. Moreover, that both Action and Performance have such is confirmed by statements in Highest Yoga Tantra explaining that in Action and Performance Tantra the desires involved in the god's and goddess's respectively looking and smiling at each other are used in the path. Since these refer to meditated deities, there is no way for these tantras not to have deity yoga. Within clarification of oneself as a deity, the attributes of the desire realm are used in the path; there is no way to perform this practice within conceiving oneself to be ordinary.

However, this is not merely a case of taking the thought of Highest Yoga Tantra and superimposing it on the lower tantras. For the *Vajroshnisha (Vajroṣhṇīṣha),* an Action Tantra, clearly describes deity yoga; its continuation or supplement, called the *Concentration Continuation,* refers to that description when it says, 'Flow to the bases, mind, and sound', alluding to the four branches mentioned above. A similar description is also found in the *Vairochanabhisambodhi,* a Performance Tantra, where the term 'bases' is clearly explained as the bases for the placement of the mantra letters — the deity whom oneself is imagined to be and the deity generated in front.

Another source is the *Extensive Tantra of Vajravidarana (Vajravidāraṇāvaipulya* [?]), where meditation on the six deities involved in self-generation is explained. These show that Action Tantra in its own right has meditation on oneself as a deity — that it is not just brought over from descriptions in Highest Yoga Tantra. Thus, the *main* trainees of Action Tantra must cultivate self-generation; however, because those who cannot do so but are nevertheless trainees of Action Tantra outnumber them, most Action Tantras do not clearly present deity yoga.

The most important and difficult of the Mantra disciplines is to meditate at all times on one's body as a divine body and to view whatever appears as a deity's sport. Whether one is going about, lying down, or sitting, one must be able to maintain the continuous pride of being a deity. Similarly, whatever forms are seen, sounds heard, odours smelled, tastes tasted, or tangible objects touched must be viewed as manifestations of the wisdom consciousness realising emptiness. When this occurs in a non-artificial way, one possesses the ethics of a Mantra Bodhisattva. One must remain free from conceptions of ordinariness and of inherent existence.

The clear appearance of the divine body is a subsidiary branch of a process whose main factor is the pride of being the deity. However, in order for divine pride to become firm there must be clear appearance as that deity, whereupon the pride of being that deity is naturally generated. For one's mind ordinary appearances must be stopped. With the disappearance of the ordinary body and mind there is no longer a sense of I, but in place of that impure body and mind the mind which earlier realised emptiness is used as the basis of emanation and itself manifests as a divine form with a face, arms, and so forth. When the pure mental and physical aggregates of a deity appear clearly to the mind, the place of the designation I has become these pure appearances of mind and body. At that point one develops divine pride, a sense of an I that is designated in dependence upon the divine body and mind that are appearing to one's mind. Since this pride is merely a sense of an imputedly existent I, it is capable of acting as an antidote to the conception of self — the conception of the inherent existence of persons and other phenomena.

Once the main practitioners of Action Tantra must have this type of self-generation, there is no reason why they could not engage in the practice of causing an actual deity meditated in front of them to dissolve into themselves. Thus, Action Tantra has both self-generation and entry of a wisdom-being.

With respect to deity yoga the *Vajrapani Initiation* [a Performance Tantra] says (see p. 61) 'Mind itself is speech; speech itself is mind; divine form itself is also mind, and speech itself is also divine form'. This is like the teaching of the union of illusory body and clear light in the *Guhyasamaja (Guhyasamāja)* [a Highest Yoga Tantra] which says, 'View body as mind; view mind as body; view speech as mind; view mind as speech'. Though the *Vajrapani Initiation,* being a Performance Tantra, cannot explicitly set forth such a union, which is found only in Highest Yoga Tantra, it can be said that what it is getting at is the union of illusory body and clear light.

For instance, Chandrakirti in his *Brilliant Lamp (Pradīpoddyotana)* quotes the *Vairochanabhisambodhi,* a Performance Tantra (see p. 186), within the context of presenting the divine bodies of the stages of generation and completion. Since in the Yoga Tantras and below the topics of the stage of completion in Highest Yoga Tantra are not explained, there is no way that the *Vairochanabhisambodhi* can explicitly indicate such. However, it can be said that the doctrine of the bodies of the two stages is hidden in the *Vairochanabhisambodhi,* not in the sense of being taught non-manifestly but in the sense of being hidden without in the least being taught. Since from among the two types of hidden meanings it is this latter, the words of the *Vairochanabhisambodhi* do not either explicitly or implicitly indicate these topics, but it still can be said that they are getting at the bodies of the two stages.

In the same way, here it is not suitable to say that the *Vajrapani Initiation* indicates, either explicitly or implicitly, the union of illusory body and clear light, but it can be said that what it is getting at is such a union. In their coarse form the body, speech, and mind that we have had since beginningless cyclic existence are different entities, but in terms of the very subtle clear light and the very subtle wind that is its mount these are not different entities. Since such subtle minds and winds are topics of Highest Yoga Tantra, here in Performance Tantra this passage is teaching on the literal level that if one considers one's own body, speech, and mind to be a deity's, they will be the undifferentiable three vajras of a deity's exalted body, speech, and mind — 'undifferentiable' in the sense of having the same taste of the emptiness of inherent existence.

In essence, when a yogi views all physical movement, all verbal expression, and all thoughts and realisations as the seals, mantras, and wisdom of a deity, then he accumulates vast merit, establishing the capacity to manifest at Buddhahood in numerous Form Bodies in order to help sentient beings.

Initiations and Vows

For the achievement of Mantra it is appropriate to use the systems of Action and Performance Tantra, and not pretend that one can achieve something one cannot. For most people the attempt to practise Highest Yoga Tantra is a case of pretending such. Action and Performance Tantra, on the other hand, are very practical for many people.

In these tantras the body of the path for achieving the supreme feat of Buddhahood and the common feats of activities of pacification, increase, and ferocity is included within ten causal branches (see pp. 63–4). Of these the four-branched repetition and the concentrations of abiding in fire and in sound are called yoga with signs. This is because, although they involve meditation on emptiness and on a deity, they are yogas in which the mind realising emptiness itself does not manifest as a deity. The meditator is mainly concerned here with achieving clarity of appearance of a divine body, mantra letters, and so forth, and thus cannot *mainly* meditate on emptiness. In contradistinction to this, the concentration bestowing liberation at the end of sound is called yoga without signs because in it deity yoga is actually conjoined with meditation on emptiness. In Action and Performance as well as in Yoga Tantra, the body of the path is divided into these two yogas, with and without signs, whereas in Highest Yoga the path is divided into the stages of generation and completion.

In order to make trainees suitable vessels for cultivating these paths initiation is conferred. In Action Tantra it is permissible to confer the five knowledge initiations —

water, crown, vajra, bell, and name. However, in general it is said that Action Tantra has the water and crown initiations as well as subsequent rites granting permission to meditate on a specific deity whereas Performance Tantra has all five initiations. The tantric vows are taken only in Yoga and Highest Yoga Tantra as the vajra master initiation occurs only in them.

The initiation of a particular deity is granted in accordance with one's lineage. In Action and Performance there are two basic lineages, mundane and supramundane. Within the latter there are three — Tathagata, lotus, and vajra in order of superiority. When initiation is attained in a higher lineage, one is allowed to listen to and explain to others teachings of the other lineages as well as to engage in their meditations and approximations, but to confer initiation it is necessary to receive the initiation of that particular deity and do the necessary preliminary rites. Although the *Kalachakra Tantra (Kālachakra)* [a Highest Yoga text] says that if the Kalachakra initiation is attained one can act as a vajra master for all tantras, according to the interpretation of Gel-sang-gya-tso (bsKal-bzang-rgya-mtsho, the Seventh Dalai Lama) this is an expression of the greatness of the *Kalachakra Tantra* and is not to be taken literally. The specific initiations of the other deities are needed in order for one, as a vajra master, to grant initiation to others.

Since Action and Performance Tantra do not have the vajra master initiation, the vows to be maintained more dearly than one's own life are the Bodhisattva ones, not the tantric. These are the eighteen root vows as well as the maintenance of the aspirational mind of enlightenment. In addition, there are many tantric pledges to be kept.

Though many of these pledges are concerned with maintaining cleanliness, there are teachings in Action Tantra not to conceive of dirtiness and cleanliness; hence, Ratnakarashanti (see p. 75) says that it is suitable for practitioners even of Highest Yoga to observe the pledges of the lower tantras. Nevertheless, external activities of cleanliness are stressed in Action Tantras, which is why they are called by that name. There is a story of a yogi trying to achieve an Action Tantra deity who, though he practised a long time, could not generate even an auspicious dream. He went to see his lama, who inquired how he was doing. Upon investigation the lama found that there was nothing wrong with the way the yogi was performing the rite except that he had not bathed. The lama advised him to do so, and thereafter signs of success emerged.

Although bathing or not makes no difference to the deity, there is a difference in how the deity appears to trainees. For instance, although Manjushri is one, for those who are practising in accordance with the procedure of Action Tantra there comes to be a Manjushri associated with that tantra set, whereas for someone who is practising in the manner of Highest Yoga Tantra there is another one associated with Highest Yoga. A person whose meditative stabilisation and so forth are improved through maintaining cleanliness and so forth should use an Action Tantra rite whereas someone of very sharp faculties can achieve a deity faster with a Highest Yoga rite. The difference in deities is established in relation to the individual trainees.

With respect to the bathing rite, since the general dictum is to bathe until one becomes free of grime, our usual mode of bathing with soap and water and the wearing of clean clothes — not necessarily new — are sufficient. Beyond that, one's food must be clean; meat cannot be eaten, and smelly foods such as garlic and onion are not allowed.

Those who are seriously engaged in meditation also sometimes have to take precautions against contamination that can occur when they eat food given by another.

Some meditators here and in Tibet have said that ill effects can be immediate and that the mind is much clearer when living from what one oneself can acquire, even if it is not of good quality, without using any offerings from others. It has been said that even eating a bowl of yogurt given by another can adversely affect the mind.

Divine Approximation

Through the practice of tantra one is seeking to achieve the supreme feat of Buddhahood in order to become a source of help and happiness for all beings. Along the way common feats are also sought for the sake of enhancing the accumulation of merit necessary for attaining Buddhahood.For both supreme and common feats deity yoga is necessary, the initial process being called 'approximation' because through imagining the deity one is approaching closer to it. Without preliminary approximation the feats of lengthening the lifespan, becoming youthful, gaining the five clairvoyances, and so forth cannot be achieved. It is to achieve such feats that prior approximation is performed, called 'prior' because it necessarily precedes actualising a specific feat and using it for the welfare of others.

With regard to how to do prior approximation there are concentrations with and without repetition. Concerning concentration with repetition, one first invites a deity in front as a field or basis for the accumulation of merit through making offerings, praises, and so forth; then one meditates on oneself as a deity. These are called generation in front and self-generation.

For the first, if you have a painting or statue of a deity, you can use that as a basis of imagination by placing it in front of you. Meditate on its emptiness and then from within that emptiness imagine the many features of the place to which the deity will be invited — the ground, mountain, and lotus seat on which is an inestimable mansion of light. This is called generation of the residence — the abode of the deity.

Then, invite the deity — the resident — ask him to sit, display seals or hand gestures, and make offerings and praises. Actually, since Form Bodies appear instantaneously to a person of faith from within the sphere of the Truth Body of great bliss, there is no need to invite a deity to come here from some specific place. However, since we are bound by our conceptions of true existence, it is helpful to imagine inviting the likes of a Complete Enjoyment Body from a pure land to the place where one is meditating and thereupon to make offerings in accordance with ordinary customs. The offerings prescribed are distinctly Indian, being geared to receiving a guest in a hot country — cool water for the feet, a cool drink, a garland for the head, fragrant perfume for the feet, sprinkling of water, and so forth. These are followed by confession, refuge, admiration of one's own and others' virtues, entreaty, supplication, and prayer-wishes. The final step is cultivation of the four immeasurables — love, compassion, joy, and equanimity — called immeasurable because one is observing an immeasurable number of sentient beings and accumulating an immeasurable amount of merit through the practice.

Then, you are ready to do self-generation. Set your body in the cross-legged posture of Vairochana, for when the body is straightened the channels in which the winds course will be straightened, thereby balancing the mind. Withdraw your sense consciousnesses from observing their respective objects — visible forms, sounds, odours, tastes, and tangible objects — and set your mind inside. Raise the back of your head and bend it slightly down like a swan's; breathe naturally and gently without either panting or gasping. Open your eyes a little since, although there seems to be an immediate benefit in lesser disturbance from closing them, in time it harms by causing unclarity. Similarly, if the eyes are left wide open, they will smart later on. Aim them at the point of the nose, or, if that is uncomfortable, farther away. Generally, one leaves the teeth as usual, but here (p. 104) Buddhaguhya says to 'press teeth with teeth', most likely meaning to leave them touching. Put the tongue to the roof of the mouth for the sake of reducing the flow of saliva and yet keeping the mouth moist.

Thereupon, the altruistic mind of enlightenment is to be cultivated. This good mind of cherishing others rather than oneself should be generated if you have not yet done so and should be enhanced if you have. When you are able to have such a good mind continuously and steadily, Buddhahood is easily attained and, while you are still in cyclic existence, happiness is brought to yourself and others.

Then, you may begin the process of self-generation by way of the six deities: ultimate, sound, letter, form, seal, and sign.

Ultimate Deity

Only non-Buddhists assert that there is a self, or I, that is a separate entity from mind and body. If there were such a separate entity, it would have to be apprehensible totally separate from mind and body, but it is not. Therefore the I is designated only in dependence on the mental and physical aggregates.

Here in the first of the six deities you are to realise the suchness or final nature of the imputedly existent I. Tsong-ka-pa makes a similar presentation in his *Essence of the Good Explanations:* first he sets forth many assertions on how various systems posit the I — such as asserting consciousness as I, the continuum of the mental and physical aggregates as I, and the continuum of consciousness as I. Then he says that in our own Prasangika-Madhyamika system there is nothing among the five mental and physical aggregates — forms, feelings, discriminations, compositional factors, or consciousnesses

— which can be put as I, and thus the I is only designated in dependence on the aggregates. He adds that when the Madhyamika view of emptiness is found in relation to such an imputedly existent person rather than the person in general, there is a great difference. In this Action Tantra, the *Concentration Continuation*, one is directed to realise the suchness, or emptiness, of such an imputedly existent I.

The self that is merely designated to mind and body has two natures, conventional and ultimate; its final nature is the ultimate one — the suchness of self which is free from all signs of dualistic elaborations. A mind that knows one's own nature to be beyond the limits of dualistic elaborations in accordance with its actual mode of subsistence ascertains suchness. Emptiness is called suchness because the nature of phenomena is exhausted as just such, as nothing else. The contemplation of suchness as equally the nature of yourself and the deity being meditated on is called the ultimate deity.

Just as one's own nature or mode of being is ultimately free from all elaborations of the conception of inherent existence and is essentially at peace since the self is only nominally existent, so is the status of the deity being meditated. Though the bases of this emptiness of inherent existence — oneself and the deity — are different, their mode of subsistence — their mere absence of inherent existence, their suchness — are the same and should be viewed as undifferentiable like a mixture of water and milk. All phenomena are of the same taste in their final nature, emptiness.

Sound Deity

Stay within meditative equipoise on suchness as long as you can and then within the sphere of emptiness use this mind which realises emptiness as the basis of emanation and manifest a flat clear white moon disc at the place where, in the later steps, you will manifest as a deity. Above the moon disc the sounds of the mantra of the deity as whom the meditator will later appear reverberate in space.

Letter Deity

First one meditated on emptiness; then, one imagined that the wisdom mind manifested as a moon disc and as the sounds of the mantra. After setting in equipoise for a little time while contemplating these, the sounds of the mantra appear in the form of letters set in order around the edge of the moon. This is the letter deity, a manifestation of the exalted wisdom realising emptiness.

Imagine that from the moon and the mantra letters light rays are emitted, from the points of which emerge forms of the deity to be meditated. These deities emanate clouds of offerings to the Buddhas, Bodhisattvas, and so forth, as well as clouds with a rain of nectar. It falls on the beings in cyclic existence and purifies them, giving a good body to those who need it, coolness to those suffering from heat, the warmth of the sun to those suffering from cold, food and drink to the hungry and thirsty — emanating to each just what he or she needs, affording beings the basis for practising the path as well as teachers to instruct them in the essential paths of the four truths, the two truths, and so forth. They are caused to ascend the paths and attain the final happiness of Buddhahood.

Form Deity

Then, the emanated deities and the beams of light are withdrawn back into the moon and mantra letters which turn into the form of the deity being meditated. The deity has now been generated.

The meditator is not separate from the deity, but appears *as* the deity. Earlier all appearances were withdrawn and emptiness contemplated; now the only appearance is of pure mind and body. The impure are not considered to be non-existent, but their appearance has been purposely withdrawn. The basis giving rise to the thought 'I' is now just this pure mind and body.

Seal Deity

The next step is to bless various important places in your divine body through touching them with hand gestures, called seals.

Sign Deity

At this point you can invite the wisdom-being [the actual being] who dissolves into the pledge-being [yourself imagined as the deity]. This completion of deity generation, involving a combination of clear appearance and pride of being that deity, is called the sign deity.

Meditation on [or cultivation of] the six deities is like faith or love meditation in that the mind is being generated into the entity of the object meditated. When faith or love are meditated, those two are not the object observed but the entity into which the consciousness is being generated. Meditation on impermanence or emptiness, on the other hand, means to take these as the object and meditate on them. Thus, there are two types of meditation — *of* a subjective aspect and *on* an objective aspect. Meditation on the six deities is the former, for first one generates a wisdom consciousness knowing the sameness in suchness of oneself and the deity — the ultimate — and then causes it to appear as the sounds, letters, and finally the form of the deity.

Within that yoga there are two modes of cultivating the six deities — by way of concentration and by way of meditative stablisation. In the first, one contemplates the six deities in series and then, inspecting the colour of the deity, the hand symbol and so forth, corrects their appearance — adjusting clarity and so forth. In the mode of meditative stabilisation, however, one observes a single object, the general body or the deity's face, for instance, and without any adjustment remains one-pointedly on that object.

First in cultivation by way of concentration one visualises the divine form in stages by way of the six deities, making adjustments for clarity and so forth. Then, engaging in cultivation by way of meditative stabilisation one remains in one-pointed meditation, stopping breath and distraction for the sake of keeping the mind from coming under the influence of scattering and excitement. This stopping of breath and distraction is called stopping vitality and exertion (*prāṇāyāma*); one binds 'vitality', that is to say, wind — the breath that is inhaled and exhaled through the nose as well as the winds that course through the hair-pores of the head and body, the male and female organs, eyes, and so forth — and stops 'exertion', which here means 'mindfulness' not in the usual sense of keeping a virtuous object in mind but in the sense of taking an object other than that of the meditation to mind — in other words, distraction.

Since wind acts as a basis or mount for consciousness, the scattering of the mind is caused by wind; hence, if the winds are restrained, the mind's scattering is stopped. We can confirm with our own experience that wind serves as the mount for consciousness by the fact that when the mind becomes somewhat one-pointed the movement of the breath in the nostrils lessens. Even with a little stability of mind, the breath becomes more relaxed and less obvious.

Though meditation by way of concentration — in which the divine body is contemplated in series — involves preventing distraction to other objects, the mind is not kept one-pointedly on a single object. Rather, one is reviewing in stages the face, arms, and so forth of the divine body, and thus a series of minds is being generated. However, in meditation by way of meditative stabilisation, one stops the movement of the mind and holds it on one object. Thus, the stopping of 'vitality and exertion', or breath and distraction, is explained at the point of meditative stabilisation and not for the earlier serial meditation by way of concentration.

Here in Action Tantra the stopping of vitality and exertion is done for the sake of keeping the mind from being distracted to other objects, whereas in Highest Yoga Tantra another practice of holding the winds is done to stop the movement of the winds in the right and left channels and cause them to enter the central channel. There it is not just for the sake of stopping distraction.

To review the process: you first gain a clear appearance of yourself as a deity whereupon arises the 'pride' which is a sense of being that mere I designated in dependence on the clearly appearing divine body. Then, within that clear appearance and pride you one-pointedly observe the mental appearance of the general divine body or a particular part — the face, for instance — holding the breath as long as possible and keeping the mind from straying to other objects. Then when exhaling, loosen the mode of observation and more relaxedly view the general divine body, loosening mindfulness and introspection a little.

When you get tired, it is appropriate to repeat mantra. However, for a beginner the main part of the meditation revolves around the six deities, which should be cultivated carefully and leisurely. This is because clear appearance of oneself as a deity must be achieved for the sake of amassing the two collections of merit and wisdom, achieving firm meditative stabilisation, and transforming all physical and verbal actions into powerful aids for others' welfare. Hence, before repeating mantra, the yoga of non-dual profundity (realisation of emptiness) and manifestation (appearance as a deity) should be sustained, developing clarity within observing the divine form and ascertaining its lack of inherent existence. When, having done this one-pointedly, you become tired, then for the sake of resting begin repeating mantra.

There was an Am-do lama, Jay-dzun Jam-yang-tsul-trim-chö-gi-nyi-ma (*rJe-btsun 'Jam-dbyangs-tshul-khrims-chos-kyi-nyi-ma*), who said that since we usually recite the instructions for a rite of deity generation quickly and then immediately repeat mantra, we are taking mantra repetition rather than meditation as the main part of the session. He joked that once the technique for resting is used for the basic session, there is no way to rest when tired except to leave the session. His point was well taken, for the Indians meditated in the main session and then when tired passed on to repetition as a second level of practice for the sake of resting. Tsong-ka-pa also says that in the approximation phase meditation is chief, mantra repetition is secondary. It is not sufficient to recite the memorised rite and then count mantra.

There are three types of repetition, the first of which involves reciting a mantra within the context of observing the form of the letters of the mantra on a flat moon disc at the heart of the deity visualised in front of yourself. The moon is a manifestation of the mind realising emptiness and thus is called 'mind'. The letters of the mantra, set around the edge of the moon with the seed syllable of the deity in the middle, are called 'sound'. The 'base' where these are set is the deity meditated in front of yourself; the second 'base' is yourself clarified as a deity.

These are the four branches of repetition — mind, sound, and two bases — to be maintained while repeating mantra. As if reading the letters of the mantra at the heart of the deity in front, repeat the mantra.

When the mind becomes one-pointed, cease reciting the mantra orally and begin mental repetition — holding the breath during the recitation and then, when exhaling, viewing your own divine body. Then, when you are tired, undo the process of visualisation in reverse order, passing from observing the forms of the letters to the moon, then the body of the deity in front, and then your own divine body. This, in turn, is left through passing backwards through the process of self-generation — observing the forms of the letters on the moon at your own heart, then the sounds, moon disc, sameness in nature of yourself and the deity, and your own suchness — finally setting in meditative equipoise on emptiness. Then, even when leaving the session, you should rise within a sense of divine pride, maintaining it throughout all activities.

The second type of repetition is done within the context of observing the form of the mantra letters at your own heart. From within the former meditation, the moon and letters at the heart of the deity in front are transferred with an inhalation of breath to your own heart, whereupon repetition is performed. With exhalation, stop the repetition and observe the divine body in front to which the moon and letters again move with the outgoing breath. Then with inhalation repeat the process. As before, this can be done with both whispered and mental repetition — the latter being more subtle.

Then, pass to an even subtler object by mainly observing the sounds of the letters, though not entirely leaving off observing your own divine body with moon and mantra letters at the heart. Later on in the concentrations of abiding in fire and in sound, one concentrates on the mantra sounds as if listening to someone else recite them, but here one is as if listening to one's own recitation. Again, this can be done with whispered or mental repetition, the latter being necessary when the breath is held since oral recitation would be impossible.

These are the three types of repetition — observing the forms of the mantra letters (1) in the heart of the deity in front, (2) in your own heart, and (3) observing the sounds of the mantra. Each of these in turn has two forms, whispered and mental repetition. For each of the three types, whispered repetition is done first and then mental while the breath is held. The process becomes subtler and subtler and should be done in order. If one knows how to meditate, the meditations of Action Tantra are very profound, its progression of stages accomplishing a withdrawal of winds which enhances meditative stabilisation.

The first type is said to have three objects of observation — the deity in front, moon at its heart, and mantra letters; the second type, two — moon and mantra letters at one's own heart; and the third, one — the mantra sounds. These refer to the *main* objects of observation on which the mind focuses and should not be taken as meaning that the other factors do not remain vividly appearing to the mind. One must remain undistractedly on whatever the object is at that point.

When facility is gained with those concentrations, you pass on to the concentrations without repetition — abiding in fire, abiding in sound, and bestowing liberation at the end of sound. The concentration of abiding in fire bestows feats in the sense of empowering and stabilising the mind. The concentration of abiding in sound is the time of achieving a fully qualified calm abiding (*shamatha*) — an effortless and spontaneous meditative stabilisation induced by physical and mental pliancy. The yoga of concentration on the end of sound is a cultivation of a union of calm abiding and special insight (*vipashyanā*) observing suchness, whereby the liberation of Buddhahood is eventually attained. These three concentrations are all performed within vivid and continuous visualisation of oneself as a deity.

With regard to the concentration of abiding in fire, you must cease the conception of inherent existence in the sense of not giving it a chance to be produced. Still, it is necessary to maintain conception of a conventional deity, that is to say one with a face, arms, and so forth. Previously, during the repetition of mantra while observing the sound of the letters, it was as if you were listening to the reverberation of the sounds of your own recitation, whether whispered or mental. However, here you are to listen to the mantra sounds as if someone else were reciting them. Therefore, that the concentration of abiding in fire is said to be without mantra repetition means that it is free from the aspect of *one's own* repetition, not that it is free from mantra sounds altogether.

These sounds are 'heard' from within a tongue of flame imagined at the heart — all this within the clear appearance of your own body as a deity's. Your own mind is as if inside the tongue of flame, appearing in the form of the mantra sounds resounding as if by their own power. This is like the practice on other occasions of the mind's taking the mind as its object of observation — a factor of the mind taking the general mind as its object. Here the mind is appearing as the sounds of someone else's repetition and is simultaneously listening to those sounds.

In the previous meditations all forms and sounds were appearances of the mind realising suchness; thus, all forms seen and sounds heard were appearances of the mind. Within that, one was as if listening to the mantra repeated by oneself; hence, there still was a sense of a listener and the listened. However, here in the concentration of abiding in fire one's own basis of designation is as if dwelling inside the tongue of flame, and it itself is appearing as the sounds being listened to in that same place.

The external sign of proficiency with the concentration of abiding in fire is to become free from hunger and thirst— meditative stabilisation itself having become your sustenance.

Then, you should pass on to the concentration of abiding in sound. Here you imagine a *subtle* moon at the heart of your divine body. This is because the smaller the object is the easier it is to eliminate scattering and excitement and the brighter the object is the easier it is to eliminate laxity. If the object observed is too large, it is difficult to eliminate conceptions; therefore a small object of observation is required.

Earlier, in the concentration of abiding in fire, you imagined a tongue of flame at the heart in which the sounds of the mantra resounded. Now, in that flame on the moon place a small divine figure with a tongue of flame at its heart in which the mantra sounds reverberate. Then, leave off one-pointed concentration on that — without leaving it altogether — and focus on the mantra sounds. As before, you are as if listening to the mantra recited by someone else. When exhaling, view the outer divine body.

These unusual objects of observation in the concentrations of abiding in fire and in sound are for the sake of achieving clear appearance and thereby avoiding laxity. For, even if the earlier meditations involved the appearance of bright mantra letters and so forth, here one imagines fire itself, even the name of which evokes a bright appearance, thereby helping in relieving the mind of laxity — any looseness in the mode of apprehension of the object. The uncommon purpose of the concentrations of abiding in fire and in sound is not concerned with ascertaining the meaning of non-inherent existence but with withdrawing the mind and achieving a fully qualified calm abiding that is conjoined with a bliss of physical and mental pliancy.

As was explained earlier [in *Tantra in Tibet*] the three lower tantras — Action, Performance, and Yoga — have unusual techniques for achieving the special insight realising emptiness. Since, to do this, calm abiding must first be achieved, the three lower tantras have methods superior to those of the Perfection Vehicle for inducing calm abiding. These are techniques such as the stopping of the breath and the observation of a divine body, as well as subtler internal objects such as fire and sound. These generate the capacity quickly to achieve calm abiding — a state in which the mind can remain one-pointedly on its object of observation as long as one wants, free from even subtle laxity and excitement, and conjoined with physical and mental pliancy.

Since with its attainment you have a fully qualified meditative stabilisation (*samādhi*), you can then switch the object of observation to emptiness in accordance with the concentration bestowing liberation at the end of sound. It is now possible to analyse the nature of phenomena with the powerful, penetrating, steady, serviceable, and undistracted mind of calm abiding. However, if you analyse too much, it will harm the stability factor of the mind, and similarly if you stabilise too much it will harm the analytical factor. Therefore, you need skilfully to alternate analytical and stabilising meditation, through which a state arisen from meditation with emptiness as the object is generated. This is a union of calm abiding and special insight realising emptiness, the yoga of signlessness, and the beginning of the path of preparation.

The mode of procedure in the three lower tantras is to attain calm abiding first and then alternate analytical and stabilising meditation whereby special insight is achieved. However, in the stage of generation of Highest Yoga

Tantra even during the period of achieving calm abiding one can engage in more and more intensive analysis without harming the stability factor. This is due to special objects of observation — such as an entire mandala within a tiny drop — and special places of meditation within the body — essential channel points. During the stage of completion in Highest Yoga Tantra, however, one mainly uses stabilising meditation during the session for the sake of drawing the winds into the central channel; nevertheless, between sessions analysis on emptiness is still done. It seems that some persons have misapplied this predominance of stabilising meditation during the stage of completion — the highest point of the path — to the beginning stages, recommending non-analysis and thereby confusing the process of the path.

In Action and Performance Tantra analytical and stabilising meditation — with emptiness as the object — must be *alternated* after achieving calm abiding. Gradually, analysis itself comes to induce even greater stability, whereupon alternation is no longer needed and a union of calm abiding and special insight is attained. Through using the above-mentioned special objects of observation and so forth the four levels of the path of preparation — heat, peak, forbearance, and supreme mundane quality — proceed faster than in sutra, whereupon the path of seeing, the initial direct cognition of emptiness, and the first of the ten grounds are simultaneously attained. However, the three lower tantras do not set forth any techniques for proceeding more quickly than in the Perfection Vehicle with regard to the abandoning of obstructions and advancing over the ten grounds. Thus, from among the five paths — accumulation, preparation, seeing, meditation, and no more learning — the profound distinguishing features of the three lower tantras are concerned with the first two. Whereas in the Perfection Vehicle the paths of accumulation and preparation take one period of countless great aeons, in the three lower tantras it can be done in one lifetime or even in a few years. Yoga Tantra has the further profundity of subtler objects of observation much like the *Guhyasamaja* [a Highest Yoga Tantra].

In the concentration bestowing liberation at the end of sound one leaves even sound and focuses on emptiness, free from the two extremes of inherent existence and no nominal existence. One is no longer mainly concerned with developing clear appearance but is mainly meditating on emptiness. Still, this does not mean that the divine body, sounds, and so forth necessarily no longer appear. Rather, to the *ascertainment factor* of the concentration on the end of sound only emptiness — a negative of inherent existence — appears. However, sounds and so forth may still appear to what is called the appearance factor of that consciousness. This means that although the sounds and so forth may appear, the mind is ascertaining or realising only emptiness. This is the union of the two truths in Mantra — one consciousness appearing in the form of divine body or speech and simultaneously realising emptiness.

These meditations depend on initially developing clear appearance of a divine body — clarity being developed through familiarising or taking to mind again and again the features of the object. For instance, if one takes to mind again and again the features of a person whom one desires, that person will eventually appear as if before one's own eyes. Thus, an object of meditation does not have to be true for clear appearance to emerge; rather, the sole factor is familiarisation. This is established in Dharmakirti's *Commentary on (Dignaga's) 'Compendium of Prime Cognition' (Pramāṇavarttika)*.

When clear appearance of the object — divine form or speech — is achieved, one's consciousness is non-conceptual with respect to that even if it is conceptually realising emptiness, as is the case with the early forms of the concentration on the end of sound. To realise emptiness conceptually means to know it through a generic image of it, not directly or nakedly as is done at the beginning of the path of seeing. Thus it seems that the one consciousness would have to be non-conceptual with respect to the divine body and conceptual with respect to the suchness — emptiness — of that body.

Clear appearance of the object and within that an intense subjective clarity are important. Many people nowadays seem to be confusing subtle laxity with meditation. In subtle laxity the mind is stable but without an intense mode of apprehension. Tsong-ka-pa explains at length in his *Stages of the Path Common to the Vehicles* that mere stability of the mind — an ability to stay on the object — is not sufficient. Here in Mantra also clarity of the object — the divine form — as well as subjective stability and clarity, free from even subtle laxity, are needed. In Action Tantra such vivid and steady meditative stabilisation is achieved through the concentration of abiding in sound, which though it is blissful, clear, and non-conceptual as well as being conjoined with the force of realising emptiness is not sufficient. It is still necessary to cultivate the concentration bestowing liberation at the end of sound; unlike the former, it is capable of cutting the root of cyclic existence because it takes only emptiness as its object of apprehension. In this way the concentrations with and without repetition provide profound means for speedy progress on the path.

Performance Tantra

Like Action Tantra, Performance Tantra has three supramundane lineages — Tathagata, lotus, and vajra. According to Bu-dön, the *Vairochanabhisambodhi* is a tantra of the Tathagata lineage; the *Extensive Tantra of Hayagriva,* which was not translated into Tibetan, is of the lotus lineage; and the *Vajrapani Initiation Tantra* is of the vajra lineage.

Initially one's continuum is ripened through initiation — the means of ripening — whereupon one works at keeping the vows and pledges in pure form. Specifically, one must properly maintain the correct view of emptiness and the altruistic mind of enlightenment, not losing these even for the sake of one's life. These are again and again said to be the root of the vows and pledges. Tsong-ka-pa's description of the Bodhisattva vows and the reasons why the tantric ones do not apply in Performance Tantra are found in his *Explanation of the Ethics Chapter* and *Explanation of the Root Infractions,* which thereby become subsidiaries of the *Great Exposition of Secret Mantra* and should be studied in detail.

With respect to the yoga of Performance Tantra, the *Vairochanabhisambodhi Tantra* speaks of thoroughly pure and impure divine bodies and yogas with and without signs. Thoroughly pure divine bodies are mainly entities of the realisation of emptiness, having the aspect of the ultimate, whereas the 'impure' mainly have the aspect of the conventional, a deity with face, arms, etc. A path without signs has the full qualifications of an undifferentiability of method and wisdom, due to which the Truth and Form Bodies of a Buddha are achieved in dependence on it. A path or yoga with signs, even though involving emptiness and deity yoga, is unlike yoga without signs in that it is not *mainly* concerned with meditation on emptiness. Thus, the yoga without signs occurs when the capacity for meditation in which a divine circle is observed and its non-inherent existence is ascertained has developed to a high degree; emptiness yoga is then predominant.

In Action Tantra, yoga without signs begins with the concentration bestowing liberation at the end of sound and thus with the attainment of a union of calm abiding and special insight observing emptiness. There, yoga without signs is deity yoga that has reached the level of a state arisen from meditation, such being gained simultaneously with the attainment of a union of calm abiding and special insight. Here in Performance Tantra it seems that yoga without signs refers to yogas on the occasion of mainly cultivating the view of emptiness, whereas those on other occasions are yogas with signs, in that they are mainly concerned with dualistic appearances, although they do involve meditation on emptiness.

Just as in Highest Yoga Tantra a divine body meditated on the stage of generation is called an impure divine body and one meditated on the stage of completion is called pure, here in the *Vairochanabhisambodhi,* a Performance Tantra, the divine bodies of the yogas with and without signs are respectively called impure and pure. Though the *Vairochanabhisambodhi* does not indeed indicate, either explicitly or implicitly, the bodies of the two stages in Highest Yoga Tantra, its thought is aimed at those, and thus it can be cited as a source for the two bodies in Highest Yoga Tantra, as was done by Chandrakirti (see pp. 185–6).

In Performance Tantra the yoga with signs is in two types, external and internal, with each having four branches as in Action Tantra — self-base, other-base, sound, and mind. At the beginning of the process of deity meditation and mantra repetition one meditates on emptiness, settling the non-inherent existence of oneself and the deity through a reasoning such as that of dependent-arising — the fact that both oneself and the deity arise in dependence on their respective bases of designation. One's own final nature and the final nature of the deity are the same, an emptiness of inherent existence.

To perform deity yoga one does not just withdraw ordinary appearances and then appear as a deity but causes the mind realising emptiness itself to appear as a deity. Thus, it is essential initially to meditate on emptiness, cleansing all appearances in emptiness. One then uses that wisdom consciousness realising emptiness as the basis of emanation of a divine body. This must be done at least in imitation of a consciousness actually doing this, for meditation on a truly existent divine body, instead of helping, will only increase adherence to inherent existence. Meditated properly, the appearance of a divine figure is the sport of the ultimate mind of enlightenment, first in imitation and later in fact.

In one mode of procedure the deity appears in full form instantaneously; in another, the wisdom consciousness first manifests as a moon and seed syllable which transform into the divine form. This latter is like the procedure in Highest Yoga Tantra in which one contemplates, 'The root of all phenomena included in the environment and the beings within it — mere wind and mind, appearing as a moon — am I'. Although Performance Tantra does not have such an explanation of wind, the basic thought is the same in terms of the mind. One first generates the view realising emptiness — at least in imitation — whereupon that mind ascertaining emptiness serves as the basis of emanation, appearing as a moon. This is said to be like the rising of a water bubble from water, for just as a water bubble is different from water but still has a nature of water, so the form of the moon disc is different from the exalted wisdom realising emptiness and yet does not pass beyond being the sport or nature of that exalted wisdom consciousness.

The moon disc with seed syllable on top of it then changes into the body of the deity, here the great Vairochanabhisambodhi; this is the first branch, the self-base or generation of oneself as a deity. The second branch, or other-base, is the imagination of a deity similar to oneself in front, a second Vairochanabhisambodhi facing oneself. Then, the third and fourth branches, mind and sound, consist of imagining a moon disc — the nature of which, again, is the wisdom consciousness realising emptiness — in the heart of the deity in front with the form of the mantra syllables set upright around its edge facing inwards. One then engages in repetition. That is the external four-branched repetition.

The internal four-branched repetition involves generating oneself as Shakyamuni with Vairochanabhisambodhi at his heart inside an upright moon disc which is like a two-sided mirror. The internal Vairochana has a moon at his heart with the mantra letters standing upright around its edge facing inwards. Meditation is done in this way until calm abiding is attained, at which point yoga without signs is begun.

The yoga without signs is cultivated within clear imagination of one's body as a deity's and is preceded by the four branches of repetition. The mode of meditation is first to reflect on the body as something not affected by good and bad since it is composed of matter; except for serving as a basis of consciousness, the body itself cannot feel anything. Then one analyses whether or not the body inherently exists in the way it appears to exist so solidly. Through using a reasoning such as the body's not being an inherently existent one or many, one realises its emptiness of inherent solidity.

The mind is similarly analysed to discover its emptiness of inherently existent production, abiding, and disintegration. Then, the I that is designated in dependence on body and mind should be analysed and settled as not inherently existent.

Buddhaguhya describes this process as beginning with identifying the subject, one's own divine body with the two factors of clear appearance and divine pride, and then settling its emptiness by any of three techniques:

1. the reasoning of its not being either an inherently existent one or many, or the reasoning of its not being produced from self, other, both, or neither;
2. a stabilising meditation on the meaning of emptiness;
3. eliminating all conventional appearances [such as a divine body] and concentrating solely on the ultimate, the emptiness of inherent existence.

The first technique is based on an analytical reasoning as done in Madhyamika. The second must refer to a stabilising meditation on an emptiness which one has ascertained earlier through analysis; however, repeated analysis would have to be done in order to enhance one's understanding, for stabilising meditation alone — without the factor of great bliss as in Highest Yoga Tantra — is not sufficient. This is because the mode of procedure for developing special insight in the three lower tantras — Action, Performance, and Yoga — is the same as that in sutra, alternating stabilising and analytical meditation.

The third is a case of viewing appearances themselves — wherever the mind alights — as empty of inherent existence, in contrast to the first technique, in which the emptiness of a particular subject is being ascertained through a reasoning such as the lack of its being an inherently existent one or many. This is like the teaching on the Great Seal (*Mahāmudrā*) in the Ga-gyu-ba (*bKa'-rgyud-pa*) order that the more thoughts one has, so much more are the Truth Bodies, or emptinesses, realised.

In all three cases it is necessary to alternate stabilising meditation and analytical meditation, for only in the stage of completion of Highest Yoga Tantra can mere stabilising meditation on emptiness be done, the difference there coming from the feature of great bliss. Thus, by merely cultivating non-conceptuality and non-analysis it is impossible to enter into the yoga of signlessness. Even after emptiness has been realised, powerful and repeated analysis is needed. Merely to set one's mind on the meaning of emptiness as realised earlier is the mode of cultivating calm abiding observing emptiness; in order to cultivate special insight it is necessary to analyse again and again. These two modes of meditation — stabilising and analytical — are alternated until analysis itself induces even greater stablisation, at which point stabilisation and wisdom are of equal strength, this being a union of calm abiding and special insight.

In Performance as well as in Action Tantra the meditative stabilisation which is a union of calm abiding and special insight is used to gain feats for the sake of aiding sentient beings and accumulating merit quickly. These are gained in dependence on (1) external substances, as in the case of the feat of the sword which is used for flying to lands of Knowledge Bearers where tantric practice is maintained; (2) internal imagination of discs representing earth, water, fire, or wind; or (3) achieving a meeting with a special deity such as Manjushri. Unlike Yoga Tantra, however, Action and Performance do not present means for actually transforming one's body [while still on the path] into a similitude of a divine body. In Yoga Tantra techniques are taught for the sake of actually transmuting this body into one of a Knowledge Bearer or of a tenth ground Bodhisattva.

II

The Great Exposition of Secret Mantra

The Stages of the Path to a Conqueror and Pervasive Master, a Great Vajradhara: Revealing All Secret Topics

TSONG-KA-PA

Parts Two and Three

Translated and edited by Jeffrey Hopkins
Associate editors: Lati Rinbochay and
Denma Lochö Rinbochay

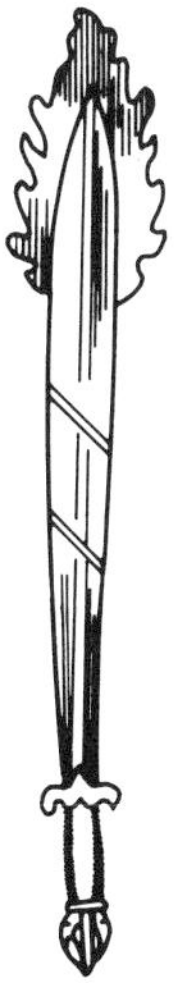

Introduction

The presentation of the stages of the path in Action and Performance Tantras has two parts: (1) analysis of whether Action and Performance have self-generation and entry of a wisdom-being and (2) individual explanations of their stages of the path.

1

Controversy about Deity Yoga in Action and Performance

The analysis of whether Action and Performance Tantras have self-generation and entry of a wisdom-being [the deity's dissolving into the meditator] has two parts: masters' [varying] assertions and the correct position among them.

Masters' Assertions on Whether Action and Performance Tantras Have Self-Generation and Entry of a Wisdom-Being

Most earlier Tibetan lamas [mistakenly] said that although Action Tantras entail meditation on a deity in front of oneself, they do not involve generation of oneself as a deity. They also [wrongly] claimed that in Performance Tantras, except for generating oneself as a pledge-being [symbolic of the actual deity] and generating a wisdom-being [the actual deity] in front of oneself, there is no entry of a wisdom-being into oneself. They held this because the *Wisdom Vajra Compendium*[1] [a Highest Yoga Tantra] says:

> One who is terrified [of single-pointed cultivation of deity yoga] and is very cleanly, who lacks the excellent bliss of a wisdom-being and pride in oneself as a deity, who is not an object of the unusual practice [of using desire in the path], and who practises with thoughts on the features of defects [such as birth, ageing, and so forth] abides in Action Tantra.

[Many Tibetans wrongly assumed that] this passage explains that Action Tantras do not involve self-generation and entry of a wisdom-being [whereas it indicates that *some* Action Tantras do not involve these in order to accommodate within their paths those unable to practise them]. Also, they claimed that the *Vairochanabhisambodhi Tantra* and the *Vajrapani Initiation Tantra* [both Performance Tantras] set forth generation of oneself as a deity but not entry of a wisdom-being into oneself.

Shridhara's *Innate Illumination, Commentary on the Difficult Points of the 'Yamari Tantra' (Yamāritantrapañjikāsahajāloka*[2] [a Highest Yoga text which agrees with this wrong interpretation]) says:

> Even in the Action and Performance systems [practitioners] do not engage in achievements and means of achievements over a long time. [Rather] these arise from imagination because they complete feats through the power of deities that are found in paintings and so forth [that is, they imagine a deity in front of themselves from whom they, as ordinary beings, receive feats]. The Yoga Tantras have this feature: Through one's own deity yoga [of self-generation] one observes a deity as found in paintings and so forth and achieves concordant feats.

Jinadatta [wrongly] describes Action and Performance Tantra in a similar way in his *Commentary on the Difficult Points of the 'Guhyasamaja Tantra' (Guhyasamājatantrapañjikā)* [a Highest Yoga text]. Also, the *Explanation of the 'Condensation of the Samvara Tantra' (Chakrasaṃvaratantrarājashambarasamuchchayanāmavṛtti)* [a Highest Yoga text] which is said to have been written by Indrabhuti [wrongly] says:

> From the approach of Action and Performance Tantras within the Secret Vajra Vehicle, [practitioners] depending on only a permission [rite] for practising knowledge mantras seek to actualise a goal achieved through observation with signs — imagination having a view of oneself and a deity as different.

These commentators [wrongly] assert that both Action and Performance Tantra do not involve self-generation.

[*The Opposite Assertion*]

The *Concentration Continuation*[3] [one of the four main general Action Tantras] says:

> The secret mantra concentrations
> Are said to be supremely secret.

Buddhaguhya's commentary[4] says:

> 'Secret' means unrevealed. The meaning is that though the secret mantra concentrations [such as deity yoga] are the essence of the branches for achieving all secret mantras [that is, feats], they are not taught in clear detail in the individual tantras. This is in order to accommodate migrators who are trainees but unable to perform earnestly the branches of concentration, such as withdrawal [of the mind from external objects] and [stopping] vitality and exertion [breath and distraction]. These are mostly set forth in a non-manifest manner in all [Action Tantras]; I will explain them later.

Thus, Buddhaguhya says that the mantra concentrations, such as deity yoga which he is yet to explain, are the essence of the causal branches for achieving feats.

However, these are not taught clearly in other Action Tantras in order to accommodate within those tantras those who could not cultivate deity yoga one-pointedly through methods such as holding the winds inside, which he is yet to describe. Buddhaguhya explains that these concentrations are, however, mentioned in an unclear way in other tantras.

His *Commentary on the 'Concentration Continuation'*[5] says:

> The activities to be done during the concentrations of secret mantra repetition are set forth in the *Susiddhi Tantra (Susiddhi),* the *Questions of Subahu (Subāhu-paripṛchchhā),* the *Compendium of Imaginations* [?], and so forth, which are compendiums of the general rites of all Action Tantras. These [activities] are also described in tantras of specific [lineages and deities] such as the *Vairochanabhisambodhi: the Empowerment of Emanations,* the *Vajrapani Initiation Tantra,* the *Essence of Enlightenment* [?], the *Scriptural Division of the Knowledge Bearers (Vidyādhārapiṭaka* [?]), and so forth. In some they are explained non-manifestly; in some, clearly. For instance, the *Susiddhi Tantra*[6] says:
>
> > When reciting with repetition,
> > Except for knowledge mantra and deity
> > Do not apprehend in thought at all [other]
> > Meditations though cherished as supreme.

Also, Buddhaguhya[7] says:

> The *Vairochanabhisambodhi* [a Performance Tantra] clearly explains that, when doing repetition, mantra training is done through training in the four-branched repetition [which involves self-generation as one of its branches]. The *Vajrapani Initiation* [a Performance Tantra] says, 'Manjushri, when a practitioner of

mantra spontaneously achieves the pride of a deity, he dwells in proximity to all secret mantra [feats]'. The *Scriptural Division of the Bearers of Knowledge Mantras* says, 'One should concentrate on a deity [as found] in a painting and so forth:

> Contemplate [the deity] with swaying ear-rings
> And the movement of the small [jewel-] bag ichneumon.[8]
> When striving at repetition in this way
> Imagine in stages the feet and so forth'.

The *Compendium of Imaginations* teaches familiarisation with the selflessness of phenomena and deity yoga in a great many passages; therefore, I will not cite them here. In such tantras the bodies of deities and the repetition that is performed prior to secret mantra concentration on sound [that is, before the concentrations of abiding in fire and in sound] are described.

Buddhaguhya says that meditation on a divine body, concentration performed while observing a mantra, meditation on the suchness of oneself, and so forth, are explained either clearly or unclearly, completely or incompletely, in [Action] Tantras. He says that the four-membered repetition is taught very clearly in the *Concentration Continuation* [an Action Tantra] and in the *Vairochanabhisambodhi* [generally considered to be a Performance Tantra].

The master Buddhaguhya asserts that the deity yoga of the four-membered repetition and so forth is similar in both Action and Performance Tantras. He says that the *Vairochanabhisambodhi,* for instance, can be an Action Tantra depending on the trainee; therefore, except for dividing Action and Performance Tantras by way of their trainees, he does not divide them from the viewpoint of the tantras themselves.[9]

Varabodhi's *Clear Realisation of Susiddhi (Susiddhi-abhisamaya)*[10] says:

> Do not think that the stages of achieving a deity are not taught in Action Tantras. Though the Blessed One did not teach these in most, they are taught as main subjects in the *Vajrapani Initiation* and the *Ten Principles (Dashatattva* [?]). In brief, all feats depend on a secret mantra deity and on suchness; if these are deficient, activities of pacification and so forth will not be achieved. These can be understood through a guru's explanation and through brief analysis of the features of tantras.

Here Varabodhi cites the *Vajrapani Initiation* [a Performance Tantra] as a source for the existence of deity generation in Action Tantra; this makes clear his assertion, like Buddhaguhya's above, that the deity yogas of Action and Performance Tantras are similar. With very good reasoning he says that since the achievement of the manifold activities of pacification and so forth depend on deity and emptiness yogas, even Action Tantra must involve deity meditation.

Correct Position Among the Assertions as to Whether Action and Performance Tantras Have Self-Generation and Entry of a Wisdom-Being

Question: Which among these different systems should be held here?

Answer: The assertion that there is no generation of oneself as a deity in Performance Tantra is not right. If the *Vairochanabhisambodhi* and the *Vajrapani Initiation* are not considered to be Performance Tantras, it would be impossible to find one. If they are, then, since they clearly set forth self-generation, the assertion that Performance Tantras do not have such is wrong. Also, the third chapter of Aryadeva's *Lamp Compendium of Practice (Charyāmelakapradīpa)* says, 'The *Vairochanabhisambodhi,* a Performance Tantra, says . . .'. Thus, Aryadeva calls it a Performance Tantra.

Also, it is thought of the *Samputa Tantra (Saṃpuṭa)* and the *Hevajra Tantra (Hevajra)* [both in the Highest Yoga class] that [Action Tantras] involve using in the path the desire of male and female deities' observing each other.[11] Therefore, it must also be asserted that Action Tantras have self-generation as a deity.

Question: Is this generation of oneself as a deity [just] carried over from [the thought of] other tantras [such as the *Samputa* and *Hevajra*] or does it come from Action Tantras themselves?

Answer: With respect to this, some latter-day scholars [such as Bu-dön *(Bu-ston)*[12] wrongly] say:

> Just as it is said that Action Tantras do not have self-generation and entry of a wisdom-being, so it is in fact. Still, Buddhaguhya and Varabodhi say that Action Tantras have self-generation but do not refer to entry of a wisdom-being.
>
> [*Possible 'reasons' for this assertion*]
>
> 1. The master Nagarjuna speaks of self-generation and entry of a wisdom-being as well as initiation in his *Means of Achievement of the Retention of the Thousand-Armed and Thousand-Eyed Avalokiteshvara (Sahasrabhujāvalokiteshvarasādhana)* [which is *based* on an Action Tantra]. Also, self-generation, entry of a wisdom-being, and so forth are explained in other *Means of Achievement*

which are *based* on Action Tantras such as the *Means of Achievement of Mahakarunika* by the master Padmasambhava, the *Means of Achievement of the Eleven-Faced Avalokiteshvara (Bhaṭṭārakaryaikādashamukhāvalokiteshvarasādhana)* by Lakshmi, the *Means of Achievement of Sitatapatraparajita (Sitātapatrāparajitāsādhana)* which is said to be by Chandragomin, the *Means of Achievement of the Five Guards (Pañcharakṣhāviddhi)* by Ratnakarashanti and Jetari [separate texts with the same title], the *Means of Achievement of Vimaloshnisha (Vimaloṣhnīṣhadhana* [?]*)* by the Foremost Elder Atisha, the *Ocean of Means of Achievement (Sādhanasāgara)*, the *One Hundred and Fifty Means of Achievement*, the *Hundred Means of Achievement*, etc. [Thus it should be analysed whether Buddhaguhya and Varabodhi mistook *Means of Achievement* based on Action Tantras for presentations of such tantra].

2. Buddhaguhya and so forth assert that even the *Vairochanabhisambodhi* and so forth are Action Tantras; therefore it should be analysed whether [their position] is based on a mixing of Action and Performance Tantras.
3. Or, perhaps [their position] is based on explanations by other masters that it is suitable to apply the format of Yoga Tantra to Action and Performance rites as is taught in the *Compendium of Principles (Tattvasaṃgraha)* [a Yoga Tantra]:

> The essence, seal, mantra, and knowledge
> Explained in the four sections [of this tantra]
> Are all achieved through whatever mode one wishes,
> [The rites of Yoga Tantra] itself or [the others].

4. Or, just as deities similar to [Highest Yoga ones] such as Pratisara, Marichi, and Parnashabari, as

> well as their mantras, appear in Action Tantras, so Sambhuta, etc., [usually associated with Action Tantra] also appear in Highest Yoga Tantras. Hence, it should be analysed whether the thought of Highest Yoga is being carried over to Action Tantra or whether the latter has self-generation in its own right.

[To refute the second hypothesis:] It is not that Buddhaguhya did not find a clear description of self-generation in Action Tantra and thus took the *Vairochanabhisambodhi* and *Vajrapani Initiation* [Performance Tantras], etc., as his sources. For Buddhaguhya asserts that the four-branched repetition is clearly taught in the *Vajroshnisha Tantra,* which is an Action Tantra.

The *Concentration Continuation*[13] [which is a continuation of or supplement to the *Vajroshnisha*][14] says, 'Flow to the bases, mind, and sound,' and Buddhaguhya's commentary says:

> This means that the characteristics of the branches of repetition and so forth, such as bases, mind, and sound, are not explained here because they were explained in this tantra [the *Vajroshnisha*] at the beginning. The characteristics which were explained there are these: 'Sound' is [the forms of] mantra letters. 'Mind' is the manifestation of a moon disc which is the base of the mantra. One 'base' is the entity of a Tathagata body. The second base is one's own [appearance in the] form of a deity. Furthermore, it should be known that since the characteristics of [stopping] vitality and exertion [breath and distraction], withdrawal [of the mind from external objects], and so forth were explained earlier in just this *Vajroshnisha Tantra,* they are not described here in this section called the *Concentration Continuation* which is related [with the *Vajroshnisha* as its continuation or supplement].

Thus, since the assumption of the form of one's own deity and so forth were explained earlier in the *Vajroshnisha Tantra,* they are not set forth here in the *Concentration Continuation* which is part of it. Also, there is no one who does not assert that the *Vajroshnisha* is an Action Tantra.

Buddhaguhya asserts that the four branches described here and in the *Vairochanabhisambodhi* are similar. His commentary on the *Concentration Continuation* says:

> For instance, the *Vairochanabhisambodhi Tantra*[15] says:
>
> > 'Letter' is the mind of enlightenment [appearing as a moon].
> > The second ['letters'] are called 'sounds' [the forms of the letters on the moon].
> > 'Base' is to imagine one's own body
> > As that of one's deity,
> > That called the second base
> > Is a perfect Buddha [imagined
> > In front], the best of the two-legged.
> > 'Vitality' is explained as wind,
> > 'Exertion' is mindfulness.
>
> Here [in the *Concentration Continuation*] one should view in a similar way the characteristics of the bases and so forth that were explained earlier [in the *Vajroshnisha Tantra*].

Therefore, if the meaning of the 'bases' [in the passage from the *Concentration Continuation*], 'Flow to the bases, mind, and sounds', could not refer to the base of generating oneself as a deity, one would have to assert that the two lines in the *Vairochanabhisambodhi,* ' "Base" is to imagine one's own body/ As that of one's deity', would not indicate generation of oneself as a deity since there is no difference between them.

[To refute the fourth hypothesis:] In some *Imaginations of Marichi* self-generation is indeed clearly described, and the terms 'stage of generation' and 'stage of completion' [which are exclusively found in Highest Yoga Tantra] are indeed used. If these are taken as Action Tantra, it is clearly wrong. If they are accepted as included within Highest Yoga [as is correct], they cannot serve as sources for the existence of self-generation in Action Tantra.

The *Concentration Continuation,* as well as Buddhaguhya's commentary, is very clear with respect to Action Tantras' having self-generation in their own right. This can also be known through Buddhaguhya's quoting in his *Commentary on the 'Vajravidarana Tantra' (Vajravidāranānāmaṭīkā)*[16] descriptions in the *Extensive Tantra of Vajravidarana* of meditation on the six deities (see p. 109).

[To refute the third hypothesis:] Anandagarbha's *Illumination of the 'Compendium of Principles' (Tattvālokarī)*[17], commenting on the early part of that text, says:

> Those who adhere to the rites of both [this] and Action and Performance Tantras, etc., should, through their [respective] rites, achieve the great seal and so forth which are explained here [in the *Compendium of Principles*]. To indicate this meaning, [that text] says:
>
> > The essence, seal, mantra, and knowledge
> > Explained in the four sections [of this tantra]
> > Are all achieved through whatever mode one wishes,
> > [The rites of Yoga Tantra] itself or [the others].

Essence, seal, mantra, and knowledge are explained respectively in [the descriptions of] the great mandala, retention mandala, doctrine mandala, and action mandala in all four sections of the *Compendium of*

Principles. These are said to be amenable to achievement through both the rites of Yoga Tantras themselves and the rites of Action and Performance Tantras. Therefore, it is clear that from the viewpoint of the *Compendium of Principles* also self-generation, entry of a wisdom-being, and so forth are suitable [to occur in Action and Performance Tantra since it says that their rites may be used].

[To refute the first hypothesis:] Also, it is clear that in consideration of the similarity of the deities and mantras, such as Marichi, that are described in both Action and Highest Yoga Tantras and using them only as illustrations, the *Ocean of Means of Achievement* and so forth frequently treat rites of generation and so on for deities explained in Action and Performance Tantras like Highest Yoga [and, therefore, are not suitable sources for Action and Performance. It is clear that Buddhaguhya and Varabodhi were not relying on such texts.][18]

Question: Then, what is the meaning of the passage from the *Wisdom Vajra Compendium* (p. 47)?

Answer: As Buddhaguhya says (p. 49), there are several types of trainees of Action Tantras who are frightened and terrified by the activity of single-pointed cultivation of deity yoga, who are not receptacles for using in the path deeds of desire — this being unusual or contrary to the world — who achieve the path through practices involving thoughts on features of faults such as birth, ageing, and so forth, in conjunction with the conception of true existence. It is said [in the *Wisdom Vajra Compendium*] that such trainees do not have generation of oneself as a deity or entry of a wisdom-being, but this does not apply to each and every trainee of Action Tantra, as in the case of the *Vajroshnisha Tantra* [which presents these]. Because such trainees are predominant in both Action and Performance, deity yoga is not obvious in them, and even those tantras that have it are not extensive. Nevertheless, the *chief* trainees of Action and Performance Tantras are not those who either do not like or are not able to cultivate one-pointedly a deity yoga by way of restraining vitality and exertion [breath and distraction], and so forth.

In accordance with the master Varabodhi's explanation (p. 52), even common beings practising Action and Performance Mantra are said to achieve the great feats of the sword [for flying in the sky], the pill [for immediately becoming youthful], and so forth, as well as the manifold activities of pacification [such as of evil spirits or illness] and so on. The *Vajrapani Initiation Tantra* clearly says that the achievement of these depends on deity and emptiness yogas:

> When a practitioner of the Bodhisattva deeds engaging[19] in the Secret Mantra approach causes himself to have the form of his own deity and with a mind free from doubt generates the pride [of being a deity] and whether going, standing, or sitting is always immovable [in this clear appearance and pride of a deity] though moving about, O Shantimati, he is endowed with the ethics of a great Bodhisattva who is practising the Bodhisattva deeds of the Secret Mantra approach.

Then it says that when he makes effort at yoga and acts in accordance with the ways shown by the deity, he is abiding in the conduct. When he performs the activities of repetition, burnt offering, and so forth within that conduct, he is performing the deeds. When, making effort at the yoga of non-difference with a deity and holding the bases of the training, he practises the Mahayana, he attains feats of Secret Mantra. Just after that, it says,

'Furthermore, a great Bodhisattva, a Bodhisattva practising the Bodhisattva deeds who engages in the Secret Mantra approach, should always abide in signlessness [deity yoga conjoined with the view of emptiness].' At the end of that, it clearly says:

> Abiding in the conduct,
> Ethics, deeds, and bases
> Of the training laid down
> By the perfect Buddha,
> A mantrika achieves mantra [feats].
> The past Conquerors became Buddhas
> Through non-conceptual wisdom,
> They taught that secret mantra [feats]
> Are achieved in the non-conceptual.
> The pure fruit of that is
> To become clear light by nature.
> For one who abides in thought
> Feats do not arise.
> Therefore abandon thought
> And think a mantra form.

'Abandon thought' refers to the eradication of thought conceiving self [inherent existence] through the wisdom of selflessness; it does not mean to stop any and all types of thought. 'Think a mantra form' means to meditate on a deity. The measure of firmness in deity yoga is indicated by 'whether going, standing, or sitting is always immovable though moving about'. When one has attained the capacity to hold the mind on the divine body in all types of behaviour — whether in meditative equipoise or not — without moving to something else, one has the capacity to remove the pride of ordinariness.

Although the two masters, Buddhaguhya and Varabodhi, do not describe entry of a wisdom-being into oneself [in their commentaries on Action and Performance Tantra], such entry is suitable, for it is described by many Indian scholars and adepts. Were it unsuitable, it would have to be because [a trainee of these tantras] holds himself and the deity — the wisdom-being — as separate and does not believe in holding them as one. However, this is not the case, for it is said that through the power of believing one's own body, speech, and mind to be undifferentiable from the deity's exalted body, speech, and mind all one's physical actions and movements are seals and all one's speech is mantra. In this way the *Vajrapani Initiation Tantra* says:

> A son or daughter of lineage[20] who has seen a mandala, who generates the mind of enlightenment, who is compassionate, skilled in means and in teaching the ways of letters — the door of Secret Mantra — should think thus, 'Separate from speech, there is no mind. Separate from mind, there is no speech. Separate from mind, there is no divine form. Mind itself is speech; speech itself is mind; divine form itself is also mind, and speech itself is also divine form.' If a mantra practitioner believes in this way that these are undifferentiable, he attains purity of mind. At those times when he has a pure mind, he always views in all ways his own body to be the same as the deity's body, his own speech to be the same as the deity's speech, and his own mind to be the same as the deity's mind; then, he is in meditative equipoise.
>
> When at all times in all ways
> A mantrika is in equipoise,
> Then he enters into a state of
> The sameness of body and so forth.
> Abiding in the state of sameness,
> Whatsoever movements of his limbs
> And whatsoever words spoken
> Are seals and secret mantras.

This is also similar in Action Tantra because, when generation of oneself as a deity occurs, one must apply the pride that is the thought that one is the actual deity being generated, whether it is Vairochana or any other.

Therefore, to view one's body as a deity, one's speech as mantra, and one's mind as absorbed in suchness is not a distinguishing feature of Highest Yoga. It is definitely required also in the lower tantra sets.

2

Structure

The individual explanation of the stages of the path in Action and Performance Tantras has two parts: (1) the general structure and (2) the actual stages of the path.

General Structure of the Path in Action and Performance Tantras

The *Concentration Continuation*[21] [an Action Tantra] says:

> Through effort to achieve secret mantra
> In three periods, this subtlety
> Is always known, O Brahma. The rites
> Of the ten branches are the activities.

It is said here that those who make effort at achieving mantra [deity yoga and all surrounding activities] know, that is, actualise, the conduct of knowledge mantra which has the nature of deity yoga and is subtle [hard to realise] in that it is known through concentration in three sessions [every day]. Thereupon, feats [special yogic powers described in chapter 9] are achieved. The branches [of this process] are included in ten topics which Buddhaguhya's commentary[22] explains as:

1. place of practice,
2. self principle,
3. knowledge of mantra principle,
4. repetition principle,

5. concentration of abiding in fire,
6. concentration of abiding in sound,
7. concentration bestowing liberation at the end of sound,
8. rites of engaging in mantra practice,
9. rites of burnt offerings,
10. initiation rites.

The self, knowledge mantra, and repetition principles[23] are the concentrations of the four-branched repetition [described in chapters 5, 6, and 7]. The concentrations of abiding in fire, abiding in sound, and bestowing liberation at the end of sound are the concentrations of the three principles which will be explained later [in chapter 8]. Those two groups of concentrations are the chief paths. The rites of engaging in mantra practice [described in chapters 4 and 7] are rites prior and subsequent[24] to practising those two groups of concentrations. Conferring initiation [briefly mentioned in chapter 2] makes [a trainee] into a receptacle suitable for cultivating these paths. [Rites of] burnt offerings [mentioned in chapter 8] are performed when effecting the achievement [of feats after preliminary approximation] and when engaging in activities [of pacification of illness, demons, etc., increase of wealth, lifespan, wisdom, etc., control of resources, power, etc., and ferocity — expelling harmful beings, etc. — after achieving such feats].

When through these approaches one gains ability, one achieves the manifold activities [of pacification, increase, and so forth that enhance progress on the path through amassing merit by helping others] whereby one completes the practices of enlightenment. In this way the meanings of both Action and Performance Tantras are included in the causal process of their trainees' enlightenment.

The Four General Action Tantras

From among the four general Action Tantras, the *Questions of Subahu* teaches the three [supramundane] lineages — Tathagata, vajra, and lotus — and the six lineages — [adding to those the three mundane lineages] Panchika, wealthy, and worldly. It also teaches their secret mantras, divisions of actions, and methods of pleasing. It condenses what was extensively explained and not condensed in some tantras, explains clearly what was taught only briefly in others, and teaches what was not mentioned in yet others. It for the most part does not clearly describe the four-branched concentration and the concentrations of the three principles [abiding in fire, abiding in sound, and bestowing liberation at the end of sound] but clearly and extensively describes the remaining rites for achieving mantra as well as how to achieve the groups of activities [see chapter 9].

The *General Secret Tantra (Guhyasāmānya)* mainly teaches the topics concerning making [trainees] into receptacles, for it shows how to draw the three thousand five hundred mandalas of the three [supramundane] lineages and teaches the general rites for conferring initiation and so forth. The *Susiddhi Tantra* is not very clear on the six concentrations [the three principles of self, knowledge mantra, and repetition as well as the three concentrations of abiding in fire, abiding in sound, and bestowing liberation at the end of sound] but clearly teaches the rites for achieving mantras [feats], the ways of achieving the groups of activities, burnt offerings, pledges to be kept, and so forth which are common to the three [supramundane] lineages. *The Concentration Continuation* teaches very clearly the six concentrations in general and in particular their branches, such as restraining vitality and exertion *(prāṇāyāma),* as well as the latter three concentrations [abiding in fire, abiding in sound, and bestowing liberation at the end of sound]. These are also common to the three [supramundane] lineages.

The Main Headings

When one understands the presentations of these, one knows well how the meaning units of the individual Action Tantras and Performance Tantras are brought together. It is convenient to condense them under four headings:

1. the topic of conferring initiation, thereby making a receptacle suitable for cultivating the path;
2. the topic of keeping pledges and vows which are the basis for achieving feats;
3. the topic of approximation for the sake of generating ability;
4. the topic of achieving feats for the sake of effecting one's own and others' welfare once one has attained ability.

Though there are many [texts describing] means of achieving deities based on Action and Performance Tantras, the texts of Buddhaguhya and Varabodhi appear to be good commentaries that accord with what occurs in these two tantras. Therefore, here I will explain Action and Performance Tantra in accordance with them.

Action Tantra

3

Pledges and Vows

The presentation of the stages of the path in Action Tantra has four parts: (1) how to become a receptacle suitable for cultivating the path, (2) having become a receptacle, how to maintain purity of pledges and vows, (3) how to perform prior approximation while abiding in the pledges, and (4) how to achieve feats once the approximation is serviceable.

How to Become a Receptacle Suitable for Cultivating the Path

Since I fear that the mandala rites together with the initiations would make this text very long, I will not write about them here. In my *Explanation of the Root Infractions* I have already described, with respect to Action and Performance Tantras, mere entry into a mandala and the initiations that are conferred on one who has entered. [Persons who have faith but are unable to keep the Bodhisattva vows and tantric pledges are allowed to enter a mandala but are not conferred initiation. They are allowed to enter because viewing a mandala with faith cleanses sins accumulated over many aeons and plants predispositions for becoming a suitable receptacle in the future. Persons able to keep the Bodhisattva vows and tantric pledges are conferred the water and crown initiations in Action Tantra, with the addition of the vajra, bell, and name initiations in Performance Tantra.][25]

Having Become a Receptacle, How to Maintain Purity of Pledges and Vows

In my *Explanation of the Root Infractions* I have extensively indicated the vows taken at the time of conferring initiation [these being the Bodhisattva vows since the tantric ones are limited to Yoga and Highest Yoga Tantra],[26] the root infractions of those vows, and so forth. Therefore, I will describe here the other pledges.

The 'Chapter on Knowledge Mantra Discipline' in the *Susiddhi Tantra*[27] says:

> I will explain the discipline
> Of repeating secret mantra,
> Through abiding in which repeaters
> Will quickly attain the feats.
>
> A wise practitioner does not despise
> Any of the secret mantras
> Or any of the gods or any
> Great being of repetition.
>
> A wise person does not fabricate
> Secret mantra rites or secret mantras
> And does not deride persons
> Who have a bad disposition.
>
> Even if the guru who reveals
> The mandala becomes of bad deeds,
> He never derides him
> With speech or with mind.
>
> A wise person does not use
> Knowledge mantras in anger
> For suppression or for binding,
> Cutting, defeating, or fierceness.
>
> He does not assume a secret mantra
> Unless another grants permission.
> Though he knows the rite he does not give secret
> mantras
> To one without reverence and respect.

One who is skilled in tantra does not give
Secret mantras, seals, the details of rites,
Or explanations of tantras and mandalas
To one who has not entered a mandala.

Do not eat or step over any
Of the varieties of seals,
All likenesses of weapons
And of sentient beings.

An intelligent practitioner
Does not deride the medicines,
He does not let filth touch them
Nor let his foot pass over them.

Those of the Mahayana and the intelligent
Should not debate [out of competitiveness].
Having heard [about] the strong Bodhisattvas
One should not disbelieve [their powers].

Never compete with practitioners
Through the use of mantras.
Do not engage in fierceness
Having angered at small faults.

One abiding in a repetition rite
Should not sing, dance, or play,
Nor wear garlands and colours
For the sake of gaining beauty.

Completely abandon
Stepping over [others], jumping,
Running, making clamour,
And physical bad forms.

An abider in true practice
Should forsake false, cruel, altered,
Harsh, and divisive speech,
And not make much senseless talk.

Do not live with or
Argue with Forders,[28]
Nor repeat secret mantra with those
Of bad lineage such as butchers.

When the intelligent repeat,
Except for just a mantra servant,
They do not talk at all
With others without purpose.

Do not annoint the body with oils,
Also do not eat sesame.[29]
One wanting feats should completely
Forsake turnip, garlic, salts,

As well as the different
Varieties of sour condiments,
Sour yeast,[30] peas, sesame yeast,
Sesame candy, and red beans.

A repeater of secret mantra
Should forsake all foods of bringers of harm,[31]
All sacrificial food,
Kṛsara and milk-soup.

Do not mount chariots and so forth,
Nor step on lotuses and the like.
Do not let your foot touch
Food which has been thrown away.

A repeater of secret mantra
Should abandon all acts of charm,
Holding shoes and umbrellas [for show],
And all adornment[32] of the body.

Do not rub a foot with a foot,
Nor rub a hand with a hand.
Do not dispose of faeces and urine in water,
Nor dispose of it near water.

Do not eat in just the hands,
Nor in a bronze bowl.
Also do not eat from leaves.[33]
The wise eat not desirous food.[34]

A wise practitioner
Does not sleep with others
On beds or couches in uncleanliness
Nor supine, nor with face down.

Do not eat again and again,
Nor very little nor too much.
Do not not eat at all,
Do not eat what you doubt.

Do not take pleasure in the strange,
Nor look at any amusements,
Do not desire with a mind of attachment
Unbridled behaviour[35] with regard to women.

An abider in a repetition rite
Should not at all use food and activities
Without physical, verbal,
And mental restraint.

A wise householder repeater
Does not wear clothes of dyed colour,
He also does not at all
Wear old or smelly clothing.

Do not deride yourself,
Do not dislike yourself,
Do not become depressed,
Nor let illness overpower.

Except in response [to one's guru]
You should not leave off secret mantra.
With obscured mind deride not [mantra repetition]
Nor let your firmness be loosened.

A repeater should say a secret mantra
Without his mind's straying to anything else,
Without many thoughts and without
Thoughts of desire for the unclean.

Do not perform rites for [expelling] demons
Nor protections or reversals.
A repeater should not perform poisonous rites,
With his own mantra or through others.

Except when they are needed for practice
Do not use secret mantras in other ways.
Do not use secret mantras for
Competition or for testing prowess.[36]

The intelligent should repeat three times
And should bathe three times [every day].

Also:[37]

A practitioner should especially
Do worship on the eighth,
Fourteenth, and fifteenth, and
For half the month of magical display.[38]

He should respectfully make efort
In repetition, burnt offering, offering,
Likewise in keeping the vows,
And particularly in the meritorious.

Also:[39]

A repeater should always think of the sayings
In the discipline of knowledge mantra,
'Do this, do not do that',
And the vows of the precepts.[40]

Night and day[41] you should forsake
Desire for your own pleasure,
Be without slothfulness toward
'Having done these, this should be done.'

At night individually confess
Deeds done without awareness during the day,
Those done at night confess in the morning,
Thoroughly rejoice in what was done well.

A practitioner should earnestly abide
In repetition, burnt offering, cleanliness,
Superior knowledge mantras, self-restraint,
And the discipline of knowledge mantra.

It is said that *kṛsara* (p. 72) is a stew of boiled black sesame, red bean, and rice mixed together.

It is unsuitable to bestow a mantra on one who has not entered a mandala. The *General Tantra* says:

If one not having seen well
A mandala repeats a mantra,
He will not attain the feats and
After death will fall to a bad state.

Whoever shows to him
Rites of mantras and seals
Falls from his pledges and goes
To a hell of grieving beings.

Therefore, it is in all ways unsuitable for one who has not entered a mandala of any of the four tantras and received initiation to achieve a deity and so forth based only on a rite of permission. It is also unsuitable for a mantra to be granted to such a person. With regard to the way to purify the sin if such is done, the same text says:

If you fall from the pledges
Just explained, you should repeat
Your essence mantra
A hundred thousand times.

Or it is suitable to repeat a thousand times
The retention mantra of mental non-obscuration,
Or perform a burnt offering of pacification,
Or it is suitable to enter a mandala.[42]

You should make effort in these ways and purify [the sin].

Ratnakarashanti's *Precious Lamp, Commentary on the Difficult Points of the 'Krishnayamari Tantra' (Kṛṣhṇa-yamāripañjikāratnapradīpa)*[43] [a Highest Yoga Tantra], after setting forth those pledges, says:

Though I have gathered these pledges from Action Tantras, yogis of the Great Yoga [Highest Yoga Tantra] should keep whatever are suitable in accordance with their area, time, and thought. Those who say that they are yogis of the great yoga and wish to be unclean and unrestrained are not right. For even Action Tantras say that in accordance with one's thoughts and so forth:[44]

> Being clean is suitable, being unclean is suitable,
> Eating food is suitable, not eating is suitable,
> Bathing is suitable, not bathing is suitable,
> Through being mindful of one's deity, achievement comes.

Such statements of looseness occur, but mostly yogis of even the Great Yoga do not transgress the above-mentioned pledges.

Thus, not only are these to be kept by those who have received Action and Performance initiations but also by those engaging in Highest Yoga. Therefore, identifying these and the root infractions, one should strive to be totally unpolluted by root infractions, and even if one is polluted by other faults they should be confessed and purified. It is said that one should not be heedless of faults but at night amend those which occurred during the day and in daytime amend those which occurred at night.

4

Preliminaries

The presentation of how to perform prior approximation while abiding in the pledges has two parts: reasons for prior approximation and its stages.

Reasons for Prior Approximation

The *Concentration Continuation*[45] says:

> The concentrations of secret mantra
> Are said to be supremely secret.
> Achievement will not occur without them
> For even the great ascetic sages.

Thus, it is said that if they do not have the two concentrations [with and without repetition] which will be explained [in this and the next four chapters], even sages striving at mantra and having ethics, disciplined conduct, and asceticism do not achieve [feats of pacification, increase, and so forth].

The 'Chapter on Feats' in the *Vairochanabhisambodhi Tantra* says:

> If one wishes to attain
> The great waves of wisdom
> Or the five clairvoyances[46]
> Or the feats of holding the knowledge mantras
> Or long life becoming a youth,
> As long as this approximation
> Is not done, so long are these not attained.

This fact is similar in both Action and Performance Tantras.

Therefore, the 'Chapter on the Character of Mantras' in the *Susiddhi Tantra* says:

> After analysing one's lineage,
> Nature, powers, and activities
> Approximation to secret mantra[47]
> Agreeable to one's own mind is begun.

Thus, you should attain well an initiation in a mandala of the three lineages [Tathagata, lotus, or vajra], come to possess the Bodhisattva vows and mantra pledges, and become skilled in the stages of what to do. You should assemble in complete form the place, companions for practice, and so forth, with their qualities as taught in the *Susiddhi Tantra* and the *Questions of Subahu Tantra.* Then, you should perform the preliminary approximation cultivating the two concentrations [with and without repetition] together with their branches.

With respect to initiation, the *General Tantra* says:

> One who has been conferred initiation well
> In a mandala of the Tathagata lineage
> Becomes a master of the mandalas
> And so forth of all three lineages.

If initiation is obtained in a mandala of the Tathagata lineage,[48] you become a master of all three lineages. With initiation of the lotus lineage, you become a master of the lotus and vajra lineages, and with that of the vajra lineage, you become a master of just that lineage. You still must receive the oral transmission of the meditation and repetition of the mantra being practised.

Stages of Approximation

This section has two parts: concentrations with and without repetition.

Concentration With Repetition

This section has three parts: how to perform the preliminaries to the four-branched repetition, the actual concentration, and how to conclude[49] it.

How to Perform the Preliminaries to the Four-Branched Repetition

This section has four parts: (1) what to do initially in the place of dwelling, (2) how to bathe outside and enter the place of practice, (3) having enrobed and sat on the cushion, blessing the offerings, and (4) protecting oneself and the place.

What to Do Initially in the Place of Dwelling
Making the seal and reciting the mantra of the general lineage.[50]

Daily, when you have risen from bed in the early morning for the first session and at the beginning of other sessions, you should construct the pledge seal of whichever of the three lineages you are practising and then utter the [respective] secret mantra.

Tathagata Lineage
Having turned up the palms, bend the two forefingers a little (seal 1). Having placed this on the head, say:
Oṃ tathāgata-udbhavaye svāhā.

Lotus Lineage
Join the palms; then form them in the manner of a blossoming lotus (seal 2). Having placed this at the heart, say:
Oṃ padma-udbhavaye svāhā.

Vajra Lineage
Reverse and join the palms; join the two thumbs and two

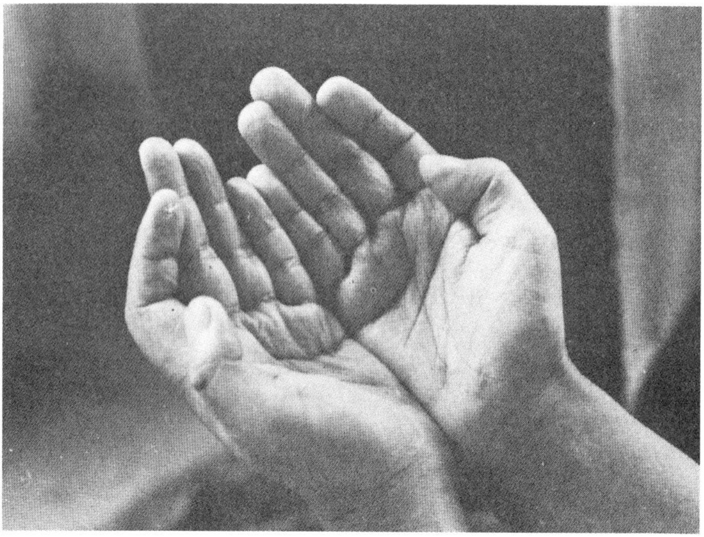

Seal 1

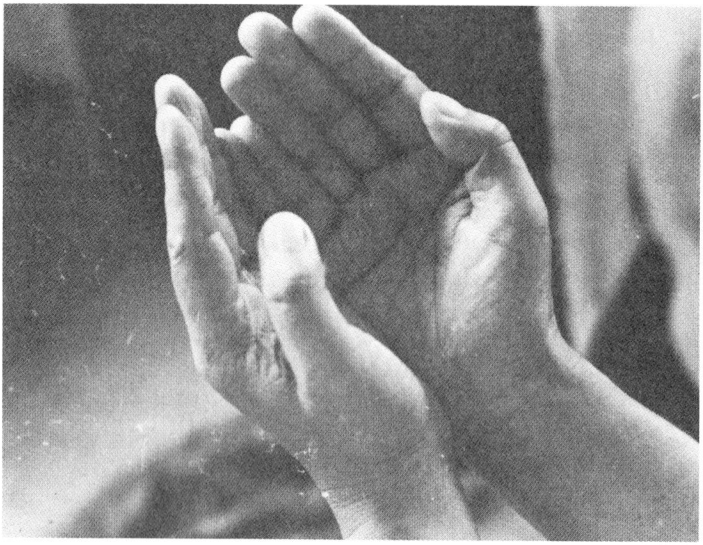

Seal 2

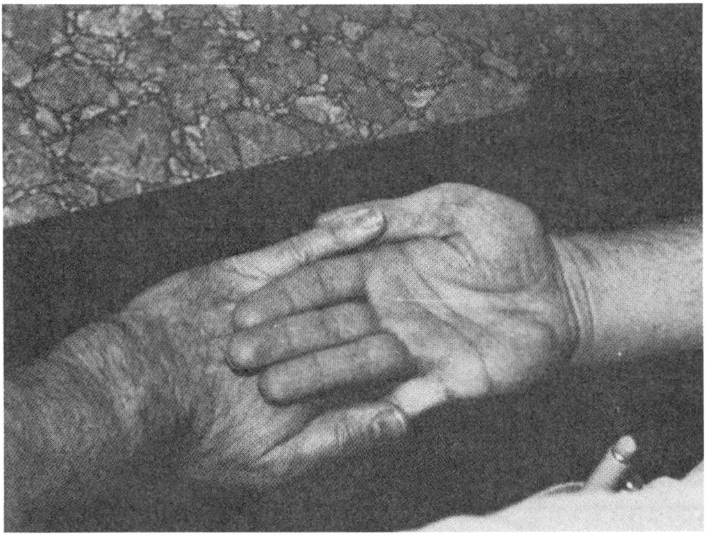

little fingers (seal 3). Having placed this at the navel, say: *Oṃ vajra-udbhavaye svāhā.*

Respectively, these are the seals and mantras of the Tathagata lineage such as Ushnishavijaya, the lotus lineage such as Avalokiteshvara, and the vajra lineage such as Vajravidarana.

Homage to the Buddhas and Bodhisattvas. Then, observing all the Buddhas in the ten directions, bow down at their feet with this mantra:
Oṃ sarva-tathāgata kāya-vāk-chitta-vajra-praṇamena sarva-tathāgata-vajra-pāda-vandanaṃ karomi.

Offering Yourself. Then, offer your body, saying:

> 'If until I am in the essence of enlightenments, I totally and thoroughly offer myself at all times to all Buddhas and Bodhisattvas abiding in the ten directions, may the great Buddhas and Bodhisattvas please take me. Please bestow upon me the unsurpassed feat [Buddhahood].'

Refuge and altruistic mind generation. Then, take refuge and generate the altruistic mind of enlightenment with:

> To Buddha, Doctrine, and Supreme Community
> I go for refuge until enlightenment.
> To achieve the welfare of myself and others
> I will generate the mind of enlightenment.
>
> 'Listen, O Buddhas and Bodhisattvas
> Abiding in the ten directions,
> I now for the sake of perfect enlightenment
> Will generate the mind of enlightenment.

Protection through secret mantra and seal. Then create protection with the seal and mantra of the Fierce Unobscured One.[51] The seal is to interlace the fingers of the two hands, making a fist; align and straighten the two

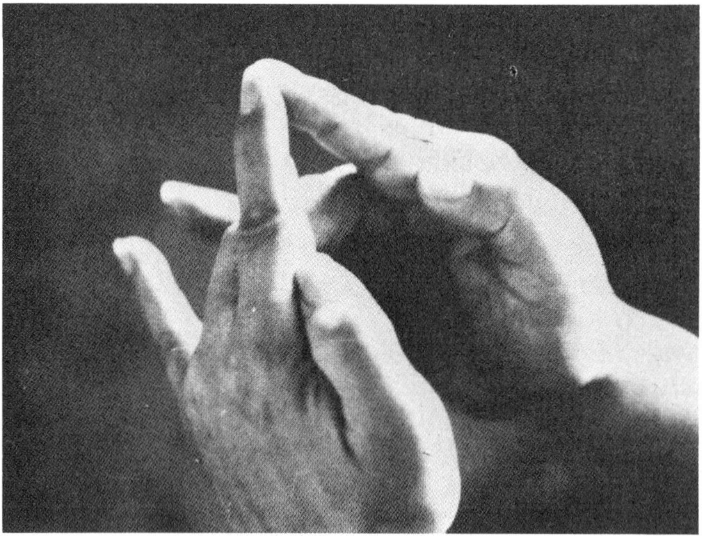

little fingers. Set the two thumbs beside the forefingers, the tips of which are joined (seal 4). The mantra is: *Oṃ vajra-krodha mahābālā hana daha pacha vidhvaṃsaya uchchhuṣhma krodha hūṃ phaṭ.*

Create protection with this mantra also when eating, drinking, urinating, and defecating.

Reflection on purity. Then, think that these letters with inter-connected flames — *ma* which is the entity of Vairochana on a moon at one's heart and *ha* which is the entity of Achala at one's head — are stirred. Say:[52]
Oṃ svabhāva-shuddhāḥ sarva-dharmāḥ svabhāva-shuddho 'haṃ.
Believe that [all phenomena are][53] naturally pure.

Going outside. Then, come out of the dwelling place; use the tooth-stick [for cleaning the teeth] and so forth. Collect and remove [the dirt and dust] in the temple and so forth.[54]

How to Bathe Outside and Enter the Place of Practice[55]

Then, in order to bathe go to a shore where beings do not gather and where there is no fright.

Picking up earth. Interlace the fingers of the two hands on the outside and bend them. Align and straighten the two forefingers, placing the two thumbs at their base (seal 5). Touch this seal to clean earth, and say:[56]
Oṃ nikhanavasude svāhā.

Pick up the earth, and dividing it into three portions, put these in a clean place. With respect to that, first construct whichever of the three pledge seals indicated earlier (pp. 79–81) is appropriate and then pick up the earth.

Self-protection. Then, create self-protection through Amritakundali. Pressing the nails of the little fingers with the thumbs, form the remaining fingers into a symbol of a vajra. Then, crossing [the arms], place these on the

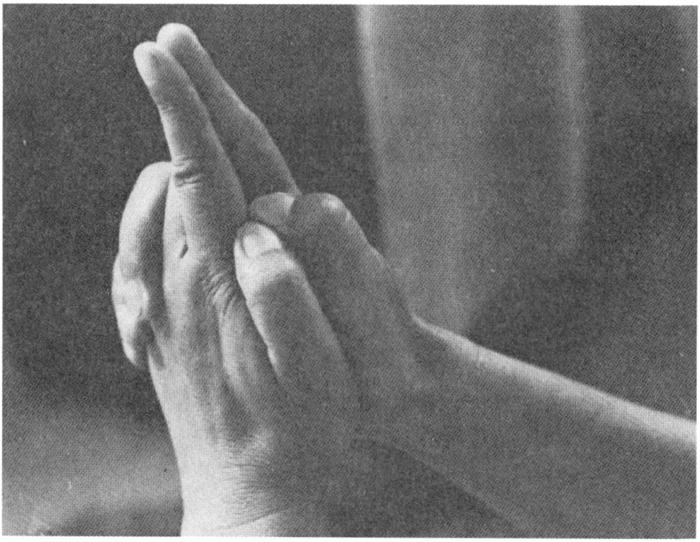

Seal 5

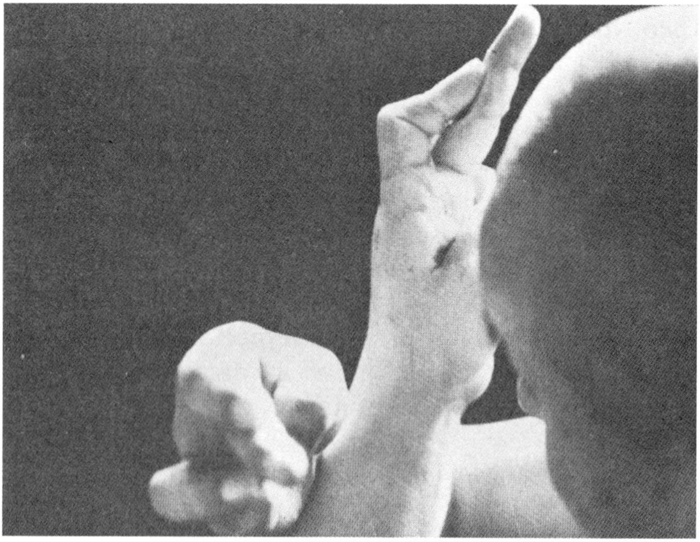

Seal 6

shoulders (seal 6). Press the lower lip with the upper teeth and look with a fierce gaze. Say:
Namo ratnatrayāya, namaṣhchaṇḍa-vajrapāṇaye, mahā-yakṣhasena-pataye, namo vajra-krodhāya, tadyathā oṃ hulu hulu tiṣhṭha tiṣhṭha bandha bandha hana hana amṛte hūṃ phaṭ.

Expelling obstructors in the body. Say:
Oṃ hana hana amṛte hūṃ phaṭ.

Bind the two fists inside; having let out and straightened the forefingers, cast this from the head to the feet (seal 7). Thereby, expel obstructors from the body.

Creating vajra armour. Then say:
Oṃ vajra-agni-pratipataye svāhā.

Having turned up the palms, set the two ring-fingers between the two interlaced little fingers. Align and straighten the two middle fingers, and bend the forefingers to the third joint of the middle fingers. Joining the two thumbs, place them in the centre (seal 8). Making

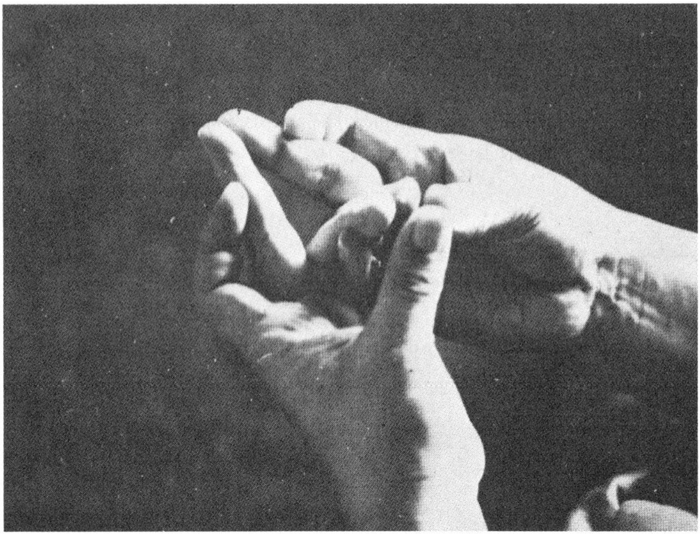

Seal 8

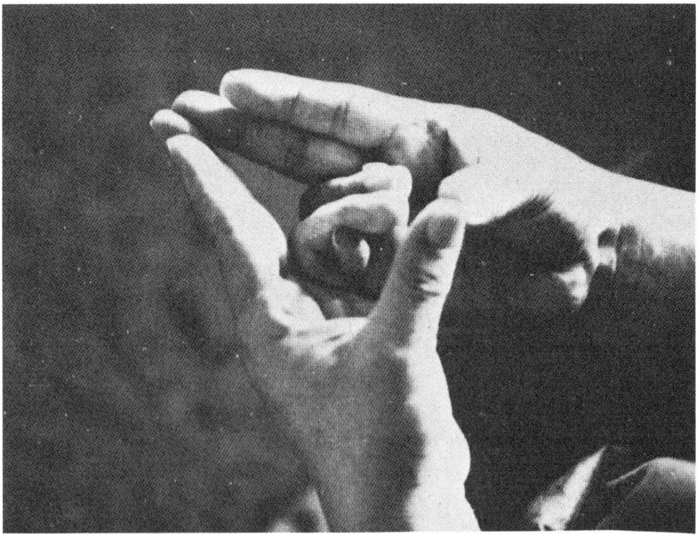

Seal 9

this seal, put on the vajra armour [to prevent obstructors from entering].

From that seal make the seal of vajra armour. Having spread out the two forefingers, form them in the manner of a vajra (seal 9). Say:[57]

Namo ratnatrayāya oṃ khakili hūṃ phaṭ.

Make the armour [in the sense of imagining vajra armour], touching the head, the tops of both shoulders, heart, and neck.

Dispelling obstructors. Then say:[58]

Namo vajrāya hūṃ hana dhuna matha vidhvaṃsaya udsarāya phaṭ.

Press the two middle fingers of the left hand with the thumb, and forming the forefinger and little finger in the manner of a circlet, stick them in the middle joints of the

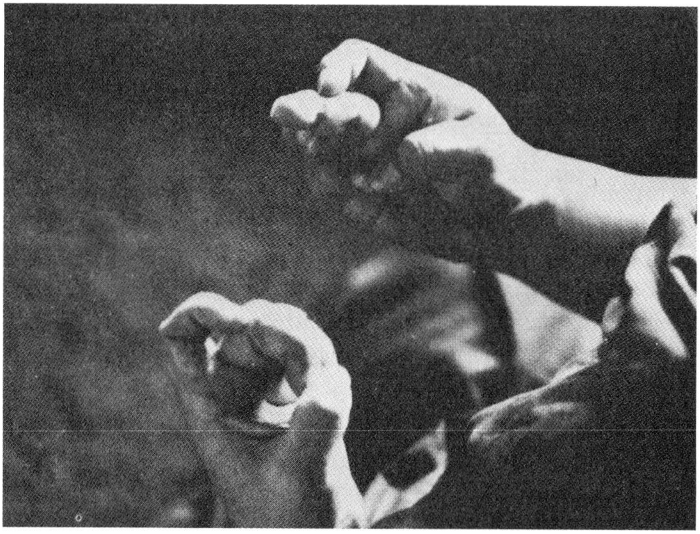

middle fingers. Form the three middle fingers of the right hand in the manner of a vajra and place this in the area of the waist (seal 10). Touch earth or water with this seal of dispelling obstructors. Since [Varabodhi] explains that this dispells obstructors, first touch earth and water.

Casting mantra into the water. Then, cast this mantra into the water:
Namo ratnatrayāya, namaṣhchaṇḍa-vajrapāṇaye, oṃ hana hana vajra vajraṇaha.

Sprinkling the earth. Say:
Oṃ kīlikīla vajra hūṃ phaṭ.

With the thumb of the left hand press the nail of the little finger, and form the remaining fingers into a symbol of a vajra (seal 11). Touch this seal of Kilikila to the water, and sprinkle the earth with the water.

Mantrafying the earth. Then, pick up one portion of the earth, having mantrafied it seven times with:
Oṃ vajra hara hūṃ.

Wearing the bathing cloth, enter into the water just to the disappearance of the navel, and bathe [washing below the navel with the first portion of earth].[59]

Ablution. Then, wash the hands with the second portion of earth. Say:
Oṃ shruti smṛti dharini hūṃ ha.

Having turned upward the palm of the right hand, place the forefinger at the base of the thumb and put the thumb at the centre joint of the forefinger (seal 12). Perform ablution [of the tops of the shoulders, mouth, nose, eyes, and ears] with this seal of Sarasvati. The *Questions of Subahu* says to perform ablution[60] at this point; it seems that the master Varabodhi holds that just the seal and mantra serve as ablution.

Protecting and tying up the hair. Then, say:
Oṃ susiddhikari svāhā.

Tying up the hair on the head, create protection.

Seal 11

Seal 12

Mantrafying, circling, and rubbing earth on the body. Pick up the third portion of earth, and mantrafy it:
Oṃ bhūr jala hūṃ phaṭ.

Turning it to the right, face it to the sun, and then rub it on the [entire] body.[61]

Stirring the water. Then, recite:
Namo ratnatrayāya, namaṣhchaṇḍa-vajrapāṇaye, mahā-yakṣha-sena-pataye, namo vajra-krodhāya daṃṣhṭotkaṭa bhairavāya tadyathā, oṃ amṛtakuṇḍali khakha khāhi khāhi tiṣhṭha tiṣhṭha bandha bandha hana hana, garja garja, visphoṭāya visphoṭāya sarva-vighnāṃ vinayakāna, mahā-gaṇa-pati jivita antakarāya svāhā.

Having turned upward the palm of the right hand, bend the middle and ring fingers, and press them with the tip of the thumb. Bend slightly the forefinger and the little finger (seal 13). Stir the water with this seal of water-stirring.

Offering to the Three Jewels. Say:
Oṃ rate rate buddhāya svāhā.
Offer three handfuls of water to the Three Jewels.

Pouring water on the head. Then, say:
Oṃ amṛte hūṃ phaṭ.
Pour three double handfuls on your head and wash your hands. With that mantra confer initiation on yourself with three double handfuls of water.

Inviting the deity and bathing his body. Mentally invite your own deity and ask him to reside on a lotus [imagined in front of yourself].[62] Bathe his body, saying:
Oṃ sarva-tathāgata-amṛta svāhā.
Then, if repetition is to be done in the temple, repeat the mantra[63] twenty-one times while in the water.

Importance of bathing. The 'Chapter on Repetition' in the *Susiddhi Tantra* says:

> The wise should not apply those
> Repetitions done without
> Restraint or cleanliness to the number
> Of repetitions that are prescribed.

Thus it is said that repetitions done without the cleanliness of bathing and so forth cannot fulfil the count of repetitions; therefore, you should abide in cleanliness.

If extensive bathing cannot be accommodated, it is clear that it is sufficient to bathe with earth and water until the grime is removed. The *Questions of Subahu* says:

> Five masses of earth at the anus, three to the [sexual] sign,
> Three for the left, and seven for the two hands,
> Or use earth and water until
> You become free of defilement.

Entering the temple and engaging in the pledges. Then, go up to the temple; wash the feet; facing east or north, do the ablution.[64] Enter the place and, visualising the deities vividly, do homage [as on p. 81].[65] Then, repeat this engagement in the pledges:
Oṃ viraja viraja mahāmvajri, sata sata sarate sarate, trayi trayi virdhamani saṃbhañjani taramati siddha-agretaṃ svāhā.

Having Enrobed and Sat on the Cushion, Blessing the Offerings[66]

Removing contamination. Then, pour scented water in the palm of the hand and repeat the essence mantra of the appropriate lineage [three times][67] (p. 95). Sprinkling it on top of the head, clear away defects of contamination and so forth.

Sprinkling the cushion and sitting. Having sprinkled the cushion [made] of *kusha* grass or other material together with [reciting the mantra of] Kundali (p. 85), sit on the cushion in either the lucky, lotus, or vajra cross-legged manner.[68]

Putting on the circlet and so forth. Then, affix a circlet to the wrist of the right hand and a sprinkler [made] of *kusha* grass to the ring finger of the right hand. Tie on the *ze'ukha* [a piece of red silk or cotton bound on the head] and [tie up the hair as an][69] image of the crown protrusion, as explained earlier (p. 88) [with the mantra *oṃ susiddhikari svāhā*].

With respect to the circlet, an uneven number of threads spun by a girl should be wound and tied in an uneven number of knots. Having affixed one rosary bead of the appropriate lineage [such as a seed of *putranjïva roxburghii* for the Tathagata lineage][70] in the centre, repeat the mantra of your own [respective lineage]. These are the knowledge mantras of the circlets, [the mantras of] the lineage mothers:

Tathagata Lineage
Oṃ ruru spuru jvala-tiṣhṭha-siddha-lochane sarva-artha-sādhani svāhā.

Lotus Lineage
Homage to the Three Jewels. Homage to the Bodhisattva, the great being, the Superior Avalokiteshvara.

> May I cure all illness
> Of all sentient beings
> Through [their] seeing, hearing,
> Touching, or remembering [me].

Tadyathā kaṭe vikaṭe kaṃkaṭe kaṭa vikaṭe, kaṃkaṭe bhagavati vijaye svāhā.

Vajra Lineage[71]
Oṃ kulandhari bandha bandha hūṃ phaṭ.
It is explained that when the circlet has been anointed with incense, the mantra should be repeated a hundred times.[72] Concerning the benefit of these, the 'Chapter on the Knowledge Mantra Discipline' in the *Susiddhi Tantra* says:

> Through these one will not be
> Overpowered by obstructors.
> Through saying these one will quickly
> Attain feats and become pure.

Concerning the sprinkler [made] of *kusha* grass, the *Susiddhi Tantra* says:

> One who has individually repeated
> The three syllables of the lineage essence,
> *Jinajik, ārolik,*[73] *vajradhrk,*
> Should put on his ring finger
> A sprinkler [made] of *kusha* grass.
> When a practitioner strives,
> His hands become pure through this.

The mantra to be cast in the *ze'u kha* — the skull binder made from red silk or cotton — is the mantra to be cast in clothing that will be set forth below (p. 153) Clothing should [also] be implanted with that mantra and then worn.

Holding the vajra.[74] Make a three-pointed vajra from wood pierced by lightning, *nimba (azadirachta indica),* a charred piece of funeral wood, sandalwood, or other [wood]. Wash it well; rub on red sandalwood [in a water solution] and generate [that is, imagine] it as a fierce Susiddhi [after reflecting on its emptiness]. Having invited a likeness of him, perform offering and so forth. At the initial ceremony [after making the vajra], repeat a thousand times and on other occasions seven times:
Oṃ dhuna vajra hā.

Make this petition:

> Blessed One, abide in me out of mercy. Please perform all my actions [such as protecting from obstructors].

When making offerings and so on to the action vajra, hold it with the left hand. Every day make offerings to it and mantrafy it seven times with his mantra [given just above]. The *Susiddhi Tantra* says that through holding it obstructors, false leaders, and harmers will take fright and leave.

Dispelling obstructors.[75] Then, preceded by refuge and generation of an altruistic mind of enlightenment [as done earlier, p. 82], repeat into the scented water with the mantra either of all the activities of [the appropriate among] the three lineages (p. 96) or of Kundali, explained earlier, *namo ratna-trayāya* . . . (p. 85). Clear away obstructors in the flowers and so forth through sprinkling [them with scented water]. Dispel them with scented water put in the left hand [into which] the appropriate[76] secret mantra of the lineage lord or lineage essence such as *jinajik* [for the Tathagata lineage, *ārolik* for the lotus lineage, and *vajradhṛk* for the vajra lineage has been repeated].

Generating magnificence. Then, from the seal of dispelling obstructors explained earlier (p. 87, seal 10), take hold of the [left] middle finger with the three middle fingers of the right formed in the manner of a vajra (seal 14). With this seal of generating magnificence distribute

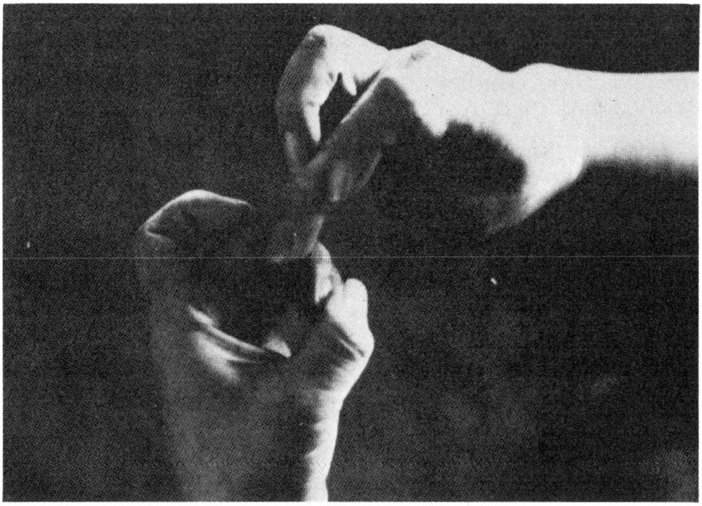

[the magnificence] on top of the perfume, flowers, and so forth and repeat the mantra of generating magnificence. Think that through these the offerings have become marvellous divine articles. The mantras of the three lineages are:

Tathagata Lineage
Oṃ tejaḥ tejaḥ sani siddhi sādhaya hūṃ phaṭ.

Lotus Lineage
Oṃ divya divya dhipaya, avesha mahāshrīyaye svāhā.

Vajra Lineage
Oṃ jvala jvalaya bandhṛ hūṃ phaṭ.

Then, bless them with the mantra of Kundali explained earlier (p. 85), and repeat the essence mantra of the appropriate lineage (p. 95).

Self-Protection[77]

Either make the seal and mantra expelling obstructors in the body[78] explained earlier (p. 85) or protect yourself with another that you know. Then repeat the mantra for all activities of [the appropriate among] the three lineages or the mantra of Kundali into the scented water and sprinkle it on yourself, dispelling obstructors. The mantra of Kundali is *namo ratnatrayāya . . . amṛte hūṃ phaṭ.* (p. 85). The mantras for all activities of the three lineages are:

Tathagata Lineage
Oṃ traṃ bandha svāhā.

Lotus Lineage
Oṃ namo mahā-shrīyāyai, sau me siddhi siddhi sādhaya, shivi shivaṃkari, abhaha, sarva-artha-sādhani svāhā.

Vajra Lineage
Oṃ kīlikīla vajra hūṃ phaṭ.

Place-Protection[79]

Circle of protection. Meditate on the circle of protection. Repeat into the scented water seven times:
Oṃ kīlikīla vajri vajri bhur bandha bandha hūṃ phaṭ.
Perform the sprinkling in all directions.

Creating the ritual dagger. Make the ritual dagger seal. Form the middle and ring fingers of both hands mutually like circlets, and join the tips [of the ring and middle fingers] at the base of each. Align and straighten the two little fingers and forefingers. Form the thumbs in the

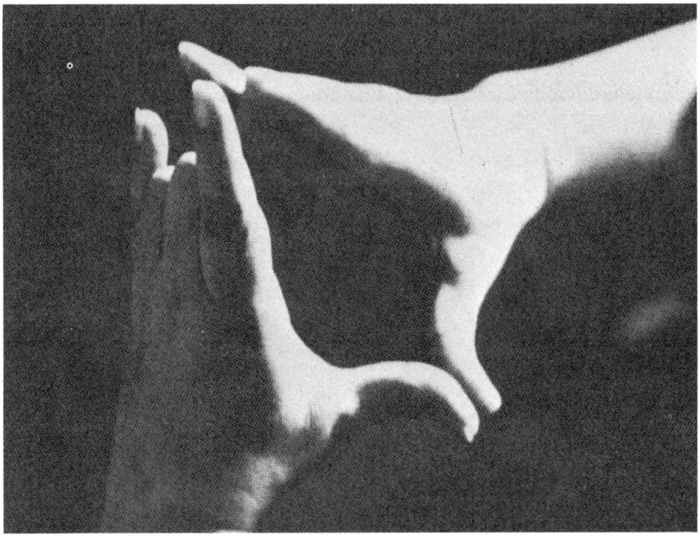

manner of a ritual dagger and set this on the earth (seal 15). Recite the mantra just explained [for the circle of protection] and implant the ōbstructors with the fierce Vajra Daggers [generated as fierce deities]. Think that thereby they have become immovable.[80]

Fumigation. Infuse them with the fumes [of powdered incense] in which you have repeated:

Oṃ susiddhikara jvalita, ananta-murtaye jvala jvala bandha bandha hana hana hūṃ phaṭ.

Think that the upper gods[81] are bound [the lower having been bound in the last step]. That mantra is a general one for the three lineages. [Otherwise] for the Tathagata lineage say:

Oṃ jvala hūṃ.

For the lotus lineage say:

Oṃ padmini bhagavati mohaya mohaya, jagad mohani svāhā.

In both the [*Susiddhi*] *Tantra* and Varabodhi's *Clear Realisation* a separate one does not appear for the vajra lineage.

Binding obstructors. Then sprinkle the area and surroundings with the scented water into which the lineage essence mantra (p. 95) has been repeated. Think that all obstructors of the directions are bound by this mantra:

Bhrūṃ oṃ amṛtodbhava udbhava hūṃ phaṭ, namo ratnatrayāya, namaṣhchaṇḍa-vajrapāṇaye, mahā-yakṣha-senapataye, oṃ sumbhani sumbha hūṃ, gṛhṇa gṛhṇa hūṃ, gṛhṇapaya gṛhṇapaya hūṃ, ānayaho bhagavān vidyā-rāja hūṃ phaṭ svāhā.

That[82] is the secret mantra of the knowledge kings of the three lineages.

Creating a fence. Then, from the dagger seal (seal 15), make the fence seal, extending the two thumbs upward (seal 16). Say:

Namo ratnatrayāya, namaṣhchaṇḍa-vajrapāṇaye, mahā-yakṣha-sena-pataye, tadyathā oṃ sara sara vajra-prakara hūṃ phaṭ.

Think that thereby a vajra fence[83] encircles [the area] without break.

Creating a latticework. Displaying the fence seal itself (seal 16) upside down, move it in a circle (seal 17). Think

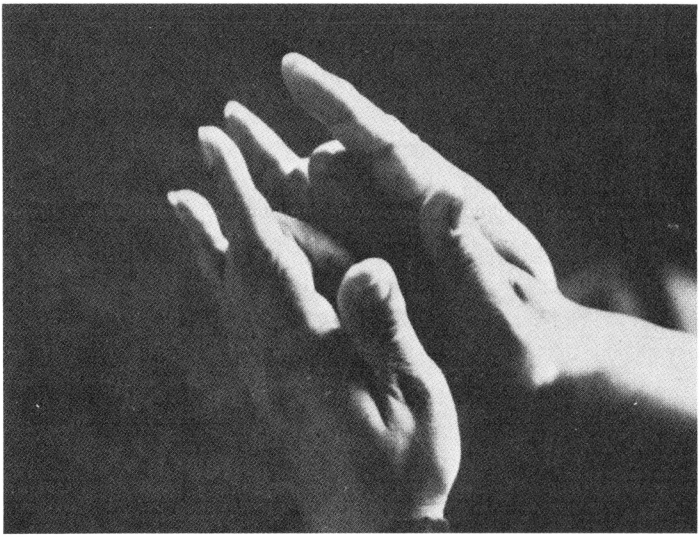

Seal 16

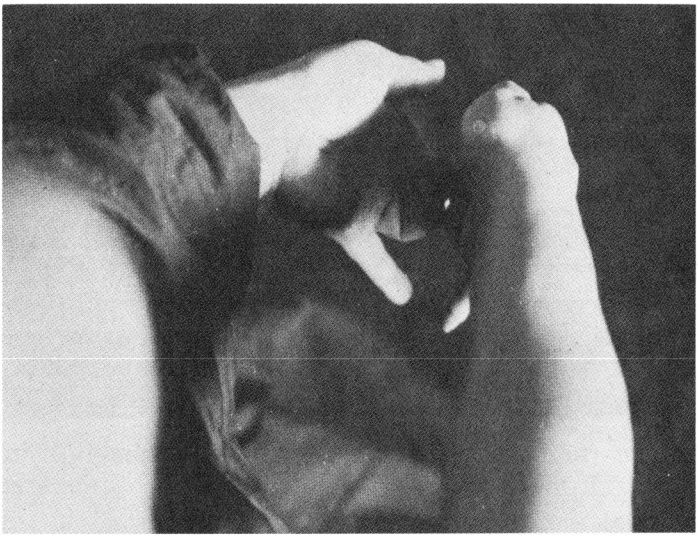

Seal 17

that a vajra latticework or tent emerges on top of the vajra fence [like a roof, saying]:
Namo ratnatrayāya, namaṣhchaṇḍa-vajrapāṇaye, mahā-yakṣha-sena-pataye, oṃ visphu-rakṣha-vajrapāṇi hūṃ phaṭ.

Then, empower these [that is, the fence and roof] with the mantras and seals of Kundali and Kilikila explained earlier (pp. 85 and 88), seals 6 and 11; for the Kilikila mantra see p. 97).[84] The *Susiddhi Tantra* explains that the two fierce ones [Kundali and Kilikila] are always associated with the fence, latticework, and daggers surrounding the house [in the sense of abiding there as protection].

Closing off the area. Then, make fists; press the nails with the thumbs. Let out the forefinger and encircle from the

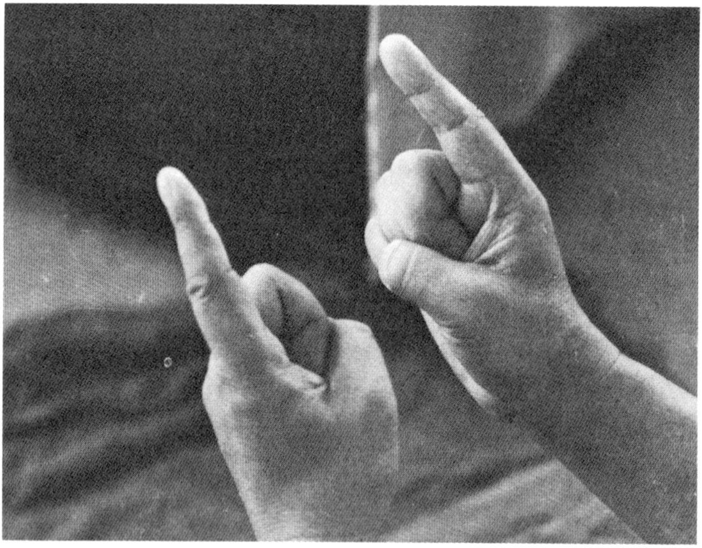

middle (seal 18). Thinking that a blazing mass of fire covers all the directions of the fence, close off the area [saying]:[85]
Namaḥ samanta-vajranāṃ, oṃ tara tara, turu turu, maṭa maṭa, bandha bandha, sarvatra apratihate, sasime

samabandha, kuru kuru tara tara samanta-vajre, samanta-vajre, kuru amale kuruṇa, maye tutaye tutaye, bara bara, kara kara sumima samanta, vidhvaṃsaye jvalāya svāhā.

5
Self-Generation

The presentation of the actual concentrations of the four-branched repetition has two parts: the concentrations of the branches of repetition and how to perform repetition in dependence on the branches.

The Concentrations of the Branches of Repetition

The *Concentration Continuation*[86] says:

> The intelligent who dwell in yoga
> Contemplate the presence of a Sugata
> Only having first made offerings
> To the image of the deity's body.

Thus it is explained that initially offerings are made to a deity [generated or imagined in front of the meditator], after which one generates oneself as a deity. Buddhaguhya's commentary says:

> Offering is just an illustration; hence, observing cleanliness, protecting oneself and the place, inviting the deity, and so forth should be performed because without having done these there is no way to make offering to the deity. [The rites of] cleanliness and so forth [through to offering] can be known from[87] all [texts on knowledge mantra, etc.].

Buddhaguhya asserts the stages [of practice] this way [with generation of a deity in front first and self-generation afterwards], but Varabodhi's *Clear Realisation of Susiddhi* explains that first one generates oneself as a deity and then invites the deity and makes offering and so forth. Though the former appears to be more convenient for stages of meditation (see p. 113), I will explain [the process] in accordance with Varabodhi since at this point I am mostly depending on his text.

The explanation has two parts: (1) generating oneself as a deity and (2) offering and so forth to the wisdom-being invited in front.

Generating Oneself as a Deity

Straighten your body and leave it that way.[88] Reverse the senses from the varieties of objects to the inside. Having made your neck like a peacock's, gently breathe in and out. Open your eyes just a little and aim them at the point of your nose. [Gently] press teeth with teeth, and touch your tongue to the palate.

Observing all the [various] groups of sentient beings, generate the great compassion, which involves assuming the burden of freeing them from suffering. Then, strive to generate the mind of enlightenment which is the thought, 'For their sake I will attain highest enlightenment', and [within that aspiration] amass the collections of merit [through cultivating deity yoga, etc.]. For all achievements of virtue while abiding in that attitude induce omniscient wisdom, and virtues blessed with this attitude induce limitless happiness even in cyclic existence.

Ultimate deity. Then the *Concentration Continuation*[89] indicates cultivation of an ultimate mind of enlightenment [a wisdom consciousness directly realising emptiness in the continuum of a Bodhisattva] with:

Afterwards, freed from the limbs [suchness
Is] not discriminated, thoroughly
Devoid of discrimination, and subtle. Unmoving
And clear mental analysis remains in its presence.

[After offering and so forth to a deity invited in front, you should reflect on the ultimate deity, your own suchness which is freed from the branches, or senses, in that the senses do not ultimately exist. It is not discriminated by others in that it is not apprehended by others and thus is formless. It is thoroughly devoid of discrimination in that it does not apprehend forms and so forth; it is subtle, for it is without inherent existence. One's mental analysis should remain in the presence of the suchness of self in the sense of revealing it; that analysis should be unmoving — stable and free of excitement — and clear — free of laxity.]

The self imputed by the [non-Buddhist] Forders (*Tīrthika*) does not exist even conventionally; therefore, a self is merely imputed to just these five aggregates [forms, feelings, discriminations, compositional factors, and consciousnesses. The stanza above] should be interpreted [as indicating] how [the step of realising] the suchness of such a self should be done.

The time [for contemplating this] is after making offering and so forth to the invited deity [if you are following Buddhaguhya's order of first generating the deity in front]. How is it done? When an analytical consciousness concerned with the ultimate [that is, emptiness] makes investigation, [the self] is not discriminated or apprehended by the eye consciousness and so forth of others' continuums. Also, that the self discriminates or apprehends others is abandoned, for the branches such as eyes are freed, that is, are not ultimately established. By refuting through this that subject and object truly exist, [suchness is this] emptiness of duality. This is how oneself should be considered.

One nevertheless might think that like a dream consciousness there is undeniably an appearance of [external] objects due to internal error and that a consciousness empty of duality truly exists. Since one might think this, [suchness] is said to be 'subtle' because the non-inherent existence [of all phenomena, external and internal] is very subtle. Through this, it is shown that the ultimate suchness of self is free from all signs of the elaborations [of inherent existence].

The mode of meditation is indicated by the line and a half, 'Unmoving/And clear mental analysis remains in its presence', which will be explained below (pp. 168–71). Furthermore, Varabodhi's explanation[90] appears to be similar in meaning to Buddhaguhya's.

Just as the suchness of self is ultimately free from all [conceptual and dualistic] elaborations, so is the suchness of the deity. Therefore, create the pride of the sameness of oneself and the deity in terms of non-conceptual perception of the undifferentiability of those two, like a mixture of water and milk. Concentrate without appearance [of the two as different] until your knowledge is very definite. This is the ultimate deity.

Meditating thus on the emptiness of all [coarse and subtle] selves of persons and other phenomena is the same essential as when, in other tantras, prior to meditating on a deity, one says a mantra, such as *svabhāva* . . .[91] and meditates on its meaning.

Sound deity. Rising from that,[92] imagine the resounding of the tones of the mantra of the appropriate deity; this is the sound deity. It does not appear in Varabodhi's *Clear Realisation of Susiddhi,* which at this point describes meditation on that mind [of the ultimate deity] in the aspect of a moon disc. Both masters [Buddhaguhya and Varabodhi] are similar in this respect [in that Buddhaguhya also describes in the next step a moon disc which is an appearance in form of the ultimate deity above which the sounds of the mantra resound].

Letter deity. Then, think that [the mind realising the ultimate deity] appears in the sky in the aspect of the written letters of the mantra of the appropriate deity. Think that the mind having the aspect of [realising] the suchness of oneself and the deity as undifferentiable has become a moon disc and that on it [the letters] are set in order [the sounds of the letters mixing with the form] like very pure mercury adhering [that is, mixing completely with] grains of gold.[93] This is the letter deity.

Except for only a description in Varabodhi's *Clear Realisation of Susiddhi*[94] of [the mantra here as] 'the mantra to be repeated' neither of the two masters clarifies the point. However, it is apparent that [not just a long mantra but also] a short one such as *oṃ bhrūṃ svāhā* which is explained in the *Ocean of Means of Achievement* as the mantra of Vijaya of the Tathagata lineage or *oṃ mārichyai maṃ svāhā* for Marichi of the Tathagata lineage is also sufficient. The same should also be understood for Avalokiteshvara [*oṃ maṇi padme hūṃ*] and so forth of the lotus lineage and for Vidarana and so forth of the vajra lineage.

Form deity. Then, Buddhaguhya says no more than that light emits from the moon; however, according to Varabodhi's explanation,[95] forms of the deity being meditated emerge at the points of variegated lights that have arisen from the moon and mantra. They fill all the sphere of the sky and through emanating great clouds of offerings make splendid offerings to all the Conquerors. Also, they emanate great clouds from which a rain-stream of ambrosia descends, extinguishing the fires of the hells and satisfying those [beings with whatever they want]. Then, the light as well as the divine bodies return and enter the moon disc which is one's mind. Meditate on this as the appropriate deity [that is, the moon as well as the letters are transformed into the deity's physical form] and create the pride of non-difference from yourself. This is the form deity.

It is also suitable to consider extinguishing the suffering of the hells as just an illustration [of relieving others' misery] and to apply this to other sentient beings [hungry ghosts, animals, humans, demi-gods, and gods — relieving them of their particular miseries and satisfying their wants through a rain of ambrosia].

Seal deity. Then, with respect to the seal deity, Buddhaguhya's *Commentary on the 'Concentration Continuation'* says, 'Having risen from that, make the seals of the gathering [a point four finger-widths above the hair line], crown of the head, and so forth as well as their branches [that is, mantras]'. Thus, in accordance with the individual tantra's explanation to construct the seals of the crown protrusion, hair-treasury [one coiled hair in the middle of the brow], eye, etc., and to recite mantra, bless the crown and so forth of the appropriate deity from among the three lineages, touching those places with the seals and mantras. This is the equivalent of blessing the eyes and so forth in other tantra sets [through the imagination of letters or deities in those places].

If you do not do it that way [using the specific seals and mantras for those places, you may use the general mantra and seal of the lineage].[96] Varabodhi[97] says, 'Then, having constructed the pledge seal of one's own deity, bless the heart, the point between the brows, neck, and tops of shoulders.' Hence, it can be done with the [general] pledge seals and mantras of the three lineages explained earlier (pp. 79–81). You should understand that for Vijaya, Sitatapatraparajita, and Manjughosha, for instance [who are of the Tathagata lineage], it should be done with the seal and mantra of the Tathagata lineage [and similarly with those of the lotus and vajra lineages for their deities].

Sign deity. With respect to the sixth deity, Buddhaguhya's *Commentary on the 'Concentration Continuation'* speaks of 'aspected conventional meditative stabilisation' and 'conceptual deity'.[98] In other places the term 'sign deity' is used. This should be understood as meditating on just the deity [as which you have been] generated.

Sources

Buddhaguhya[99] describes meditation in this manner by way of the six deities in commentary on the meaning of the *Concentration Continuation* where it says:

> Having set oneself thus,
> Meditate with the mantra minds.

'Mantra minds' are the six deities, called the six aspects of secret mantra. 'Meditate' is explained as [meaning] to suffuse the mental continuum with these. [The six deities are not described in the *Concentration Continuation* itself but] are clearly set forth in the *Extensive Vidarana Tantra* which Buddhaguhya's *Commentary on the 'Vidarana Tantra'* cites:

> Having first bathed, a yogi
> Sits on the vajra cushion
> And having offered and made petition
> Cultivates the six deities.
> Emptiness, sound,[100] letter, form,
> Seal, and sign are the six.

Buddhaguhya says, 'Making oneself into Vajrapani by way of the six clarifications — the emptiness of the Buddha or Bodhisattva who has entered [oneself], etc. . .'.

This is the equivalent of deity generation by way of the five clarifications in other tantras [Yoga and Highest Yoga].

With respect to this mode [of self-generation by way of cultivating the six deities] Buddhaguhya's *Commentary on the 'Concentration Continuation'*[101] says, 'These are the general stages for cultivating the minds of secret mantra; they likewise should be applied to descriptions in other forms.' Buddhaguhya thus asserts that [the six deities] should be used in all the various generation rites of deity yoga in Action Tantra.

Modes of Meditation

There are two types of meditation on the six deities (see also p. 164):[102]

1. With concentration (*dhyāna*): engaging in many observations by way of many aspects, contemplating the six deities in series or contemplating the colour, hand symbol [and so forth] of the deity in series;
2. with meditative stabilisation (*samādhi*): dwelling on the body of the deity as contemplated [formerly] with concentration but [now] by way of one aspect, not many, for meditative stabilisation is described as one-pointedness of mind.

The *Concentration Continuation*[103] says:

> Meditate with the mantra minds. Restrained,
> Dwell in meditative stabilisation.
> Thoroughly restrain vitality and exertion.

'Meditate with the mantra minds' and 'Dwell in meditative stabilisation' indicate the two modes of meditation. The rest speaks of restraining vitality (*prāṇa*) [breath] and exertion (*āyāma*) [distraction] when meditating with meditative stabilisation.

The stages of the latter are these: Position the body so that it has the essential points explained earlier (p. 104). Having meditated through to the form deity[104] without the distraction of thought elsewhere, assume the pride of clear appearance as the deity. This is to be done prior [to meditative stabilisation]. The wind [energy] that emerges and enters through the eyes, ears, nose, mouth, navel, male or female organ, anus, and head and body hair-pores is [called] vitality. Exertion refers to 'mindfulness' [not in the usual sense of keeping a virtuous object in mind but] in the sense of becoming distracted to another object of observation which you have taken to mind. Therefore, bind these two in this way: stop the exhalation and inhalation of breath; withdraw inside movements of the breath throughout the body like a turtle's retracting its limbs and drinking water with the tongue by means of the upwards-drawing wind. Also, withdraw inside the usual intense movement of the non-equipoised mind out through the senses. Nevertheless, leave your eyes a little open, raise your face a little, and set yourself in one-pointed meditative equipoise, observing your own body clarified as a deity. The observation should be done like that of a person dwelling in a cave and looking outside [in the sense that one is as if inside the divine body, observing it from within].

The passage from the *Vairochanabhisambodhi* quoted earlier (p. 56) establishes that the meaning of vitality and exertion (*prāṇāyāma*) is as given above. In another way, vitality (*prāṇa*) is as described above, but here *āyāma* means to *stop* exhalation and inhalation and sever the continuum of their movement.

Hold [your breath] in that way with whatever capacity you have [all the while observing one aspect of the divine body]. Then, when unable, let the breath out gently; relax, viewing yourself clarified as a deity and then act again as before [stopping breath and distraction and observing the same one aspect of the divine body]. The method for resting when tired from meditating will be explained later [in chapter 7].

Here, in order for the divine body to appear clearly, meditative stabilisation in which the mind remains for a long period [on one object] must be generated. Since the horse of the mind is wind [that is to say, since the mind rides on currents of energy], Buddhaguhya's *Commentary on the 'Concentration Continuation'* speaks of holding the wind, referring to its being easier to hold the mind to one object when the wind is held:

> The mind — the king — surrounded by a retinue of mindfulness, meditative stabilisation, mental engagement, and so forth is considered as being mounted on the horse of vitality (*prāṇa*). When the horse of vitality [wind] is held, the mind — the king — as well as the retinue will definitely be held. For another [text] says, 'Vitality [wind] is to be stopped. When it is stopped, one's mind as well as mindfulness, intellect, mental engagement, and so forth will definitely be held.'

Although concentration also requires restraining [vitality and exertion], it operates on many objects of observation and, therefore, does not require restraining like that necessary for meditative stabilisation to operate on one object. Therefore, the *Concentration Continuation* says, 'Restrained,/Dwell in meditative stabilisation'(p. 110) with regard to meditative stabilisation and not concentration.

To what point should this be performed? According to the *Vajrapani Initiation Tantra* quoted earlier (pp. 59–61), it should be performed until attaining the capacity to stop — by means of the clear appearance of the deity as well as by means of the pride of being a deity in all modes of behaviour — the pride of ordinariness. Therefore it is not sufficient just to hold the mind to the appearance of a divine body; once the pride [of being a deity] is made firm, the mind must also be held to that; both [clear appearance and pride] are necessary. These points will be explained in detail on the occasion of the stage of generation in Highest Yoga Tantra.

In Highest Yoga the wind yoga of holding the winds is prescribed after deity yoga has become firm; however, here it is said that it should be done simultaneously with holding the mind on the divine body. [In Highest Yoga Tantra the holding of the winds, or the stopping of vitality and exertion, specifically refers to stopping the movement of the winds in the right and left channels and thus is performed during the stage of completion and after attaining steady clear appearance of the deity in the stage of generation. Hence, even in Highest Yoga Tantra the stopping of vitality and exertion *as explained in the lower tantras* for the sake of withdrawing the mind inside and setting it on the appropriate object as long as one likes is also performed in connection with the early stages of holding the mind on the divine body.][105]

Although the master Varabodhi did not explain these [two types of meditation], I have described them in accordance with the master Buddhaguhya's clear exposition of the meaning of the [*Concentration Continuation*] *Tantra*. They appear to be very important.

It is convenient to do this combination of wind yoga and holding the mind on the divine body as found in the six deities *after* inviting the wisdom-being [the deity in front], offering, praising, and so forth [since one is then free to remain withdrawn]. It is not convenient to invite the wisdom-being afterwards [since one would have to be disturbed from single-pointed equipoise]. Therefore, on the occasion of initial practice, the order should follow Buddhaguhya [performing generation in front first and self-generation afterwards].

On occasions when one has performed prior approximation and then bestows initiation [on another], or performs a rite of cleansing [others' obstructions, etc.] related with a vase, or achieves feats for oneself or others [such as increasing wealth] and so forth, whichever of the two orders is done appears to be the same. If self-generation is done after [generation in front], perform the offering and praising to [yourself generated as a deity] in accordance with what is prescribed by other masters who composed *Means of Achievement* for Action and Performance Tantras. [Offering and praising would be done twice, once for the deity generated in front, as explained in the next chapter, and again for oneself after generating oneself as a deity.] When self-generation is performed beforehand, it is permissible to perform the offering and praising [of the two deities — the one generated in front and oneself] at the same time if these are not done separately.

During self-generation other masters say to meditate on one's own appropriate deity completely [with retinue and so forth]. However, according to these masters [Buddhaguhya and Varabodhi] the main deity of the individual lineage is sufficient on the occasion of self-generation during initial approximation. When achieving one's own and others' aims once prior approximation is finished, it is better — during self-generation — to meditate on the deity in complete form as explained [in the rite with surrounding figures, etc.].

[In connection with self-generation] it is suitable to perform the entry of the wisdom-being [that is, the dissolving of the actual deity into oneself imagined as that deity], conferring of initiation [on oneself by an invited initiation deity], seal implanting [the affixing of the seal or sign of the lineage through imagining the lineage lord at the crown of the head after initiation], and so forth as explained by other masters. However, there also is no contradiction in acting in accordance with these two masters' not describing these.

6

Generation in Front

The presentation of how to make offering and so forth to the wisdom-being invited in front has six parts: (1) generation of the residence, (2) inviting the resident deity and asking him to sit, (3) displaying seals, (4) offering and praising, (5) confession and so forth, and (6) cultivating the four immeasurables.

Generation of the Residence[106]

In front of yourself in the direction where a painting [of the deity] or the like has been arranged, imagine a ground of many precious substances covered with golden sand. Bless it [that is, make it magnificent] with:
Oṃ chalavī hūṃ svāhā.

On top of it, imagine a great ocean of milk [that is, of white colour] free from such faults as scum and adorned with flowers such as lotus, and *uptala,* with many flocks of precious birds flying overhead. Bless these with:
Oṃ vimala-dhaha hūṃ.

In the centre, imagine the square Mount Meru, adorned from its four sides with sets of stairs made from gold, silver, sapphire, and topaz. All over it are wish-granting trees well grown and adorned with a thousand flapping victory banners. On the top of the mountain imagine a lotus stalk adorned with many precious substances, having petals of various jewels, golden corolla, and anthers of topaz with silver lines surrounding the top of its centre. Many *yojanas* in breadth, the lotus stalk rises out of the centre of Mount Meru, and from it hundreds, thousands, ten thousands, and ten millions of lotus latticeworks emerge.

From the [position] of palms in homage interlace [the fingers] and press the left thumb with the right (seal 19).

Seal 19(a)

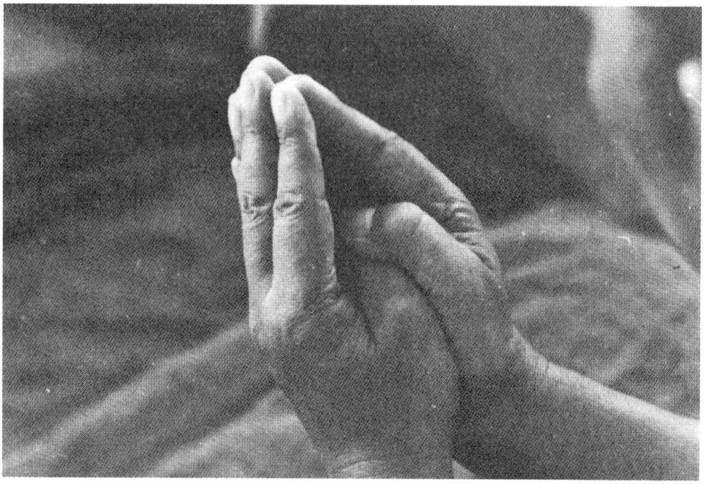

Seal 19(b)

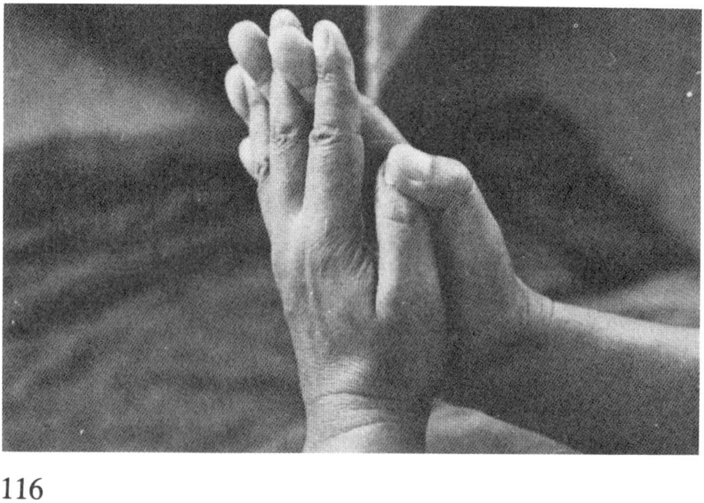

Bless [the imagined residence], repeating a hundred times:[107]
Namaḥ sarva-tathāgatānāṃ sarvathā udgate spharaṇa-himaṃ gaganakhaṃ svāhā.

Also, mentally imagine a canopy [appearing] above the residence in an instant.

Although Varabodhi's *Clear Realisation of Susiddhi* does not mention meditation on an inestimable palace [as a residence for the deity] at this point, it does later,[108] saying, 'Ask him to come again, together with an inestimable palace.' Therefore, an inestimable palace should also be generated. [One first imagines an empty inestimable palace into which the deity comes with his own palace which fuses with the former, much like a wisdom-being fusing with a pledge-being.] Furthermore, it can be generated all at once in the centre of the former lotus just as were the others [the land, ocean, trees, and so forth] without being generated from syllables. Or it can be generated from *bhrūṃ* [imagining the syllable which turns into the palace]. It is similarly permissible to generate a second lotus [inside the palace] as the deity's seat.

These two masters [Varabodhi and Buddhaguhya] do not speak of generating an inestimable palace or of other seats in self-generation, but other masters' *Means of Achievement* mention thrones supported by lions, etc., seats of living beings [such as a deer], generation inside a reliquary for Vijaya, and so forth.

Inviting the Resident Deity and Asking Him to Sit[109]

Preparing an oblation

Invitation must be done with oblation [like drink offered to a visitor]. It must, therefore, first be achieved [that is, it must be prepared, cleansed of obstructors, and made magnificent]. The oblation vessel can be of gold, silver, stone, wood, or other substances; a copper vessel is auspicious in common for all [activities, whether of pacification, increase, or ferocity]. In such a vessel offer oblation of [ground] barley and milk for pacification [of illness, demons, and so forth] and high feats (see p. 175), of [ground] sesame and yogurt for increase and middling feats, of cow urine and rice with *kodrava* [a common grain] or blood for ferocity and low feats. A mixture of [ground] parched rice, fragrant incense, white flowers, *kusha* grass, and sesame in pure water is auspicious in common for all activities [pacification, increase, and ferocity].

Set out [whatever has been chosen] and suffuse it with incense. Bless the oblation, repeating seven times either the mantra of the knowledge king (p. 98), the essence mantra of the general lineage (p. 95), the mantra of all activities of the individual lineage explained earlier (p. 96), or the mantra of inviting a deity [to be explained two paragraphs below].

Inviting the deity

Then, face in the direction where the painted figure or the like is. Bow down (as on p. 81) and kneel on the ground. Construct the seal of invitation by intertwining the fingers, turning the palms upward, aligning and straightening the two forefingers, and beckoning with the two thumbs (seal 20). Say:

> Due to [my] faith and [your compassionate] pledges
> Come here, come here, O Blessed One.
> Accepting this oblation of mine
> Be pleased with me through this offering.

At the end of the mantra [described in the next paragraph], add *ehyahi.*[110] Holding the vessel, offer it in a line with the head for the Tathagata lineage, and in a line with the chest and navel for the other two lineages [lotus and vajra respectively]. Think that because of this

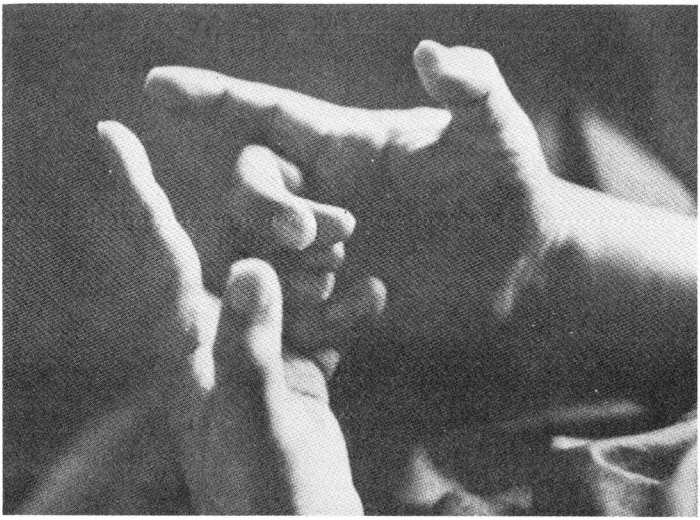

Seal 20

wisdom-beings similar to those [imagined deities] come [that is, the actual deities come to receive the offerings].

With respect to the mantra, invite a male deity with the mantra of the knowledge mantra king (p. 98); invite a female deity with the mantra of the knowledge mantra queen. Or do it with [the deity's] individual mantra. Or the *Susiddhi Tantra* says that invitation with the general essence mantra of the lineage, such as *jinajik ehyahi* for Vijaya [of the Tathagata lineage and similarly *ārolik ehyahi* for the lotus lineage and *vajradhṛk ehyahi* for the vajra lineage] is supreme.

Furthermore, the 'Chapter on Invitation', in the *Susiddhi Tantra*[111] says that when the deity to be invited is standing, sitting, or bent to one side, one should assume that form and then make the invitation with oblation. Also, it says that, if the oblation has not been obtained as prescribed [in the rite], one should ask for the deity's patience and make the invitation with whatever has been obtained.

With regard to how many deities to invite, the *Concentration Continuation*[112] says [to do it with full retinue]:

> Abide always to fulfil concentration
> Approaching the body of a Conqueror
> With all the many knowledge Mantra and Fierce Ones
> As well as Secret Mantra Ones and so forth.

Buddhaguhya's commentary[113] on this says:

> Imagine the body of a Tathagata in front of yourself. Imagine that in an instant the sphere of space is pervaded and the perimeter surrounded by Knowledge Mantra Ones, Secret Mantra Ones, Fierce Ones, male and female Emissaries, and so forth. You also abide in their centre with divine pride. Also those Knowledge Mantra Ones and so forth always remain in the presence of the Conqueror. Thereby, through performing deity yoga the mantrika also approaches a Conqueror.

Offering a Seat

Then, [offer a seat to the deity with the appropriate seal and mantra]. The seal of the lotus posture (seal 21) is to display the pledge seal of the lotus lineage which was explained earlier (seal 2, p. 79). The seal of the vajra posture (seal 22) is from the seal of the lotus posture to form the three fingers like a vajra. The seal of the heroic posture (seal 23) is from the seal of the lotus posture to join the middle fingers as one. The mantras respectively are:
Oṃ kāmalāya svāhā,
Oṃ vajra-asani hūṃ phaṭ,
Oṃ vajraka hūṃ phaṭ.

In accordance with the explanation to offer an appropriate seat, offer such and ask the deity to sit. Or, offer a seat while reciting the stanza:[114]

Seal 21

Seal 22

It is good that the compassionate Blessed One has come,
I am meritorious and fortunate.
Taking my oblation, please pay
Heed [to me] and grant [my request].

Or:

From compassion for myself and migrators,
As long as I make offering
May the Blessed One please remain [here]
Through your powers of magical creation.

Displaying Seals[115]

Then, say:
Shaṃkare samaye svāhā.

Display the pledge vajra seal: press the nail of the little finger with the thumb of the right hand, and form the remaining fingers like a vajra (seal 24).

Then, displaying the seal of the [appropriate among the] three lineages, say [the appropriate among] the three essence mantras, *jinajik, ārolik,* or *vajradhṛk.* With respect to the seals, for the Tathagata lineage make the two hands into fists together, and display the two thumbs (seal 25). For the lotus lineage insert the left thumb inside and display the right thumb (seal 26). For the vajra lineage display the left thumb (seal 27).

Then construct the great pledge seal of the lineage (seals 1-3) and revolve it. Do it thus, for this is said to afford great protection from all evil deeds by obstructors who arrive after [the achievement of deities due to one's own karma and conceptions], etc. If this is not done, drive away these obstructors by repeating the mantra of the appropriate Fierce One into white mustard seed [which is then scattered].

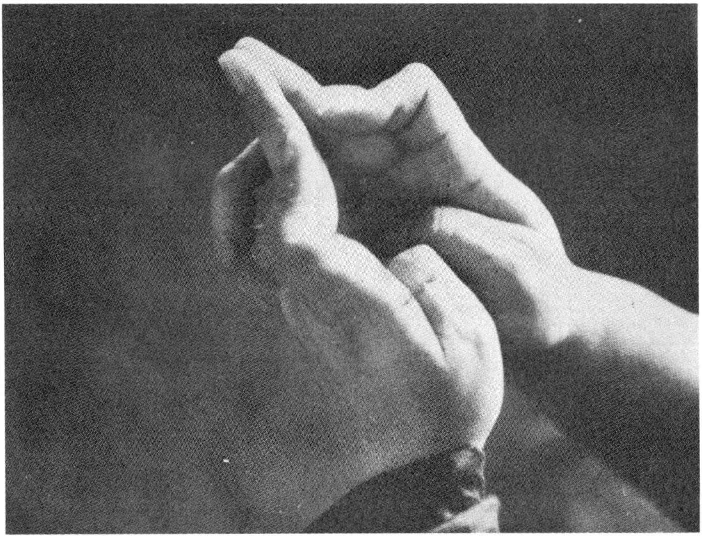

Seal 23

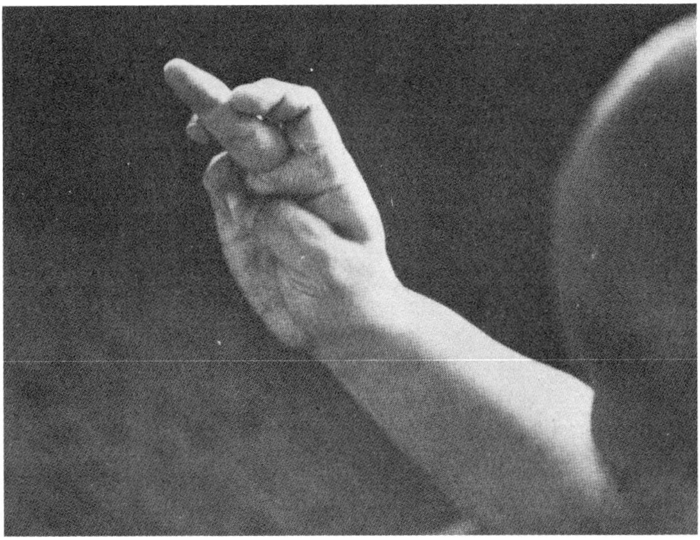

Seal 24

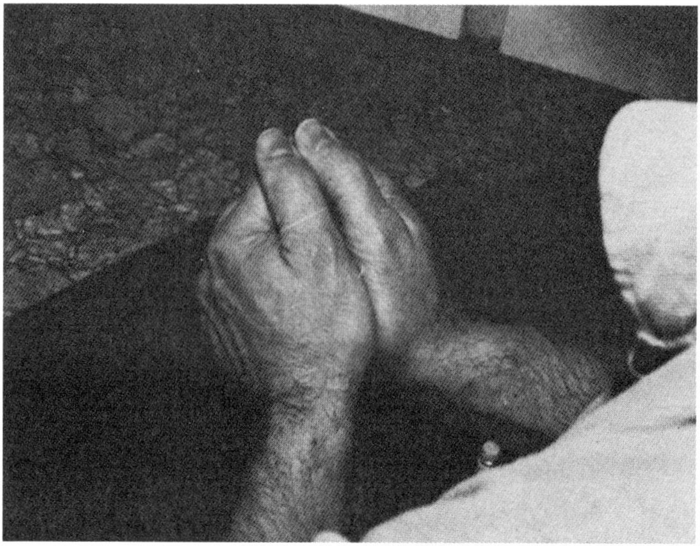

Seal 25

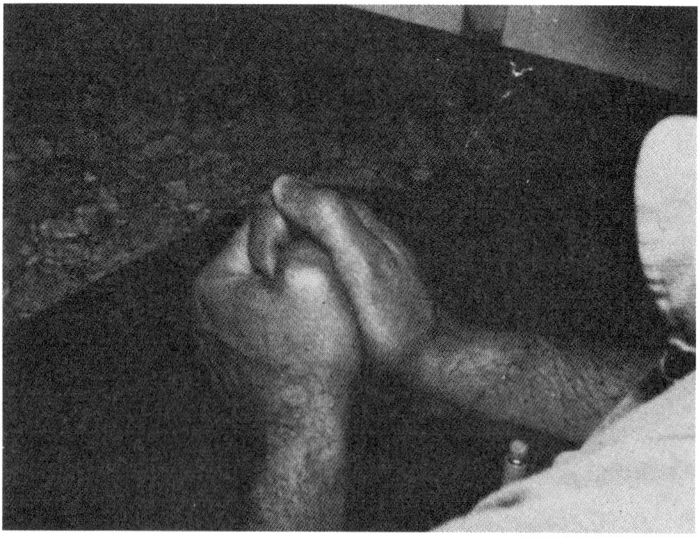

Seal 26

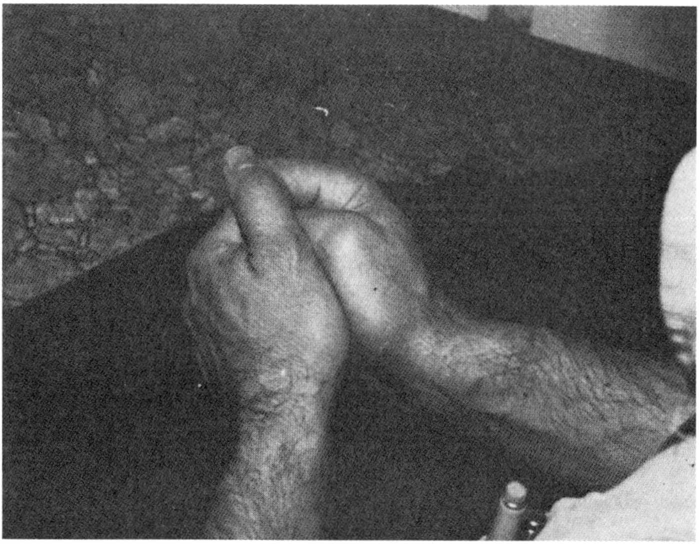

Seal 27

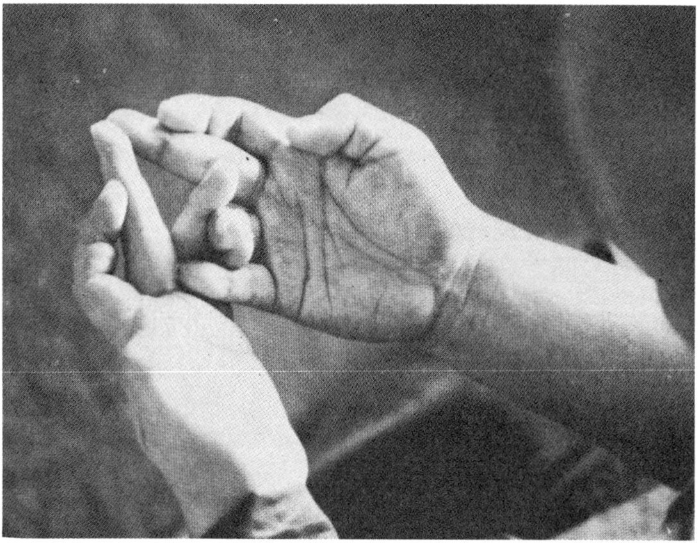

Seal 28

Offering and Praising

Presenting Offerings[116]

As before (pp. 95–6), perform the dispelling of obstructors, cleansing, and generation of magnificence with respect to the articles of offering. Since the *Susiddhi Tantra* says to cleanse them while repeating the [eight] mantras of presenting offerings [as given below] or the mantra of the appropriate particular lineage, these are also necessary.

Offering oblation. Then, construct the seal of oblation: interlace the little fingers and the ring fingers inside; bend the forefingers to the third joint of the two middle fingers which have been aligned and straightened. Join the two thumbs to the sides [of the hands] (seal 28). Say:[117]

> You have come blissfully, Blessed One.
> Come here and please be seated.
> Receiving my oblation also,
> Please take pleasure in mind from this.
> I have respect for you.

At the end of the deity's mantra, offer oblation, saying:[118]
Arghaṃ pratīchchha svāhā.

Offering a foot-bath. Construct this seal: make the forefinger and thumb of the fisted right hand like a pincers, take a flower from the vessel for bathing the feet, and gradually release the fingers (seal 29). Putting 'foot-bath' in place of 'oblation' in the above stanza, offer the foot-bath with:
Oṃ pravarasatkaraṃ pratīchchha svāhā.

Offering a bath. Then actually offer a bath to the reflection of the image in a mirror if one is obtainable. If not,

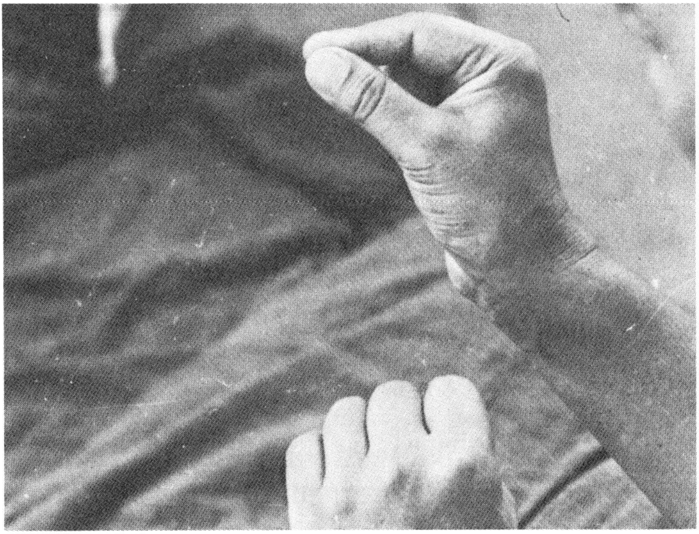

Seal 29(a)

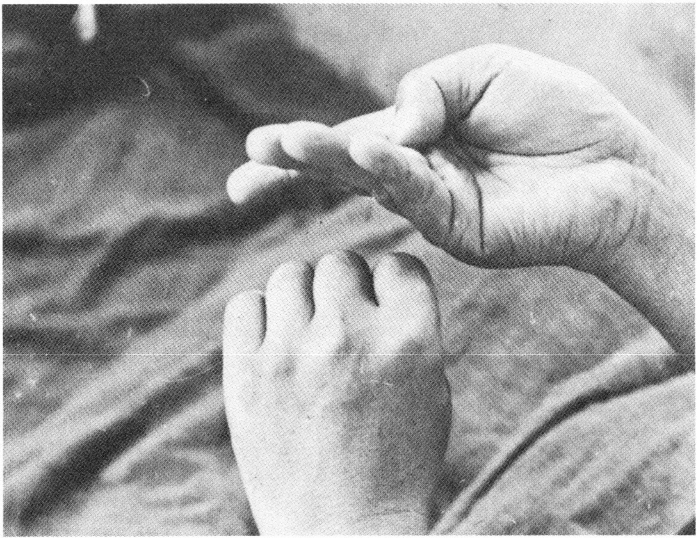

Seal 29(b)

make the seal of washing the body: having turned up the palms, join the tips of the forefingers and tips of the thumbs (seal 30). Say:
Oṃ sarva-devatā-achinta-amṛta svāhā.

Imagine washing the deities' bodies with great clouds of perfumed water [which have risen from][119] many precious gold vases and so forth filled with fragrant perfumes.

Offering clothing, adornments, and music. Then, mentally offer clothing and adornments. Offer music, and mentally raise up melodies of praise.[120]

Offering perfume. Then, make the seal of perfume: with the left hand hold the wrist of the right hand which is making [the seal of] bestowing refuge (seal 31). Offer the perfume:

> I offer with faith these perfumes
> Of wholesome divine substances
> Arisen from the clean, most clean.
> Receiving them, be pleased with me.
> *Āhara āhara sarva-vidyādhari pūjite svāhā.*

Except for the lamps, use this mantra of offering for the other three [flowers, incense, and food] also.

Offering flowers. Make the flower seal: interlace the fingers of both hands; make the forefingers into one inside the hand and form them in the manner of a bracelet; put the thumbs, formed in the manner of a lotus, beside them (seal 32). Offer flowers with:

> I offer with faith these flowers
> Of auspicious divine substances
> Grown from the clean, most clean.
> Receiving them, be pleased with me.
> *Āhara āhara sarva-vidyādhari pūjite svāhā.*

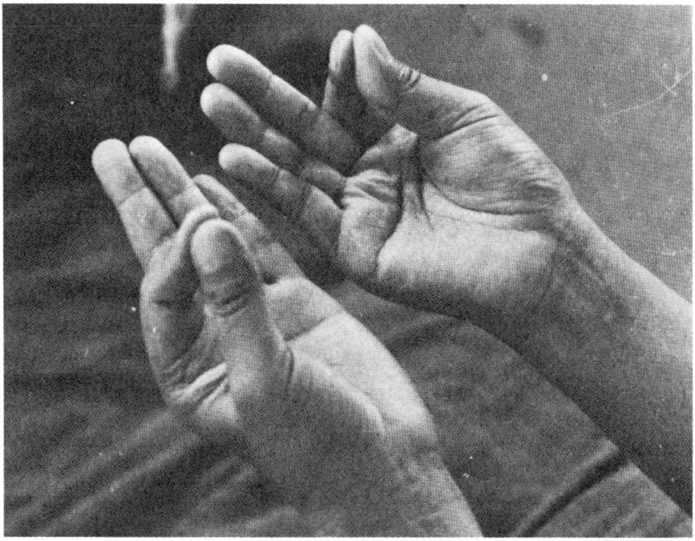

Seal 30

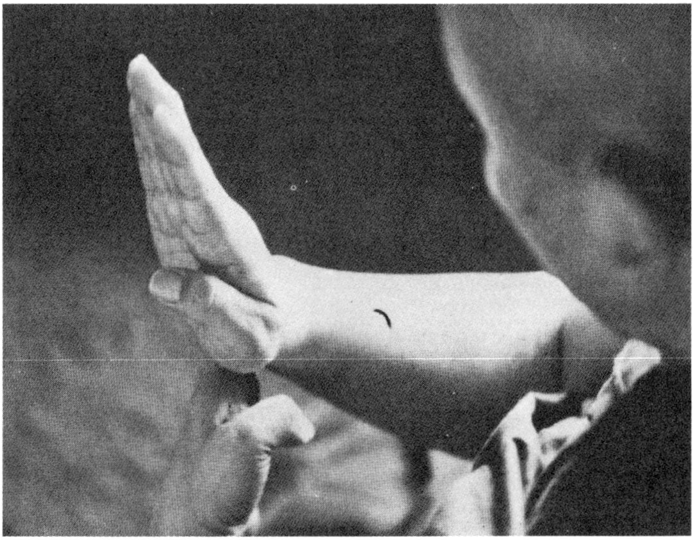

Seal 31

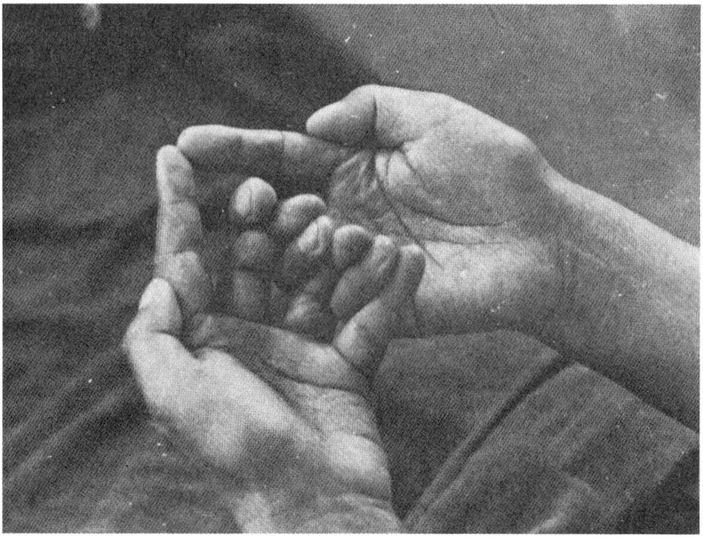

Seal 32

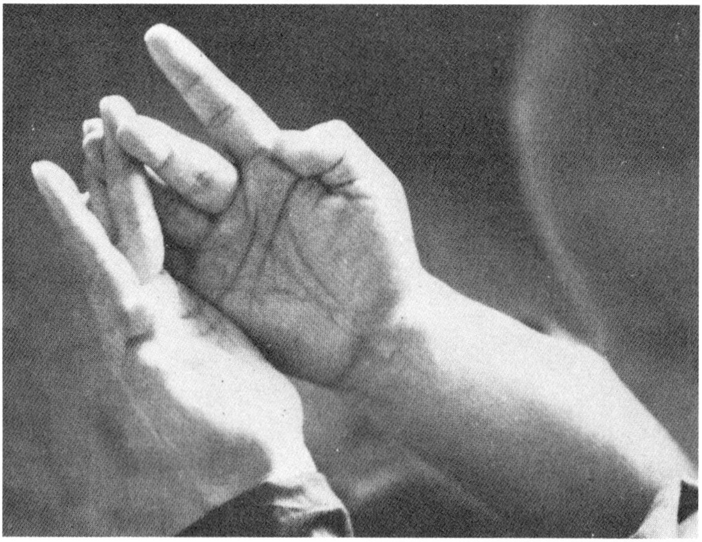

Seal 33

Offering incense. Make the seal of incense: join together the little, ring, and middle fingers of both hands. Bend the ones in front at the base of the nails of the others; stretch the two forefingers at an angle, and put the two thumbs at their side (seal 33). Offer incense with:

With faith I offer divine
Substances made with perfume,
Pleasant essences of the forest.
Receiving them, be pleased with me.
Āhara āhara sarva-vidyādhari pūjite svāhā.

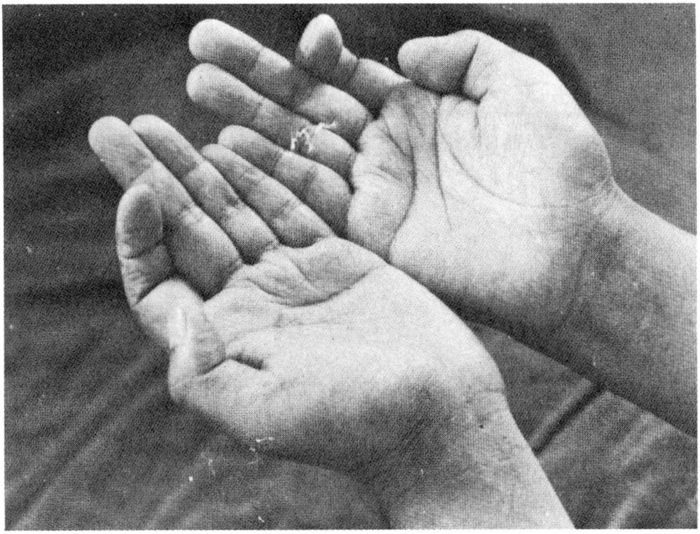

Offering food. Make the seal of divine food: from cupped palms, bend the forefingers slightly (seal 34). Offer food with:

I offer with faith these foods
Of mantra, pleasant
Essence of medicines.
Receiving them, be pleased with me.
Āhara āhara sarva-vidyādhari pūjite svāhā.

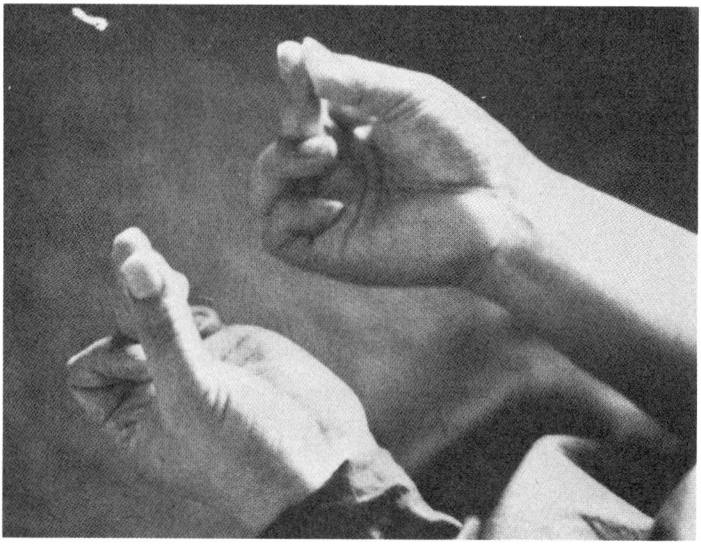

Offering lamps. Make the lamp seal: join and straighten the thumbs and middle fingers; make the hands into a fist (seal 35). Offer lamps with:

> I offer with faith these dispellers
> Of darkness, conquering harmers,
> Auspicious and virtuous.
> I beg you to receive these lamps.
> *Ālokāya ālokāya vidhādhare pūjite svāhā.*[121]

[*Comments*]
If the articles of offering mentioned for the particular deities of the individual lineages are not obtainable, mantrafy the offering articles of another lineage with the mantras of the lineage [being practised] and offer them.

If the oblation and below are not actually obtainable, [the *Susiddhi Tantra* and Varabodhi's *Clear Realisation*] say that one should make the [respective] seals and mantras and, having visualised the articles of offering mentally, offer them. With respect to the flowers and so forth, paintings of them are also suitable for offering. Even with respect to actually obtained offerings, it is said that since the mind precedes everything, mental offerings have a great difference [and thus should be given along with external ones].

Having in this way made whatever offering is possible, at this time repeat one hundred times more the mantra of blessing the place explained earlier as repeated a hundred times (p. 117).

Making Praise[122]

Then, praise the Three Jewels and the lords of the three lineages with these verses from the *Susiddhi Tantra*.

Obeisance to the Three Jewels

Homage to the Tathagata,
Protector with great compassion,
Omniscient teacher, oceanic
Field[123] of merit and attainments.

Homage to the pacifying doctrine,
Through purity separating from desire,
Through virtue liberating from bad migrations,
In all ways the supreme ultimate.

Respectful homage to the spiritual community,
Liberated, teaching the path of liberation,
Completely dwelling in the precepts, excellent of fields
[For accumulating merit], possessing attainments.

Obeisance to the Lords of the Three Lineages

Homage also to Manjushri,
Bearer of the appearance of a youth,
Vividly adorned with the lamp of wisdom,
Dispeller of the three worlds' darkness.

Homage to the always merciful,
Whose name is Avalokiteshvara,
Composite of all excellent qualities,
Strongly praised by all the Buddhas.

Homage to Vajrapani,
Powerful and having fierceness,
Virtuous king of knowledge mantra,
Tamer of the hard to tame.

Also, make specific praise of the particular deity, and repeat a hundred times the mantra of bringing forth praise:[124]
Namaḥ sarva-buddha-bodhisattvānāṃ, sarvatra saṃkurumita avijñā-rāshini namo stute svāhā.

Confession and So Forth[125]

Confession
With strong contrition for sins done formerly and firm resolve to refrain from doing them henceforth, confess sins:

Tathagatas residing in all
Directions of the worlds,
Foe Destroyers, and Bodhisattvas,
I ask you to heed me.
Whatever sins I have
Committed in any lifetime,
Or, disturbed by the power of desire,
Stupidity, or anger in cyclic
Existence in former lives or this life,
Whatever sinful actions I did,
Asked others to do, or admired
Even a little, even slight ones
Unconscientiously done with
Body, speech or mind to Buddha, Doctrine,
Or Spiritual Community

Or gurus, father or mother,
Foe Destroyers, Bodhisattvas,
Or any object of giving,
Or to other sentient beings,
Educated or uneducated —
Having mentally collected all these
I bow down in great respect
To the perfect Buddhas and sons
Manifest before me now
And confess individually
And repeatedly my mistakes
With pressed palms and saddened mind.
Just as the perfect Buddhas know
The sins that I have committed,[126]
I make individual confession.
Henceforth I will not do such.

Refuge

Go for refuge with strong respect:

So that the sufferings of beings might be pacified
I respectfully go for true refuge
To Buddha, Doctrine, and Spiritual Community
As long as I remain alive.

Admiration

Set in equipoise, I take admiration
In the varieties of doctrinal usage.

Entreaty and Supplication

To generate non-conceptual knowledge
I entreat you to turn the wheel of doctrine
And not to pass away from sorrow
Until [all] trainees are satisfied.[127]

Prayer-Wishes

Just as the earlier Buddha Children
Made prayer-wishes,
I also with a virtuous mind
Plant prayer-wishes in that way.
May all beings have happiness,
Peace, and freedom from disease.
May I be capable in all activities
And also possess [all good] qualities.
May I be wealthy, generous,
Intelligent, and patient
Having faith in virtue, memory of
Former births in all lives, and mercy.

Say those with one-pointed attention to the meaning.

Cultivating the Four Immeasurables[128]

Then, observing all creatures stricken with suffering, abide in compassion which is the thought 'May they be free from all suffering'; in love which is the thought 'May they possess all happiness'; in joy which is the thought 'May they become happy with the bliss of Buddhahood'; and in equanimity which is the thought 'May they pass from sorrow with the unsurpassed nirvana of a Buddha' [which is an equanimity devoid of the conceptions of subject and object as inherently existent].

Then, say:

In order to pacify the suffering
Of limitless realms of sentient beings,
To release them from bad migrations,
Liberate them from afflictions,
And protect them completely from
The varieties of sufferings when
The discomforts of cyclic existence crowd in,
I will generate the altruistic mind of enlightenment.

May I always be a refuge
For all destitute sentient beings,[129]
A protector of the protectorless,
A support[130] of those without support,
A refuge for the unprotected,
Maker of the miserable happy.
May I cause the pacification
Of all sentient beings' afflictions.
May whatever virtuous actions I have
Accumulated[131] in this and other lives
Assume the aspects of the collections
Which are called merit and wisdom.
May whatever effort I make
By way of the six perfections
Be of benefit to all beings
Without there being any exception.
Making effort until enlightenment,
I will strive at actions temporarily
And limitlessly over lives so that
In short all the afflictions
Of all sentient beings may be
Pacified and they be freed.

Generate a mind of enlightenment that will definitely suffuse the mental continuum, thinking, 'I will attain Buddhahood in order to liberate stricken migrators.'

[*Comments*]
Meditation in this manner on a deity in front is explained by both masters [Buddhaguhya and Varabodhi] as on an invited wisdom-being [one who comes from his natural abode to the place of meditation] rather than as new generation [as was done in self-generation]. Other masters assert that the invited deity is to be taken as the basis of accumulation [of merit through offering and so forth] and that after amassing accumulations one causes the wisdom-being [the invited deity] to enter oneself generated as a deity and then performs meditation and

repetition. No more than a few describe performing [meditation and repetition] while observing a deity in front, and they explain that when one becomes fatigued from deity meditation, one should perform repetition from that point.

Since deity yoga is the main means for achieving feats, here also the mind, as was explained before, should be held on the clarification of oneself as a deity. From time to time also visualise the body of the deity like yourself in front and keep the mind on it as long as possible [within maintaining a less emphasised observation of yourself as a deity]. These two [self-generation and generation in front] are branches of the four branches of repetition; they are treated as two.

7
Mantra Repetition

The presentation of how to perform mantra repetition in dependence on the branches has three parts: (1) how to assemble the rosary and count, (2) how to perform repetition observing what objects, and (3) how to reinstate the repetition if unfavourable conditions arise.

How to Assemble the Rosary and Count[132]

You should cultivate deity yoga as explained as long as you do not tire. Then, when tired after [one-pointed] cultivation [of deity yoga], you should engage in mantra repetition.

With respect to the material of the rosary used in repetition, [seeds of] *putranjiva roxburghii (putrajīva)* are best for the Tathagata lineage, lotus hearts for the lotus lineage, and *rudrākṣha* (berries of the *elaeocarpus ganitrus*) for the vajra lineage. The *Susiddhi Tantra*[133] says that if these are unobtainable, *lung tang* [?], conch, crystal, pearl, coral, jewel, ivory, clay, various seeds, and so forth are suitable. The *Questions of Subahu* explains that lead, copper, and bronze are also suitable.

With respect to the number [of beads], you should use 1,008, 108, 54, or 21. Pierce the beads and wash them with the five cow-products [a mixture of milk, yogurt, butter, dung, and urine gathered from orange-coloured cows that eat clean grass and drink clean water].

With respect to the string, you should thread the beads with three strands wound together, spun by a girl.

Having tied the knot, you should make offerings to the gods. Then, placing the rosary in your cupped palms, bow down to the lamas and gods. Then, to initially achieve [that is, empower] the rosary repeat the appropriate mantra of the three lineages one hundred and eight times:

Tathagata Lineage[134]
Namo ratna-trayāya, oṃ adbhute vijaya siddhi siddharthe svāhā.

Lotus Lineage
Namo ratna-trayāya, namo aryāvalokiteshvarāya, bodhisatvāya, mahā-satvāya, oṃ amṛtaṃ gale sḥrīya shrīmalina svāhā.

Vajra Lineage
Oṃ kīri kīri rautriṇi svāhā.

When performing repetition [after the initial consecration], you should join the palms and pay homage to the lamas and gods.[135] Put the mantra rosary in your cupped palms, and repeat the [appropriate] mantra seven times:

Tathagata Lineage
Oṃ bhagavati siddhi-siddhaya, siddhārthe svāhā.

Lotus Lineage
Oṃ vasu-mati-shrīye svāhā.

Vajra Lineage[136]
Oṃ vajraya jatanajeye svāhā.

Then, raise the rosary to the heart; extend the middle and little fingers of either the right or left hand. Putting the forefinger behind, count with the ring-finger and thumb for all activities or with the forefinger for the fierce. The *Questions of Subahu* explains that when repeating one should hold the action vajra explained earlier (p. 94) [in the other hand], but, if it is unobtainable, one should clench a vajra fist.

How to Perform Repetition Observing What Objects

This section has two parts: repetition observing the form and the sound of letters.

Repetition Observing the Form of Letters

This section has two parts: repetition observing the form of letters at the heart of a deity visualised in front [of you] and at your own heart.

Repetition Observing the Form of Letters at the Heart of a Deity Visualised in Front

The *Concentration Continuation*[137] indicates this with:

> Flow to the bases, mind, and sound.
> Dwell on the immutable secret mantra base [the deity].
> Repeat secret mantra without losing the branches.
> If becoming tired, rest yourself.

This is interpreted as meaning that secret mantra should be repeated, and, with respect to how to do this, repetition should be performed within the context of not losing the four branches [the two bases — self-generation and generation in front — plus mind and sound] or letting them degenerate.

'Bases' [indicate] two branches; the first is creation of the pride of your being a deity, and the second is meditation of a deity in front similar to yourself. The third branch is 'mind', a moon [disc] set in the heart of the deity in front. The fourth branch is 'sound', the series [of letters] of the mantra to be repeated set [around the edge of] the moon. 'Flow to them' refers to the repeater's adhering to them by way of uninterrupted observation.

The base, in observation of which repetition is performed, must not deviate from the appearance of a deity; this is done through becoming very familiar with [such] meditation. Therefore, the text says, 'Dwell on the *immutable* secret mantra base', which is the base where the secret mantra of mind [appearing as a moon disc] and sound [the letters set around the edge of the disc] are placed [that is, the deity in front].

In brief, restraining vitality and exertion as explained earlier (pp. 110–12), simultaneously observe the three branches in front [the *deity* in front with a *moon* at the heart on which the *letters* of the mantra stand][138] within the complete form of the four branches of repetition [that is, within also maintaining pride in oneself as a deity] and perform repetition. When exhaling, view your own body meditated as a deity [without repeating the mantra], and then do as before [holding the breath, observing the deity, moon, and letters in front, and repeating the mantra].

Resting at the End of a Session

Resting is for the sake of abandoning distraction, and the base being rested is yourself — your fruition body [which is explained in the next paragraph. In brief] leave off contemplating your body as a divine body [in intense one-pointed meditation], and rise contemplating the fruition body. [This means to leave the contemplation in stages and appear again as a divine figure like an illusion, as is now explained.]

With respect to the stages of leaving the contemplation,[139] [when tired] leave off [observation of] the sounds of the mantra letters being repeated through observing the form of the letters [set on the moon at the heart of the deity in front]. Leave the letters through observing the moon without them. Leave the moon through observing only the body of the Tathagata [in front]. Leave the body in front through contemplating only your own divine body. Leave it through contemplating the form of the letters [of the mantra standing on the moon disc]. Leave them through observing their sounds. Leave them through observing the divine Wisdom Body. Leave off contemplating the Wisdom Body through contemplating the Truth Body — this being the suchness of self unapprehendable [as inherently existent]. Then, contemplate as your fruition body [the re-emergence of yourself as a deity] appearing like a magician's illusion, a mirage, and so forth. This is the meaning of resting yourself.

The other [steps in the above description] are easy to understand; the meaning of 'Leave it [your own divine body] through contemplating the form of the letters' and so forth refers to viewing the letter deity, sound deity, moon disc, creation of pride in the sameness of the suchness of yourself and the deity, and the suchness of self free of [dualistic] elaborations [in a manner similar to that] when they occurred in the initial [self-] generation [but in reverse order].

[Buddhaguhya] says that resting here is done in order to forsake distraction; therefore, [as described above] when distracted by conceptual elaborations, withdraw the observation in [reverse] order and finally set in meditative equipoise on emptiness. Then, since you are to rise like an illusion, it is not that you should not maintain the pride of being a deity when leaving the session. Other masters who composed *Means of Achievement* for deities based on Action Tantra frequently describe divine pride for all modes of behaviour.

Repetition Observing the Form of Letters at your Own Heart

The *Concentration Continuation*[140] indicates this with:

> Likewise contemplate a mental purity [moon disc],
> Possessing immutability and letters,
> Which is imagined for your mantra. It moves
> From the base [in front] to the base [yourself].

'Likewise' indicates that this is a mode of observation other than the former; a mental purity is to be contemplated. This is the moon of the heart which is called 'mental' because it arises from the mind [in the sense that it is a manifestation of the mind realising emptiness]. Since it is unpolluted by the taints of desire and so forth, is complete in all respects, and appears without taint, it is a 'purity'. It possesses the series of mantra letters which are immutable since they do not deviate from vivid appearance due to thorough meditation. Also, since the mind appearing as a moon and possessing the letters does not change nor become separate from them, it possesses 'immutability'. Such a moon is imagined as the place for setting one's mantra.

In short, restrain vitality and exertion as explained before (pp. 110–12). A moon, on which the mantra series is set, dwells in the heart of the 'base', which is the Tathagata body being meditated in front of yourself, not too distant and a little higher than yourself. The moon as well as the letters on it moves to the 'base' which is yourself[141] meditated as a deity — that is, together with the inhalation of air, it moves to your own heart. Observing it, perform [mental] repetition until the breath is exhaled. When the wind [breath] is let out, emit [the moon disc and letters] with it, and contemplate them as dwelling in the deity's heart. Again, as before, move it to your own heart and perform repetition.

Repetition Observing the Sound of Letters

The *Concentration Continuation*[142] says:

> Having again retracted the mind through withdrawal
> And restrained vitality and exertion,
> Join the mind of secret mantra to the mantra
> And begin mental repetition.
>
> Otherwise, by means of just this rite[143]
> Whispering is also suitable.
> One wishing feats of mantra knowledge
> Should not perform other repetition.

Repetition should be performed while the mind observing the sounds of a secret mantra is joined to the mantra. Furthermore, the non-equipoised mind operating as usual should again be withdrawn and retracted; with vitality and exertion [breath and distraction] restrained as before (pp. 110–12), repetition should be performed.

After initially visualising the four branches of repetition, you should not [mainly] observe the form of the mantra to be repeated or the moon and so forth, but should perform repetition within, [mainly] observing the tones. Do this not as if listening to another recite the mantra but within observing the proclamation of the mantra sounds while you yourself repeat it [in thought or whisper].

Buddhaguhya's commentary says that mental or whispered[144] repetition should be performed with the rite of just this observation of mantra tones but that, when vitality and exertion are restrained, whispered repetition is impossible [since the breath is stopped]. His commentary also relates the restraining of vitality and exertion as well as mental and whispered repetition to the two earlier [repetitions, performed while observing the form of the letters on a moon disc at the heart of the deity in front and at one's own heart, which therefore can also be understood to have mental and whispered types].

Question: If each of the three observations involves both types of repetition [mental and whispered], what is to be done first?
Answer: Initially perform whispered repetition. Then, when the mind is not distracted to other [objects], restrain vitality and exertion and perform mental repetition. [This process] is described as being done in stages beginning with the coarse. Buddhaguhya's commentary[145] explains:

> Since the first [of the three] involves observation of a deity [in front], moon, and mantra series, it has three [main] objects of observation. The second has two [main] objects of observation, just the moon and the mantra [at one's own heart]. The last observes just the sound and, therefore, has only one [main] object of observation.

One person is to perform these three in order.

Varabodhi[146] describes repetition with the mantra set in one's own heart and in the heart of the deity in front. Although no more than this appears [in his description, the meditation should proceed] in accordance with Buddhaguhya's detailed explanation of the meaning of the [*Concentration Continuation*] *Tantra.*

Other Indians who composed *Means of Achievement* based on Action Tantra also describe an observation in which one makes offerings to Buddhas and achieves the welfare of sentient beings with beams of light emanating from the mantra series. [At the points of the beams deities emerge, emanating clouds of offerings to the Buddhas, Bodhisattvas, etc., and clouds of rain relieving the sufferings of all sentient beings.]

How to Repeat
The fifth chapter of the *Questions of Subahu* says:

> When performing repetition be not fast
> Nor slow, be not loud nor very soft,
> Do not [repeat] while speaking nor while distracted,
> Lose not the vowels, anusvara, or visarga.

Also:

> Reversing quickly from the objects to which
> A lazy, desirous, and non-virtuous mind
> Is distracted and runs, apply the mind well
> To the supreme letters of secret mantra.

The *Susiddhi Tantra* as quoted (p. 50) says that when repeating one should not take to mind even high objects other than the objects of observation of that occasion, the deity and so forth.

For pacification and increase repeat softly, and for ferocity such that others would hear.[147] When you arrive at the initial and final bead [of the rosary while counting repetitions] of the mantra, pay [mental] homage to the deities. When [the full count of] the beads is finished, look with your eyes at an image such as in a painting, or at a reliquary, or the seats [on which they sit].

The periods of recitation involve a session at the morning watch [see p. 149], half-sessions at the dawn and post-dusk watches, and either a half, third, or quarter of a session or a little repetition at noon. The burnt offerings involved in repetitions prescribed for the day may be made at night, and those prescribed for the night during the day, but making them right after repetition is superior.

With regard to the number of repetitions, the *Susiddhi Tantra*[148] says:

In general perform a hundred thousand repetitions
For as many syllables as there are
When the count is fifteen or below.
Three hundred thousand repetitions are prescribed
For the count of syllables until thirty-two.
When the syllables are more than that, do ten
Thousand for prior approximation.

It is not necessary [to perform mantra repetitions] for both the central and surrounding deities as is the case with other tantras. [In Yoga and Highest Yoga Tantra separate repetitions are necessary for each of the deities surrounding a central figure].

How to Reinstate the Repetition if Unfavourable Conditions Arise[149]

If while reciting you become sleepy, yawn, sneeze, cough up phlegm, expel gas, or must urinate, defecate, etc., it is said that you should immediately set down the rosary and, having walked about [to relieve sleepiness] and so forth, do the ablution (see p. 88) and then start from the beginning of the count. Do not add [the new repetition] onto the earlier count [of that particular cycle of the rosary when the interruption occurred]. Also, if through non-conscientiousness another deity's repetition is done, you should mentally plant a petition [to your deity] and begin the repetition again.

The *Susiddhi Tantra* says that repetitions do not count when one is affected by obstructors, afflicted by illness, has become loose, non-concientious, physically or mentally depressed, misses the time prescribed for the ritual, is unrestrained or unclean. Also, it explains that if bad dreams [such as going in darkness, wearing tattered clothes, becoming dirty, being bitten by a poisonous animal, sliding down a mountain of sand] arise at night, repetition during the [next] day does not count unless one repeats the mantra of the lord of the lineage (p. 98) a hundred times [to overcome the bad signs]. It also says that though one might complete the entire count through repeating half in one place and half in another, all such repetition is to no avail.

With regard to missing the time of a rite or repetition or doing it at a wrong time, the morning period is from the dawning of half of the sun until a full-length shadow [is cast, that is, when the shadow of a stick is the same length as the stick]. At noon there is a period of eight or nine water-clock hours [192-216 minutes]. The afternoon period is from when a full-length shadow remains until half of the sun has set. Those are the periods of the day. The period of the beginning of night is from the setting of half of the sun through half the post-dusk time. The second period is from half dawn time [?] until half of the sun appears.

It is important to know the explanations in Varabodhi's *Clear Realisation*[150] that activities of fierceness, invisibility, and so forth as well as cemetery activities are performed from midnight on and that pacifications and so forth are performed at opposite times [in the morning before noon]. For it says that repetitions performed at the wrong time do not count.

[After completing a repetition rite] do as is quoted in Varabodhi's *Clear Realisation:*[151]

> When a repeater has finished repetition,
> By repeating twenty-one times
> [The mantras of] the mother and lord
> Of the lineage [the count] is always protected.

Manjughosha is the lord of the Tathagata lineage; Avalokiteshvara of the lotus lineage, and Vajrapani of the vajra lineage. Lochana is the mother of the Tathagata lineage; Pandaravasini of the lotus lineage, and Mamiki of the vajra lineage.

How to Conclude the Concentration of the Four-Branched Repetition[152]

Offering the Virtue

After the number of repetitions for the session is completed or exceeded, make the vase seal: put the middle-finger of the right hand behind the ring-finger, and put the middle-finger of the left hand behind the ring-finger; then join them [respectively]. Wrap the middle and ring-fingers of the left hand with the right forefinger, and wrap the middle and ring-fingers of the right hand with the forefinger of the left. Place side by side and straighten the two little fingers, and place the two thumbs at the centre joint of the forefingers (seal 36).

Offer the virtue:

> I offer this virtuous root of mine to the Blessed One as a cause of such and such feat. O Protector, please bestow such and such feat.

It is unrefined talk to assert that with this seal the rosary is offered [to the deity] when not performing repetition and is taken back when repeating.

Asking Forbearance and so Forth

Then, ask for forbearance for the fault of not having the circumstances to do the rite exactly according to the tantra, and make offering, praise, and so forth as before (pp. 126–34).

Requesting Departure

From the seal of invitation (seal 20) extend outside the two thumbs, making the seal of requesting departure (seal 37). At the end of your [particular] essence mantra or the general essence mantra add *gaccha* and ask the deity to depart along with the inestimable mansion.

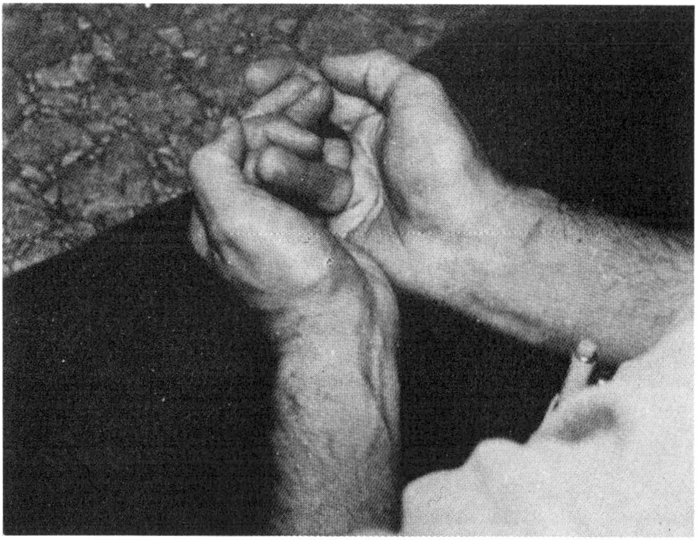

Seal 36

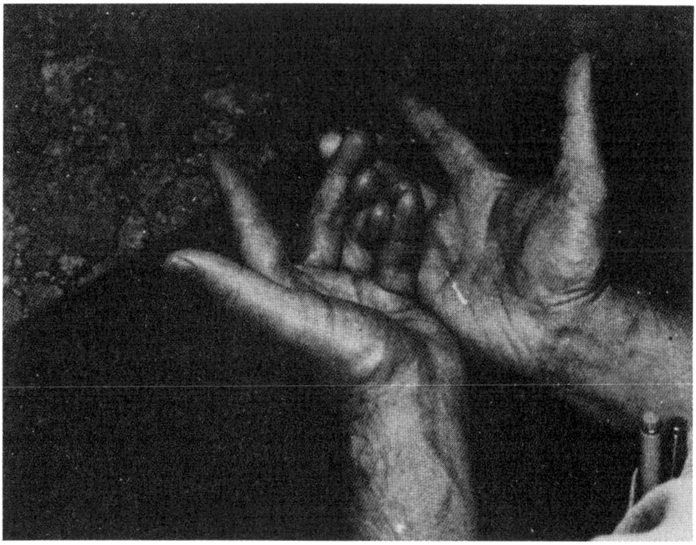

Seal 37

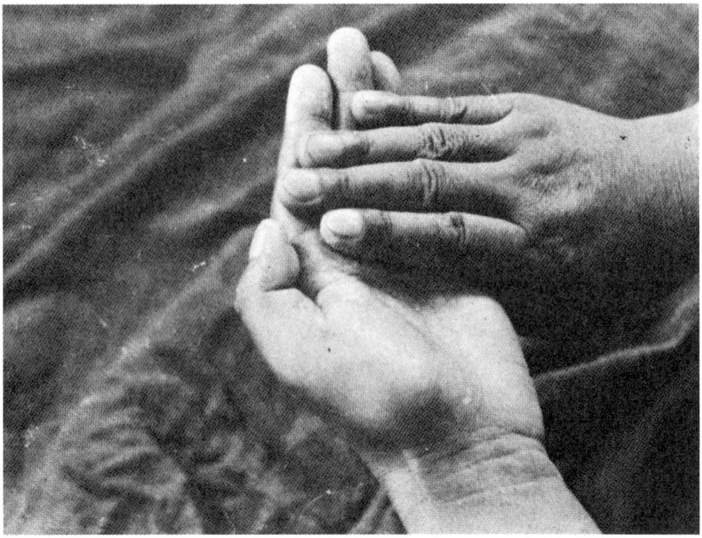

Then place the right palm on the left hand which has been turned up; join the tips of the crossed fingers to the base (seal 38); put this directly [in front]. Circle this seal of unequal limbs from the left, and free the directions and intermediate directions bound before, as well as [the upper and lower gods], with:
Oṃ hulu hulu chaṇḍali-mataṃ givi svāhā.

Between Sessions, Etc.[153]
Then [within the firm pride of being a deity] do such [activities] as reading a book of the perfection of wisdom, cultivating the six mindfulnesses [of Buddha, doctrine, spiritual community, giving, ethics, and gods], establishing mandala or bases of worship *(stūpa)*, and so forth.

The offering vessels should be washed daily; the flower offerings should be refreshed three times [daily]. Robes such as the upper one should be mantrafied and washed, scented, or sprinkled three times daily. The upper robe should always be worn when repeating, making burnt offering, offering, and so forth, except when sleeping or

reclining. Do not remove the lower robe except when sleeping or bathing, and do not let it become sullied with sweat. The mantra [to be cast in the robes] is:
Oṃ rakṣha rakṣha mānā sarva-buddha-adhiṣhṭhana ātma chivara svāhā.

Also, make food offerings (Tibetan *gtor ma,* Sanskrit *bali*) in accordance with the statement to make them for spirits on the occasion of approximation.

Tie seven knots in a red string wound by a girl [154] and dyed with poppy juice or camphor. Repeat a thousand times:
Oṃ āhara āhara bandhāni shukra-dharaṇi siddhārthe svāhā.
By tying it on the waist at night, it protects against emission.

You should perform the repettion rite as explained above, having bathed at the three times — morning, noon, and afternoon with the method [described on pp. 83–91).

Having fasted for one day each half-month, mantrafy a hundred times [a mixture of] the five cow-products — milk, yogurt, butter, dung, and urine of an orange-coloured cow — as well as kusha grass and water. Facing the east, squat, and drink it in any oblation vessel of about three 'ounces' *(srang).* The *Susiddhi Tantra*[155] says that if this is done one will be purified for a half-month and that whatever is eaten — unsuitable food and so forth — will be cleansed. The mantras of the three lineages for this are:

Tathagata Lineage
Namo bhagavate uṣhṇīshāyaṃ vishuddhe viraja shivi shantikare svāhā.

Lotus Lineage
Oṃ yashoje svāhā.

Vajra Lineage
Namo ratnatrayāya, namaṣhchaṇḍa-vajrapāṇaye, mahāyakṣha-sena-pataye, oṃ shikhi shikhi, nirmale, prabhesvare, tejo tejo vati svāhā.

8

Concentration Without Repetition

This section has two parts: The concentrations (1) of abiding in fire and in sound and (2) on the end of sound.

Concentrations of Abiding in Fire and in Sound

The *Concentration Continuation*[156] sets forth the three principles of abiding in fire, abiding in sound, and the end of sound:

> The secret mantra abiding in fire
> Bestows feats. That abiding in sound
> Bestows yoga. The end of sound bestows
> Liberation. These are the three principles.

Buddhaguhya's commentary says that meditation on the six deities and [all steps] prior are preliminaries for both concentrations [with and without repetition]. Also, he says that at this point the forms of Secret and Knowledge Mantra [deities] and so forth are to be manifested. Therefore, in order to generate these concentrations there must first be vivid appearance by way of the six deities as well as an ability to abide continuously in that vivid appearance. Furthermore, they must be done *within* visualisation of deity yoga.

Abiding in Fire

The *Concentration Continuation*[157] says:

A mantrika with intelligence binds to the self
[That is, to the mind] the phenomena arisen
From the non-distinguished [mental consciousness].
  Dwelling on what transcends
The branches [eyes and so forth], he concentrates
  without adherence.

When contemplating within adhering
To the immutable letters [that is, sounds] strung
  together,
Continual like the sounds of a bell and
Set in a series which is called 'sound',

He should contemplate [them as] abiding in fire —
  quiescent,
Free from words, having the branches [the mantra
  letters]
With a nature of having stopped vitality
And exertion as well as having forsaken sleep.

The stages of this are as follows. The first four lines indicate initial contemplation of the suchness of self. [They mean that] concentration should be performed. By whom? By a mantrika. How? He should cease adherence; here this means to cease the conception of true existence and not mere adherence to [or conception of] a conventional deity [for he still appears in the form of a deity and conceives that he is the deity]. He dwells on, that is, does not leave, [realisation of emptiness], the freedom from the elaborations [of inherent existence][158] which transcends the branches — [conventional phenomena such as] the eyes and so forth — in that these have been settled as not ultimately existent.

With respect to the mode of dwelling [on emptiness], that which is not distinguished or cannot be apprehended by the eye sense consciousness and so forth is the mental consciousness. The mind and mental factors concomitant with it are to be bound to the self — the mind — in the manner of the non-arising of entanglements, and thereby one dwells on that [freedom from the elaborations of the conception of inherent existence]. If one possesses intelligence, that is, wisdom, one can investigate suchness [the emptiness of inherent existence].

Then, upon rising from that [in the sense of ceasing to concentrate solely on emptiness], the principle of the sound deity is the appearance [of that wisdom consciousness] in the aspect of the mantra of one's deity [as if] being heard or in the aspect of its resounding. When through the yoga contemplating as one the principle of this sound deity and the suchness of self — like milk mixed in water — clarity is [attained], a mantrika abides in the deity yoga the nature of which is sound.

[The second stanza] should be put together to mean that 'one contemplates within adhering in mind' to the letters [that is, sounds] of the mantra joined or set in series. One might wonder whether the forms of the letters are to be arranged in series; therefore, it says, 'a series which is called 'sound' [that is, the sounds] of the mantra letters, 'like the sounds of a bell'. In order to make that definite, it says 'letters strung together'. 'Immutable' means that the sounds of the letters appear uninterruptedly and without fluctuation whereby they are like the continual arising of the external sounds of a bell being rung. You should concentrate on those sounds without adhering to their true existence.

[With respect to where this is imagined] contemplate a fire, burning like the tongue of flame of a butter lamp, at the heart of your [body] clarified as a deity, and think that the series of sounds described above abides there. Because it lacks the harm of heat and so forth, it is 'quiescent'. Since it is 'free from words' whispered or mentally repeated, it lacks those two types of repetition. It possesses without interruption 'the branches', which are the individual letters of the appropriate mantra.

In order to prevent excitement while contemplating in

this way, it says to stop vitality and exertion [breath and distraction] because when these are not stopped, the mind lacks equipoise, like a cow. Prevention of slackness or laxity is indicated by 'having forsaken sleep', since sleep is included in the scope of slackness. This [concentration] does not have the aspect of one's own reciting mantra mentally but is like listening to another's reciting mantra. One's own mind appears in the aspect of the tones of the mantra dwelling in the midst of the fire.

Buddhaguhya's commentary[159] says:

> Perform this concentration until the external and internal signs of no hunger or thirst and so forth occur, whereupon one can achieve what one wants.

The 'external signs' are not to be affected by hunger or thirst. The internal sign is to have generated meditative stabilisation in dependence on bliss and warmth through the force of observing fire and performing wind yoga.

Buddhaguhya's commentary[160] says that this [concentration of abiding in fire] may be performed after repetition or on other occasions by one who is practising the four-branched repetition for the sake of generating the power of mantra and of setting the mind in equipoise. Thus, since abiding in fire causes repetitions to become powerful and causes the mind to stabilise [the *Concentration Continuation Tantra* (p. 155)] says that it bestows feats [in the sense of bringing one closer to the achievement of feats].

Abiding in Sound

The *Concentration Continuation*[161] sets forth the concentration of abiding in sound:

> Place [a divine body which is] the base of the
>   immutable [mantra letters]
> In the very peaceful tongue
> Of flame with brilliant pure light
> That is in a subtle stainless moon disc dwelling
>   at the heart.
> Then contemplate the sounds while abiding in bliss.
> Or having set the [written] letters on the immutable
>   [moon disc],
> Contemplate only the sounds themselves.

A *subtle* stainless moon disc is contemplated in the heart because if it were large it would be difficult to eliminate thought [since the larger the object is, the greater is the tendency of the mind to stray]. A divine body that is the base of the immutable mantra letters is placed in the earlier tongue of flame dwelling in [the centre of] the moon disc [at the heart]. Then, leave that and concentrate [mainly] on only the mantra sounds. When exhaling, observe your own divine body [that is, the larger one, not just the one in the tongue of flame on the moon disc at the heart].

Here, when you observe the sounds, you should not [mainly] observe the deity and moon, or fire; thus this is different from the two modes of the four-branched repetition [observing the form and the sound of the letters] and the abiding in fire. This is because [as Buddhaguhya reports] other texts say that if one observes form when performing concentration on sound or being touched by wind, one's mind will be distracted.

[With regard to the variant mode of this concentration indicated by the last two lines of the quote from the *Concentration Continuation*] the mind of enlightenment realising suchness abides *solely* in an aspect devoid of [dualistic] appearance; therefore, it is called 'immutable'. Hence, the moon that symbolises it is also called 'immutable'. One observes the written syllables of the mantra on the moon disc and then, leaving that, concentrates on only the tones of the sounds.

This is different from the observation of sound in the four-branched repetition because there, having rested the mind [through observing] the divine body, one later [mainly] observes only the sounds [in the repetition observing the sounds of the letters] whereas here, having rested [through observing] the written syllables, one observes the sounds. Buddhaguhya's differentiation of them thus in his commentary is from the viewpoint of the objects of observation. However, the main difference is that formerly one observed the tones of the sounds within mental repetition whereas here one observes the tones of the mantra free from the aspect of one's own recitation [as if hearing another recite it]. For these [concentrations of abiding in fire and in sound] are again and again described as not involving repetition.

On this occasion also, Buddhaguhya's commentary sets forth wind yoga for stopping vitality and exertion [breath and distraction].

Concentration on the End of Sound

This section has two parts: the stages of leaving the state of sound and the actual concentration on the end of sound.

Stages of Leaving the State of Sound

The end of sound is the suchness free from the two extremes [of inherent existence and no conventional existence] in which one has left completely even an abiding in the mere mantra sounds. When it has been cultivated, one is freed from the two obstructions [to liberation from cyclic existence and to omniscience] and attains the liberation which has as its nature the Truth Body. The *Concentration Continuation*[162] says:

> A Conqueror knows the abandonment of the branches [states]
> Of the lords [deities] of knowledge mantra — the dependent
> Appearance with the limbs [of a deity], the one called 'sound' [whispered repetition],
> The mental one [mental repetition], and purity from words [that is, the concentrations of abiding in fire and in sound which are free from both whispered and mental repetition].

This passage indicates the stages of the path through familiarisation with which the concentration on the end of sound that bestows the liberation of the Truth Body is granted. Thereby, it clearly indicates the general stages of the path and the point where emptiness is meditated. [Realisation of emptiness was cultivated earlier at the time of the suchness of self, and a sense of it was maintained throughout all the subsequent yogas. However, here the yoga is not merely conjoined with the *force* of emptiness yoga; rather, the mind of deity yoga actually realises emptiness. Also, here emptiness is the *main* object, rather than a divine form, mantra letter, or sound.]

Buddhaguhya's commentary[163] says:

> Yogis engaging in the practice of secret mantra actualise the Truth Body through the stages of completely leaving the states of appearing with the limbs of secret mantra [a divine body], of sound [whispered repetition], of the mental one [mental repetition], and of verbal purity [the concentrations of abiding in fire and in sound which are free from whispered and mental repetition]. Therefore, it is said that if one has meditated on the end of sound — the nature of which is the element of [Superior] qualities (*dharmadhātu*) — liberation is bestowed.

[In the stanza above from the *Concentration Continuation*] 'knowledge mantra' is just an illustration; hence, it also refers to secret mantra. The lords of knowledge and secret mantras are those having the aspect of the goddess and god whom you are practising. Their 'branches' are the parts or states related with those deities. The 'abandonment' of them means to leave those states gradually.

From among the four states the first is the mantrika's appearing with the limbs of his deity in dependence on [having stopped] vitality and exertion [breath and distraction] as well as on asceticism, concentration, and so forth; this is his appearing in a divine body. The second is the branch called sound, the mantra state of performing whispered repetition. The third is the branch of mind, the state of performing mental repetition of mantra. The fourth is a purity from whispered and mentally repeated words — the concentrations of abiding in fire and in sound, in which the mind appears in the aspect of mantra sounds [as if recited by someone else]. The way to abandon these is to make the former firm and then move to the latter. Buddhaguhya's commentary [164] says:

> The stages of gradual abandonment of the coarse by one wishing for liberation are like this: having performed withdrawal, asceticism, concentration, [stopping] vitality and exertion, and so forth, one makes firm a very gross meditative stabilisation through observing the image of one's deity. Then, having thoroughly abandoned apprehension of that very coarse meditative stabilisation through[165] observing secret mantra sounds in whispered repetition, one makes firm a coarse meditative stabilisation. This apprehension of the coarse is also thoroughly abandoned through the subtle meditative stabilisation of

mental sound. Then, having also completely abandoned that, one abides in the very subtle meditative stabilisation of secret mantra imagination [free from repetition]. Having also abandoned that, one who wishes liberation earnestly performs the meditative stabilisation of observing the Truth Body.

[The stanza from the *Concentration Continuation* on p. 161] is interpreted in two ways: 'A Conqueror knows the stage bestowing liberation when emptiness is meditated after gradually leaving the four branches [that is, the four states described above].' Or: 'O Lord of Knowledge Mantra, when you leave those branches, you will become a Conqueror knowing the divisions of mantra meaning.' If the stanza is taken in accordance with the latter interpretation, it agrees with Buddhaguhya's summary exposition of the 'bestowal of liberation at the end of sound'.[166]

Question: If it is necessary also to leave off observing the divine body, why is the 'end of sound' described as merely leaving sound?

Answer: To leave the first branch [appearance as a deity] is to leave the place [or basis] of mantra *sound* because the mantrika who appears as a deity is the repeater of mantra. To leave the two middle branches [the stages of whispered and mental repetition] is to leave the compositional activity [involved in making] mantra *sound*, and to leave the last branch [abiding in fire and in sound] is to leave the very nature of mantra *sound*. Therefore, it is suitable to call the leaving of these a leaving of sound. Since not any of these appear in the face [of the ascertainment factor] of concentration observing suchness, it is said that they are left at this time [though they may still appear to the appearance factor of that concentration].

Here [with respect to the concentrations of Action Tantra] three meditative stabilisations are to be generated: observing a divine body, observing a divine speech mantra, and observing suchness — the divine mind. The first is a 'very gross' or very coarse meditative stabilisation. The second is subtler than that, and the third is very subtle. Hence, the order is definite, since they must be generated in the mental continuum in stages, beginning with the coarse.

Concerning this, initially it is necessary to generate a composite of *clarity* of the divine body and *dwelling* for a long time on it. Therefore, clear appearance must be achieved by means of concentration having many aspects because it arises from repeatedly putting in mind the aspects with which one is familiarising, as is the case with conditioning to desire or fright [whereupon their objects appear vividly to the mind. Also] if [the mind] is not set one-pointedly [on the divine body], then even though clear appearance arises, one cannot remain on a single object of observation as much as one wishes. Thus, it is [also] necessary to fixate by means of one-pointed meditative stabilisation as explained earlier (pp. 110–12).

About the way to attain a serviceable mind through such means the fifth chapter of the *Questions of Subahu* says:

> Look at the point of the nose and abandon thought.
> When though moving about one is immovable
> And a purity from states of unclarity is attained,
> The mind is certain to become serviceable.

As it says, the factor of stability, which is an immovability despite moving about,[167] must be free from laxity, for stability without an intensity of clarity does not preclude laxity.

Prior to repetition it is very important to achieve a firm

meditative stabilisation observing a deity. The *Questions of Subahu* says:

> In a person having a one-pointed mind
> Mentally arisen joy is strongly produced.
> Through joy physical pliancy is attained.
> Through suppleness of body one has the fortune of bliss.
> Through physical bliss, one-pointed mind, and meditative
> Stabilisation, repetition is then unobstructed.

In my *Stages of the Path Common to the Vehicles* I have explained the way of faultlessly achieving meditative stabilisation of one-pointed mind, the initial generation of mental pliancy from having achieved [meditative stabilisation], the generation of physical pliancy in dependence on that, the achievement of fully qualified calm abiding after that, and the generation of only a similitude of calm abiding prior to that.[168] Therefore, I will not elaborate on these points here.

In all four tantra sets the time of initially achieving a fully qualified calm abiding is chiefly when being instructed in deity yoga. Therefore, if you do not distinguish between fully qualified calm abiding and a similitude of it and do not differentiate finely the time of achieving calm abiding in accordance with how it appears in the great texts, you will not know the extent to which you must be led when initially being instructed in deity yoga.

When meditative stabilisation observing a [divine] body becomes firm, you leave that and train in meditative stabilisation observing a speech mantra. 'Leaving' should be understood as setting aside the training of continuously holding the mind on the [divine] body and mentally apprehending another object of observation. It does not preclude the later [continued] clear appearance of the deity because there are many descriptions of observing a deity during the three repetitions [observing the form of letters at the heart of the deity in front and at one's own heart and observing the sounds of the letters] as well as during abiding in fire and in sound.

Among the three types of observation of mantra, observation of the coarse means to observe the form or sound of letters and perform whispered repetition. This is a training in repetition such that only you can hear it while continuously holding the mind on the aspect of [written] syllables set on the moon or on the aspect of the tones, without scattering to anything else. When this repetition yoga — during which a mantra is repeated in speech and the mind does not scatter to anything other than the appropriate object of observation — becomes firm, you leave that training and train in the subtle. This is done until the two factors — (1) mere mental repetition without reciting the mantra in speech and (2) the mind's holding to either the aspect of the written form or the tone of the syllables without scattering to anything else — become firm. With the attainment of firmness, these are also left, and you train in the two very subtle concentrations [abiding in fire and in sound] whose nature is sound. Just your own mind realising the suchness of self appears in the aspect of mantra sounds and blazing fire — the objective factor — and it is held to this. Through sustaining such until the signs as explained before (p. 158) are attained, [the concentration of abiding in fire] becomes firm, and then it also is left, whereupon you train in the yoga of undifferentiable union of two factors — the vivid appearance of your own mind as having the aspect of the mantra tones, which are the objective factor, and the subjective factor's abiding on just the series of mantra sounds without scattering to anything else. The firming of this is the meaning of the bestowal of yoga by abiding in sound (see p. 155).

With respect to those two [concentrations of abiding in fire and in sound],for example, your own mind manifests simultaneously [during deity yoga] in the aspects of the face, arms, and so forth of a deity — the objective factor — while it abides one-pointedly on its object of observation. Similarly, here there is a steadiness of mind in which the appearance of the former letters [that is, sounds] in the series vividly manifest even when the aspects of the latter appear.

Actual Concentration on the End of Sound

Wind yoga is performed in order to stop vitality and exertion [breath and distraction] so that the mind can be held [on its object] starting from [observing] the divine body and going through abiding in sound. Through the force of wind yoga and observing fire as well as one-pointedly holding the mind on many coarse and subtle objects of observation such as a divine body, the factor of stability — as explained in the *Questions of Subahu* (p. 164–5) — becomes very firm. Also, there is generated a special joy and bliss in body and mind, as well as pliancy — physical and mental serviceability. In particular, through the force of long cultivation of wind yoga and observation of fire, bliss and warmth are generated. Based on them, powerful meditative stabilisation – blissful, clear, and non-conceptual — is generated. However, even these are not called the stage of completion [which only occurs in Highest Yoga Tantra], and because you have not yet gained a path eliminating the conception of self [inherent existence] — the root of cyclic existence — you leave abiding in sound and, cultivating the concentration bestowing liberation at the end of sound, meditate on emptiness [for the sake of achieving a union of calm abiding and special insight realising emptiness].

[The *Concentration Continuation* and Buddhaguhya's commentary] describe only briefly at this point how to cultivate this due to its having been explained earlier on the occasion of meditation on the suchness of self. Thus, the earlier description will be utilised here in explaining the concentration on the end of sound.

As explained before (pp. 104–6), the [coarse and subtle] selves of persons and other phenomena are refuted by scripture and reasoning, and one should first seek the view of the middle way, realising that all phenomena do not ultimately exist. This is because a mere non-conceptuality without having gained that view does not have even the slightest meaning of meditation on emptiness.

With respect to how to cultivate the view when it is found,[169] you must meditate within possession of the two features mentioned in the *Concentration Continuation Tantra*, immovability and clarity (see quote, p. 105). If you analyse too much with the view of selflessness, excitement is generated and [the mind] wavers. Therefore, you should single-pointedly sustain just that ascertainment — inducing firm understanding of the meaning of selflessness — and not analyse a great deal.

If, having performed such stabilising meditation, you fixate too much, [the mind] will not spread into individual analysis of phenomena and will become completely non-conceptual, unable to diffuse when it should. Since calm abiding is then predominant, the factors of calm abiding and special insight will not be equal. Also, if you fixate too much in that [state], slackness, or laxity, and lethargy are induced, whereby [the mind] becomes lax and lethargic. This is similar to the fact that when special insight predominates due to too much analysis, excitement is finally generated.

Therefore, you should perform both *analysis* training in the dexterity of analytical wisdom and one-pointed *stabilisation*. Buddhaguhya's commentary[170] says:

> Now, to indicate that the nature of the wisdom of the suchness of self is without slackness and excitement,

[the *Concentration Continuation*] says 'unmoving and clear'. Immovability is synonymous with non-wavering. This expresses that a yogi with excited wisdom should stop excitement, which is characterised by a non-pacification of movement in a mind that is accustoming to thought thoroughly analysing phenomena. Therefore, it mentions an immovable mind, pacified in the path.

Thus, having cited a scriptural source [from the *Concentration Continuation*], Buddhaguhya says that since too much analysis is a fault, one should perform stabilising meditation [at that time]. His statement that the wisdom differentiating phenomena has the character of excitement means that if one analyses too much, excitement is finally generated. How could it mean that wisdom itself is a case of excitement!

Buddhaguhya's commentary[171] also says:

Similarly, 'clear' means pure; it is synonymous with freedom from the faults of lethargy and so forth. This indicates that a yogi engaged solely in calm abiding should stop the factor of lethargy which is discordant with analysing phenomena and is characterised as a slackness of mind which is an over-fixating in equipoise even when analysing phenomena.

This means that when one stabilises too much, lethargy and laxity are finally generated and that these are factors discordant with thorough analysis of phenomena. It does not indicate that calm abiding itself is slackness and lethargy.

In the same fashion, the last of Kamalashila's [three works on the] *Stages of Meditation (Bhāvanākrama)* says:

When, due to having cultivated special insight, wisdom becomes too dominant, calm abiding is lessened.

> Thereby, like a butter-lamp set in a breeze, the mind wavers, due to which suchness is not seen very clearly. Therefore, at that time you should cultivate calm abiding. Also, when calm abiding is predominant, you will, like a person asleep, not see suchness very clearly. Therefore, at that time you should cultivate wisdom. When, like two oxen yoked as a pair, both are engaged equally, you should abide without application [of the antidotes to a predominance of either] as long as body and mind do not become adversely affected.

In accordance with his statement, you should, between calm abiding and special insight, emphasise cultivating whichever is not predominant and meditate, having caused them to become equal.

When the factor of calm abiding becomes predominant and calm abiding and special insight are not in balance, you should not hold that you have attained mastery over non-conceptual meditation. Also, you should not hold the system of the Chinese abbot [*Mahāyāna Hvashang*] for, without identifying the measure of what [in the view of selflessness] is refuted by reasoning, [proponents of the Chinese abbot's system mistakenly] think that all conceptuality whatsoever, thinking, 'It is such and such', are conceptions of true existence. Thinking that all these are refuted in the Madhyamika texts, they then [wrongly] hold that all analytical meditations involving individual investigation are hindrances to full enlightenment. The root text and commentary to the *Concentration Continuation* clearly speak to this; Buddhaguhya's commentary[172] says:

> Thus, the suchness of self has the character of being experienced as without the branches [the five senses], observation, form, or aspect, immovable and clear. However, this is asserted as not having forsaken the

path of analysis. Therefore, [the *Concentration Continuation*] says that 'mental analysis remains in its presence'. 'Mental' refers to wisdom; its operating on its object is 'analysis' and thus 'mental analysis'.

This mental analysis, characterised by the illumination of wisdom, dwells in the presence of the suchness of self; [thus, the text says that] 'mental analysis remains in its presence'. The passage explains that though the nature of self-knowledge is non-conceptual, the illumination of wisdom engages in analysis in the presence [of the suchness of self].

This establishes that the wisdom of individual analysis is not fit to be forsaken even on the occasion of meditating on suchness.

In brief, during the concentrations of abiding in sound and below, calm abiding is achieved, and with the end of sound special insight is cultivated. If during this process the wisdom of individual analysis is excessive, the former factor of stability disintegrates. Therefore, performing analytical and stabilising meditation alternately, you should attain a *union* of calm abiding and special insight.

In order to achieve the limitless varieties of activities of special feats just as they are described in Action and Performance Tantras, they must be preceded by the four-branched repetition and the concentrations of the three principles [abiding in fire, in sound, and the end of sound]. However, there is no certainty that such is needed in order to achieve many minor feats. [Great feats such as living for a great aeon require the completion of all the above concentrations to the point where a meditative stabilisation which is a union of calm abiding and special insight observing emptiness is attained, whereas lesser feats such as pacifying illness or increasing intelligence do not.][173]

9

Feats

The presentation of how [common][174] feats are achieved once the approximation is serviceable:

The *Susiddhi Tantra*[175] says:

> Very supreme activities are achieved
> Through special repetition. Even during
> Prior approximation
> Minor activities will be achieved.

The *Questions of Subahu* says:

> Having first repeated a hundred thousand according
> To the rite, engage thereon in achieving
> Secret mantra, then feats will quickly be attained.
> One is not long troubled with secret mantra rites.

Also, the *Concentration Continuation*[176] says:

> If a person knows all the principles
> Of knowledge mantras, the rite of suchness
> Of self, and the supreme principles
> Of repetition, he will attain feats.

Thus, it is said that when preceded by the yoga of the four-branched repetition, feats are achieved. Therefore, prior to achieving pacifying, increasing, or fierce activities — such as increasing wisdom and the lifespan — you must perform the approximation and then apply yourself to the activities. [Upon finishing the approximation the same rite is used in modified form in a second stage called 'achieving', or rites of burnt offering are performed, etc.; the third stage is the activity or feat itself, using it for the benefit of others.] This is the system of all four tantras.

Lineage.[177] Pacifying, increasing, and fierce activities are respectively achieved by way of [the mantras of] the Tathagata, lotus, and vajra lineages. Supreme, middling, and low feats [within the common] are achieved similarly. Pacifying activities include pacifying untimely death, illnesses, epidemics, harmers, and contagion. Increasing activities include increasing the lifespan, youth, magnificence, power, qualities [of realisation, etc.], and desired objects [such as resources]. Fierce activities include killing, expelling, [confusing], and so forth [of harmful beings].

Season.[178] During the waxing [from the first to the fifteenth] of the last month of winter, the second month of autumn, the first and second months of spring, and the first month of summer, supreme feats and pacifying activities should be achieved. There are no obstructors with respect to the first [that is, supreme feats within the common]. It is auspicious to perform pacifying activities mostly in the autumn; increasing, in the winter; fierce, in the late spring. Middling and lesser feats should be practised during the wane [from the sixteenth to the thirtieth] of those five months [last month of winter, second of autumn, first and second of spring, and first of summer].

Time.[179] The time for high, middling, and low feats and for pacifying, increasing, and fierce activities are respectively morning, post-dusk, and midnight or noon. Also, pacifying activities [should be achieved] from the first day of the month until the fifteenth; increasing, from the fifteenth to the fifteenth; fierce, during the wane.

Times auspicious for all activities are the first half of the first month, lunar or solar eclipse, and the first, third, fifth, seventh, and thirteenth days of the month as well as times of the appearance of the gar-ma-gyel (*skar ma rgyal*) constellation.

Place.[180] High, middling, and low feats should be practised respectively on mountains and so forth, lake shores and so on, and other places concordant with mantra. They should not be done in dilapidated houses, etc.

Posture.[181] Use the lotus cross-legged posture for pacifying activities; the lucky posture for increasing activities; press one foot with the other for fierce activities. Face the north, east, and south [respectively].

Agent.[182] Since each lineage also has the three feats and the three activities — pacifying, increasing, and fierce — the activities of pacification and so forth are achieved by way of the lineage lord, mother, and fierce one.

Divisions.[183] With respect to how feats are divided into three [high, middling, and low], there are many approaches. From the approach of entity, the high are knowledge-bearing [such as being able to proceed to a pure land with one's usual body], clairvoyance, knowing all treatises [immediately upon reading], and so forth. The middling are invisibility, essence-taking [empowering a pill so that all nourishment can be gained from it or so that one immediately turns into a youth], speedy feet, etc. The low are control of others, killing, expelling, and so forth [of harmful beings].

The three from the approach of lineage have already been explained (p. 174). From the approach of signs [which are external indications of having attained capacity] there are three by way of substances blazing [with fire], giving off smoke, and giving off heat.

By way of base, there are feats of (1) [enhancing] the body [so that it becomes free from disease, youthful, etc.], (2) [using] substances [such as leaves, swords, and so forth for gaining feats], and (3) [changing ordinary] resources [into marvellous ones]. By way of speakers, there are [feats achieved through] mantras [set forth] by Superiors, deities, and those above the earth [*yakṣha*, Smell-Eaters, etc.].

Though the [deity] bestowing a feat [to a particular practitioner] might be supreme, there are cases of a low feat being granted due to the practitioner's not working hard at approximation. However, if the approximation is done well, there are instances of a low [deity's] granting a supreme feat through [the deity's] requesting such from another [higher deity].

Analysing dreams.[184] Prior to [the stage of effecting] the achievement of a feat, the technique for examining omens of whether the feat will be achieved or not involves fasting on the full moon day or any auspicious day of the moon's waxing and then analysing dreams for one or three nights. You should bathe with the bath-oil of *dhātri (emblica officinalis)* and fragrant perfume, perform the ablution, put on new clean clothes, offer oblations during the post-dusk period as explained before (pp. 117–18, 126), and invite your deity.

Suffusing the offerings with white sandalwood and so forth as well as [mixed] incense, make the offering. Offer many good food offerings that contain yogurt. Offer one hundred and eight burnt offerings of butter and burnt pourings [in a fire] of *sarjarasa* sticks *(vatica robusta)* according to the activity.

Make seven knots in a string wound by a girl and, having mantrafied it seven times with the mantra of your deity, tie it around the left upper arm. Make a petition to the deity to reveal in a dream whether that which is intended to be effected will be achieved or not. Then, contemplating yourself as like your deity, lie down while reciting the deity's mantra on a mattress of *kusha* grass strewn with many flowers.

If you dream joyful dreams of the Three Jewels, your deity, Bodhisattvas, the four types of retinue [monks, nuns, male and female lay devotees], mountains, elephants, waterfalls, obtaining jewels and clothing, and so forth, then you should begin the [stage of] achievement.

Effecting the achievement. Then, to effect the achievement, do the many things that are prescribed [in the particular text] such as for achievement by means of burnt offerings or by mere repetition and meditation of mantra, etc.

Three times [each day] make offerings, confess sins, admire [your own and others'] virtue, plant aspirational wishes, read books of the perfection of wisdom, make mandalas, maintain vows, and do those things that are to be maintained three times, while changing clothes thrice daily. If, having become unconscientious, it happens that you do not perform these three times, recite your deity's mantra twenty-one times. For high, middling, and low feats fast respectively for three days, two days, or one day. I have explained these points in accordance with what the *Susiddhi Tantra* says.

On these occasions [of effecting the achievement] it is not sufficient to invite the deity in front; the deity must newly be generated. According to the two masters [Varabodhi and Buddhaguhya], to achieve a mandala [for this] or to generate a vase [as an inestimable mansion for the deity], etc., you should perform the ritual of self-generation of the six deities explained earlier and then, when performing repetition, do whichever of the first two of the four-branched repetitions [observing the form of the letters at the heart of the deity in front or at your own heart] is appropriate. For the substance of the vase, the generation rite, and so on, it is sufficient to use the usual.

The *Susiddhi Tantra*[185] explains that if on the occasion of such yoga you have less hunger, become free from a discasc, bccomc of an unusual mind, become of especially great and steady magnificence, dream auspicious and true dreams, develop a greater liking for repetition, are little fatigued, [smell] fragrant odours [without depending on external substances], are intent on good qualities, or develop greater respect for the deity, these are signs of effectiveness in repetition and meditation.

The *Concentration Continuation*[186] says that non-faith, indolence, being overcome[187] by hunger and thirst, excitement, great mental pain, doubt about the activity [which you are trying to achieve], not adhering to repetition and concentration, liking senseless talk, engaging in unsuitable actions, possession by an evil spirit, dreaming bad dreams, and so forth are causes of the deity's approaching elsewhere [that is, becoming farther away from yourself]. It says that pacifying desire, hatred, haughtiness, deceit, and so forth as well as continuous abiding in repetition are causes of the deity's approaching. These should be understood [as applying] during initial approximation.

Prior to achieving minor feats of your own and others' welfare — such as pacifying sickness — and prior to performing initiations, consecrations, and so on you must complete the prerequisite meditative stabilisation of the six deities and the number of repetitions through the approach of the four branches. [For minor feats] it is very much all right even if you have not cultivated the concentrations of the three principles [abiding in fire, in sound, and bestowing liberation at the end of sound]. Therefore, [insistence] on cultivating the concentrations of the three principles and on using all three objects of observation of repetition [the form of the letters in the heart of the deity in front and in one's own heart as well as the sounds] for [achieving] these [minor feats] is a case of not distinguishing when they are needed.

If one claims to know the meaning of Action and Performance Tantras
By knowing a portion of their meditations and repetitions
Such as fasting, bathing rites, and so forth, it is a source of laughter.
Therefore, cherish arrangement of the tantra meanings into paths.

This clear differentiation upon seeking the thought of the four general Action Tantras
And in particular of the *Susiddhi* and *Concentration Continuation Tantras*
According to the commentaries by the two Indian sages
Is the sole eye for viewing all the Action Tantras.

The second section of *Revealing All Secret Topics, The Stages of the Path to a Great Vajradhara,* called 'Stages of Progressing on the Path in Action Tantra', is concluded.

Performance Tantra

10

Outline

The presentation of the stages of the path in Performance Tantra has four parts: (1) how to become a receptacle suitable for cultivating the path, (2) having become a receptacle, how to maintain purity of pledges and vows,(3) how to perform prior approximation while abiding in the pledges, and (4) how to achieve feats once the approximation is serviceable.

How to Become a Receptacle Suitable for Cultivating the Path

One receives initiation in a mandala such as that of Mahakarunagarbhika as described in Performance Tantra and thereby becomes a receptacle for cultivating the path. Concerning this I have described mere entry into a mandala and the modes of initiation for one who has entered in my *Explanation of the Root Infractions.* Also, I will not write about the mandalas and rites of initiation because I fear it would make this text too long; these can be known from the *Vairochanabhisambodhi Tantra* and Buddhaguhya's commentaries on it[188] as well as the *Vajrapani Initiation Tantra,* etc.

Having Become a Receptacle, How to Maintain Purity of Pledges and Vows

The *Vairochanabhisambodhi Tantra*[189] says:

> The pledges are to be taught to him:
> From henceforth, child, you should not
> Forsake the excellent doctrine
> Or the mind of enlightenment
> Even for the sake of your life.
> You should not be miserly
> Nor injure sentient beings.
> The Buddha explains these pledges
> To you — a good system of conduct.
> Protect these just as you
> Would protect your own life.

Furthermore, you should act in accordance with the prescription to abide in the basis of training which is the abandoning of the ten non-virtues [killing, stealing, sexual misconduct, lying, divisive talk, harsh speech, senseless chatter, covetousness, harmful intent, and wrong views]. Regarding other pledges, since those described in Action Tantra are mostly shared [with Performance Tantra] you should keep them (see pp. 70–76).

The Mahayana vow that applies to both Action and Performance Tantra is, as the *Manjushri Root Tantra (Mañjushrīmūlatantra)* says, the Bodhisattva vow. Hence, root infractions are explained in Performance Tantra as they are in Asanga's *Bodhisattva Levels (Bodhisattvabhūmi)* and in the *Sutra on Skill in Means;* I have explained these at length in my *Explanation of the Ethics Chapter.* Furthermore, in my *Explanation of the Root Infractions* I have extensively explained about how in Action and Performance Tantra it is not fitting to hold the vows of the five lineages [since these tantras do not involve the vajra master initiation] and have also described at length the rite for assuming the Bodhisattva vows, the point at which one incurs a root infraction with regard to them, and so forth. Therefore, I will not elaborate on those points here.

How to Perform Prior Approximation While Abiding in the Pledges

Divisions of the Yoga for Prior Approximation

The *Vairochanabhisambodhi Tantra*[190] says:

> [O Vajrapani] Caretaker of the Secret, divine forms are of two types, thoroughly pure and thoroughly impure. About those the thoroughly pure are entities of realisation, free from all signs. The thoroughly impure are forms with signs — [a body with] colours and shapes. By means of the two types of divine forms two types of purposes are achieved; by means of the one with signs, [feats] having signs [Form Bodies] arise, and by means of the one without signs feats having signs also arise [that is, a Truth Body as well as Form Bodies are attained].
>
> The excellent Conquerors assert that feats
> Having signs [arise] through that with signs.
> Through abiding in the signless
> That having signs can also be achieved.
> Hence, you should rely in all
> Respects on the signless.

As it says, [the yoga for prior approximation] is of two types — yoga with and without signs.

Yoga with signs refers to deity meditation and repetition devoid of meditation on emptiness [in the sense that although it may be conjoined with the *force* of realising emptiness, the mind of deity yoga itself is not realising emptiness or is not conjoined with a mind of special insight actually realising it]. Yoga without signs refers to deity meditation and repetition involving meditation on emptiness [in the sense that the mind of deity yoga itself actually realises emptiness or, in other words, the wisdom consciousness itself appears in the form of a deity] and does not refer to meditation on emptiness alone. If yoga without signs did refer to just meditation on emptiness, it would be necessary to assert that one could be fully enlightened through emptiness yoga alone since the *Vairochanabhisambodhi Tantra* [as quoted above] says that both feats [supreme and common] can be achieved through the signless.

When that tantra teaches about thoroughly impure divine bodies, it calls them 'forms with signs', referring not just to a form with a face and arms but to a special form. Though Buddhaguhya uses the term 'deity' when he calls meditation on emptiness the 'ultimate deity',[191] here the terminology of 'deity' is used within the context of dividing the deity's *form* itself into two types [one not directly involving and the other directly involving meditation on emptiness] and in the context of [indicating] which feats are achieved. Also, Chandrakirti's *Brilliant Lamp* explains that this passage [from the *Vairochanabhisambodhi*] indicates [in a hidden way] the divine *bodies* of the two stages [of generation and completion in Highest Yoga Tantra. Therefore, it is mistaken to think that yoga without signs refers to mere meditation on emptiness.]

Mundane and Supramundane Yoga

[The yoga for prior approximation] is also divided into the mundane and supramundane [which are other names for the yogas with and without signs]. The *Vairochanabhisambodhi*[192] says:

> I have explained [the yoga] having four branches
> With external and internal application.
> This is the unsurpassed worldly imagination;

Suppressed with the word of withdrawal,
The mind which has accorded with the deity
Is taught as the supreme of whispered
Repetitions, having apprehension.

For the mentally supramundane,
Withdrawal [from external branches of repetition to
the internal] and so forth are completely abandoned.
[Oneself and the deity] are made undifferentiable in
[terms of their empty] nature
Through a mind creating oneness with the deity['s form]
And not conceiving of difference.
In no other way is [supramundane repetition] to be done.

The supramundane in this passage does not refer to a non-contaminated [wisdom consciousness in the continuum of a Superior *directly* realising emptiness] but is [a consciousness] having the aspect of selflessness [that is, realising emptiness conceptually *or* directly] or a yoga conjoined with that [in which the wisdom consciousness itself manifests in form].

Usage of the Terms 'With and Without Signs' and 'Stages of Generation and Completion'

Subhagavajra's *Stages of the Mahayana Path (Mahāyāna-pathakrama)*[193] says:

> Action, Performance, and Yoga Tantra set forth means of achievement with and without signs. The Great Yoga [Highest Yoga Tantra] sets forth the stages of generation and completion. Just these are the paths.

His description of the two stages as the system [only] of Highest Yoga Tantra and his using the terminology of the two yogas — with and without signs — for the lower tantra sets accord with the *Vairochanabhisambodhi Tantra* and are very good. I will explain the reasons later (pp. 201-2).

11
Yoga With Signs

This section has two parts, the external and internal four-branched repetitions.

External Four-Branched Repetition

There do not appear to be as many deity meditations and repetitions based on Performance as there are based on Action Tantra. Also, if one knows how to generate the yogas with and without signs in one's continuum, the subsidiary branches of the path are easier. Thus, here I will not explain the preliminary protection of oneself and the place, offering to [exalted beings who are] bases of the amassing [of the accumulations of merit], and so forth, but will describe the stages of cultivating the two yogas as well as repetition.

First Branch: Self-Generation

The first branch is to generate yourself as a deity; prior to this you should meditate on emptiness as follows:

> The Buddhas understand that my own aggregates which depend on the great elements [earth, water, fire and wind] are ultimately like space and conventionally like reflections. Since there are none greater than them, I should realise this in just the way that they perceive it. It is like this: both myself and the deity to be meditated do not have inherent existence in the sense of existing by way of our own entity because of being dependent-arisings, like reflections.

Contemplating thus, you should ascertain the absence of inherent existence of yourself and the deity.

Then:

> The two emptinesses which are the non-inherent existence of myself and the deity are undifferentiable.

You must train in this thought until firm ascertainment is gained, and then generate yourself as a deity. The *Vairochanabhisambodhi* states this clearly:

> A Bodhisattva practising the Bodhisattva deeds by way of Secret Mantra should generate his body as a [divine] physical body in the following way: there are none greater than the completely perfect Buddhas. The Tathagatas completely and perfectly realise that my eyes, ears, nose, tongue, body, mind and so forth are included in the four great elements and that even those [elements] are empty of their own entityness, included within mere nominalities, similar and akin to space, unapprehendable [as inherently existent], arisen from causes and actions *(karma)*, like reflections. Even those [elements] are continuously related as interdependent arisings. Whatever is dependently produced arises like a reflection. Thus, because of being interdependently arisen, that which the deity is I am; that which I am the deity is. This is how you should physically generate your physical form as a divine body.

In the four tantra sets the mode of meditating on emptiness prior to deity meditation is necessarily like this; without ascertaining [emptiness] by way of the view [of the middle way] it is senseless merely to utter a mantra such as *svabhāva*[194] . . . and withdraw appearance [leaving a vacuity that is not specified as being an absence of inherent existence]. Furthermore, Buddhaguhya's

Condensation of the 'Vairochanabhisambodhi Tantra' (Vairochanābhisambodhitantrapiṇḍārtha) quotes a passage from the tantra stating that one should ascertain the non-inherent existence of the aggregates and so forth through the reasoning of the lack of their being one or many and then perform deity yoga.

With respect to how to rise as a deity from within emptiness Buddhaguhya's *Condensation of the 'Vairochanabhisambodhi Tantra'* says:

> The stages of one's own conventional deity yoga are indicated here as of two types. Through transformation of the aspect of one's own mind, devoid of all appearance [and realising emptiness], into the aspect of a moon disc and so forth, one achieves appearance as one's own deity.

Thus, he sets forth one way in which [the mind realising emptiness] first [appears] as a moon and so forth and [later] a second way in which [the deity] is generated all at once without those preceding [steps]. Buddhaguhya says that these are taught in the chapter on the divine suchness and so forth in this tantra but such is missing in the tantra as translated [into Tibetan].

According to the first [of the two methods] you should contemplate the letter *aṃ* on a thoroughly complete moon disc which is a manifestation of your mind [realising emptiness]. Make light spread out from and gather back into the syllable. Then, through its transformation generate yourself as the great Vairochana with one face and two hands making the seal of meditative equipoise, with a body of golden colour surrounded by interwoven flame, sitting on cushions of white lotus and moon, with head adorned and plaited hair wound up on the top, and wearing light upper and lower garments.

Perform the blessing [of important parts of the divine

body] with mantras and hand symbols in either extensive or brief form. I will not write about these in detail (see pp. 108–9).

Second Branch: Generation in Front
Meditate on a Tathagata similar to yourself in front.

Third and Fourth Branches: Mind [moon] and Sound [letters]
Then set the mantra series to be repeated on a moon at the heart of the deity in front.

Those are the four branches of repetition. In this way the *Vairochanabhisambodhi Tantra*[195] says:

> Join the letters to the letter [a moon disc].
> Likewise they move from the base [in front] to the base [yourself].
> Very restrained you should make
> A hundred thousand repetitions in mind.
> 'Letter' is the mind of enlightenment [appearing as a moon].
> The second ['letters'] are called 'sounds' [the forms of the letters on the moon].
> 'Base' is to imagine one's own body
> As that of one's deity.
> That called the second base
> Is a perfect Buddha [imagined
> In front], the best of the two-legged.
> A mantrika contemplates with [mind]
> Abiding on a very pure moon disc.
> The letters are well set in order
> In the middle of that [moon disc].
> Upon having suppressed [the wandering mind] with the word of withdrawal.
> Vitality and exertion are thoroughly purified.
> 'Vitality' is explained as wind;
> 'Exertion' is mindfulness.
> Having restrained those two
> Perform prior approximation well.

Concerning the two 'letters' there is no clear statement in Buddhaguhya's two commentaries on the *Vairochanabhisambodhi*, but in accordance with his commentary on the *Concentration Continuation* explained earlier (pp. 141–2) they are the moon and mantra series from among the four branches. It is senseless to explain them as a moon [seat] and mantra at the time of deity generation.

Having restrained vitality and exertion [wind and distraction], one initially seeks stability with respect to the clear appearance of a divine body and then performs repetition within observing the letters. How these are done is similar to the earlier explanation on the occasion of Action Tantra.

After that passage the *Vairochanabhisambodhi Tantra*[196] says:

> Then a mantrika, very restrained,
> Should perform repetition for a month.
> The prior activity of secret mantra
> Is to put it from one base to the other.
> All the Buddhas having great fame
> Describe this as 'prior activity'.

Thus, it says to perform [repetition] for a month. 'To put it from one base to the other' means that if you become tired from observing the mantra set on the moon at the heart [of the deity] in front, you should alternate with [observing it] at your own heart.

The [earlier] statement (p. 192) to perform repetition in mind is just an illustration; hence, both whispered and mental repetition are set forth. The *Vairochanabhisambodhi*[197] says:

> A supreme yogi should analyse whether
> To repeat mentally or in whisper.

As before [in Action Tantra], with respect to these two types you should first perform whispered repetition and then, when doing it mentally, stop vitality and exertion [breath and distraction].

Internal Four-Branched Repetition

The first branch is to generate [yourself as a deity], as explained before, from any of the four — *a, ā, aṃ, aḥ* — from within emptiness. Buddhaguhya's *Condensation of the 'Vairochanabhisambodhi Tantra'*[198] describes this as generating [oneself] as Shakyamuni. He says that one should meditate on a very pure and stable moon disc, like a [two-sided][199] mirror — [set upright] at the heart of Shakyamuni — meditating until one sees one's own body as a divine one.

The second base is to meditate on Vairochana — as described before — in the [upright] moon as if dwelling in a cave. Contemplate the mantra as dwelling on a moon at his heart and perform repetition. [One's own mind meditated as the moon is the third branch, and the letters standing around the edge, the fourth.][200] It is said here to repeat the mantra one hundred thousand times. Here the need for the two repetitions [whispered and mental] and for restraining vitality and exertion [breath and distraction] when repeating mentally is similar.

After 'Describe this as "prior activity" ' the *Vairochanabhisambodhi*[201] says:

> After that offer even a few
> Flowers, incense, and so forth.
> Then also dedicate these to enlightenment
> In order to become a Buddha.
> A mantrika should perform repetition
> For a second month like that without fear.

Thus, it explains that one should perform the approximation for a month without mixing in offering flowers and so forth and for a month in connection with such. The *Vairochanabhisambodhi*[202] says:

> These counts of secret mantra which I have mostly
> Prescribed as three hundred thousand
> Are taught as the number of repetitions
> For very pure mantrikas —
> Embodied beings free from sin.
> They are not to be done in any other way.

You should meditate in this way until, in dependence on holding the mind that observes a divine body and on wind yoga, you attain calm abiding.

12

Yoga Without Signs

When you gain calm abiding observing the divine body, [moon, letters, sounds] and so forth, you should meditate on emptiness. The *Vairochanabhisambodhi Tantra*[203] says, 'In a grove, temple, cave, or place where your mind is isolated cultivate the [ultimate] mind of enlightenment, remaining until the mark [of success] arises.' Buddhaguhya's *Condensation of the 'Vairochanabhisambodhi Tantra'* explains the mark [of success] as a stable mind, [abiding] as long as one wishes in the meditative stabilisation realising all phenomena as without their own entityness.

Although a mode of meditating on emptiness is set forth prior to the four-branched repetition, it indicates how to take emptiness to mind *prior* to meditating on a deity. The stages of meditating mainly on emptiness [done at this point] are performed *after* deity yoga. Buddhaguhya's *Condensation*[204] says:

> The stages of the yoga for achieving repetition by way of familiarising with the meditative stabilisation of signlessness which has the character of the Truth Body of your own deity are as follows. As before, you should for a while actualise all the factors of the four branches of repetition, etc., and then analyse the imagined colour, shape, and so on of your deity who is non-dual with yourself, breaking them down into many particles.

The *Vairochanabhisambodhi Tantra*[205] sets forth at length how to meditate on signlessness:

> Lord of the Secret [Vajrapani], a Bodhisattva practising the Bodhisattva deeds by way of Secret Mantra who wishes to achieve the signless meditative stabilisation should contemplate in this way: From where do signs [of blue, yellow, and so forth] arise? Do they arise from my body, my mind, or my consciousness? About that, the body is produced from actions *(karma);* [thus] it should be analysed as naturally [matter and] without inherently existent activity [of giving rise to signs] like grass, or wood, or the wild aconite, as like a fool, or like a mannequin. For, if someone angers at a mannequin and destroys it with fire, poison, a weapon, water, or a diamond or burns or cuts it, it does not in the least dislike him.Though it is offered various articles of gods and humans such as food, drink, baths, fragrant ointment, garlands, clothing, sandalwood, camphor, and so forth, it does not come to like that man. Why? A man who, out of incorrect thoughts due to error aroused by his own pride, makes offering or does harm to a form empty of entityness has the nature of a child. Lord of the Secret, in that way you should cultivate mindfulness of the body as empty of inherent existence.

Thus, it sets forth ascertainment and meditation of the body as empty of its own inherent existence.

With regard to how to analyse the mind, the same text[206] says:

> Lord of the Secret, furthermore you should contemplate the mind as without entityness, free from all signs [of blue, yellow, and so forth], and empty of inherent existence. Lord of the Secret, the mind does not have the three times [future, present, and past or product-

> ion, abiding, and cessation]. You should contemplate it thinking thus, 'That which is separate from the three times is inherently without signs.' However, Lord of the Secret, childish common beings conceive of the mind as having signs; this is the same as an unreal conception. That which is unreal is not to be known as 'non-produced'. Lord of the Secret, if a Bodhisattva who is practising the deeds by way of Secret Mantra has contemplated in this way, he will attain the meditative stabilisation of signlessness. Lord of the Secret, when he dwells in the signless meditative stabilisation, he approaches and tends toward the secret mantra [feats] set forth by the Tathagata.

Thus, it sets forth how the mind does not inherently exist, that the conception of its true existence is merely a mental superimposition, that if analysis of body and mind are done in that way the meditative stabilisation of signlessness is attained, and that when this meditative stabilisation is attained feats of mantra are attained.

Moreover, Buddhaguhya's *Condensation of the 'Vairochanabhisambodhi'*[207] says:

> Having manifested appearance in colour and shape with yourself and the deity non-dual, analyse [the divine body] by breaking it down into subtle particles. Or it is also suitable to do this by way of the reasoning of its not having been produced from the start and its not being produced, or by way of the reasoning [that is, technique][208] of withdrawing vitality [wind or currents of energy] through the yoga of turning your mind inside, or by way of not taking the appearance of colour and shape to mind. In accordance with that realisation actualise mere self-knowledge of the mind, without [dualistic] appearance, free from your own divine form body, and repeat mentally whatever your knowledge mantra is.

It says to meditate on the meaning of that which is without appearance and free from the deity's colour and shape (1) at the end of analysing with the reasoning of the lack of being one or many or the diamond slivers, or (2) by way of setting the mind on the meaning [of emptiness] explained earlier (pp. 198–9) through withdrawing its running to the outside by means of the reasoning [that is, technique] of withdrawal of vitality [wind], or (3) by way of not taking to mind the elaborative appearance [of the deity's body and so forth] within mindfulness of the view [of emptiness]. You should meditate in this way.

These accord greatly with Kamalashila's [three works on the] *Stages of Meditation*, the last of which says:

> The *Cloud of Jewels Sutra* says, 'One who is skilled in this way about faults takes as his yoga meditation on emptiness in order to become free from all elaborations. Through much meditation on emptiness, when he thoroughly examines the nature of those places where his mind scatters and which it likes, he realises them as empty. When he analyses what the mind is, he realises it as empty. When he examines by what mind that is realised, he realises it as empty. Through realising such he enters into the yoga of signlessness.' This indicates that whoever does not analyse in this way will not enter into signlessness.

Kamalashila says that since the sutra explains that one who analyses by means of the wisdom of individual analysis will enter into the yoga of signlessness, implicitly [it can be understood that] if one abandons the wisdom of individual analysis, one will not enter into the yoga of signlessness.

In this tantra also it is said that one wishing to achieve the meditative stabilisation of signlessness should analyse the body and mind as not established in reality. Hence, it also indicates that if one does not analyse with the wisdom investigating the suchness of things, the meditative stabilisation of signlessness will not be produced.

Therefore it is necessary to sustain the continuum of a consciousness that ascertains the meaning of the non-inherent existence of all phenomena as settled through the view [of emptiness]. Setting in non-conceptuality a mind that does not understand the view or, despite having gained the view, sustaining mere non-conceptuality at the time of meditation without sustaining ascertainment [of emptiness] by means of the view is not meditation on emptiness. As explained earlier (pp. 168–71) you should alternate analytical and stabilising meditation since if you analyse too much by way of special insight it is unsuitable.

The Four Yogas

Thus, in Action and Performance Tantra there are four important yogas — deity, emptiness, wind, and repetition yogas. About these the two yogas of the ultimate [emptiness] and conventional deities are the main means of achieving the two Bodies [Truth and Form]. Since repetition is a branch [of the process] of arousing the mind of the deity being meditated, it is included as a branch of conventional deity yoga. Since wind yoga is a branch [of the process] of making both deity yogas stable, it is included in both. Thereby, [the four] are included in the two yogas — [conventional and ultimate or] with and without signs.

Though that is so, it is explained that these do not involve the stage of completion [which is found only in Highest Yoga Tantra]. Therefore, you should know that the generation of a blissful, clear, and non-conceptual meditative stabilisation through the force of holding the winds inside and even the yoga of signlessness which is based on that are not the stage of completion. The uncommon [features of] the stage of completion in Highest Yoga Tantra should be known without confusion. For, if you do not know in detail just what the features of the path are in these lower tantra sets, you will not know the uncommon paths of the higher.

How to Achieve Feats once the Approximation is Serviceable

The *Vairochanabhisambodhi Tantra* sets forth the achievement of the sword knowledge bearer and so forth in dependence on external substances such as a sword [for flying in space], the achievement of activities such as pacification and increase through having meditated on discs of earth, water, fire, and wind in internal places in the body, and the attainment of the meditative stabilisation of not forgetting the altruistic mind of enlightenment upon performing the achievement [of the appearance] of Manjushri and so forth whereupon those Bodhisattvas eventually stroke one's head or say 'Well done', after one has done repetition until such occurs. Many ways of achieving such feats are described.

Conclusion

If, through this good arrangement of the meanings of all the Action and Performance Tantras into these four general structures containing the paths (p. 66), the tantras appear [to you] as instructions [for practice], then you can be counted among those knowing the tantras. Since otherwise one who knows just a portion of the path does not know the essential points of the general path, those with intelligence should strive at means whereby the texts of these two tantra sets appear as instructions [for practice].

This description of the stages of the two yogas
In accordance with the explanation by Buddhaguhya,
scholar and adept,
Of the meaning of the chief Performance Tantra, the
Vairochanabhisambodhi,
Is a door for easy entry to Performance Tantra.

The third section of *Revealing All Secret Topics, The Stages of the Path to a Great Vajradhara*, called 'Stages of Progressing on the Path in Performance Tantra', is concluded.

III
Supplement

JEFFREY HOPKINS

The Need for Common Feats

Since a Mahayanist wishes to attain Buddhahood in order to help other beings, it is not sufficient merely to be liberated from cyclic existence. It is necessary to attain a state wherein the welfare of others can be accomplished effortlessly and spontaneously. This is done only with the Form Bodies of a Buddha — Complete Enjoyment and Emanation Bodies — and thus a Bodhisattva seeks the omniscience of Buddhahood.

Such omniscience is attained through removing the subtle obstructions which prevent simultaneous realisation of all knowable objects — specifically, the appearance of objects as if existent in their own right and the consequent inability to realise the two truths, emptinesses and conventional objects, in direct cognition at the same time. In order to gain the capacity to overcome these obstructions the wisdom consciousness of a Bodhisattva must be enhanced. In the Sutra, or Perfection, Vehicle a Bodhisattva does this through training in the six perfections — giving, ethics, patience, effort, concentration, and wisdom — in limitless forms over a 'limitless' time, three periods of a countless number of great aeons. ('Countless' refers to a one with fifty-nine zeros, and a 'great aeon' is composed of eighty intermediate ones — twenty each for formation of the world system, abiding of it, destruction, and vacuity.)[209] The practice of these deeds of giving and so forth empowers the mind so that eventually the wisdom consciousness realising the emptiness of inherent existence can eradicate the obstructions to omniscience. That is the Sutra mode of procedure.

The Mantra or Tantra path also has as its basis the generation of an altruistic aspiration to highest enlightenment and also involves the practice of the six perfections, but not for a limitless time in limitless varieties as is done in the Perfection Vehicle. Rather, all four tantra sets make use of deity yoga, the special tantric means for amassing the collections of merit and wisdom quickly. Highest Yoga Tantra has, in addition, techniques for generating subtler minds that realise emptiness and for using the winds or currents of energy that are the mounts of these subtler minds as the substantial cause of an actual divine body. Through this enhancement of the wisdom consciousness the obstructions to omniscience are quickly removed and Buddhahood is attained.

In the three lower tantras — Action, Performance, and Yoga — deity yoga is used to bring about the speedy achievement of many common feats and to come directly under the care of Buddhas and high Bodhisattvas, receiving their blessings, and so forth. This is done through a threefold process known as prior approximation, effecting the achievement of feats, and using the feats in the performance of activities for the welfare of others.

The initial period of deity yoga is called prior approximation because one is accustoming to a deity through becoming closer and closer to its state, whereupon the deity grants the feat, either directly or in the sense of bestowing a capacity to the mind. Actually effecting the achievement of feats is done by way of carrying out prescribed burnt offerings or repetition of mantra, etc., after the approximation has been completed. These feats are then used for the welfare of others in the third stage, which involves activities of (1) pacification such as overcoming plague or relieving others of demons, (2) increase of lifespan, intelligence, wealth, and so forth, (3) control of resources, persons harmful to others' welfare, etc., and (4) ferocity, such as expelling or confusing harmful beings.

These feats — as well as the capacity to understand all treatises immediately upon reading them, clairvoyance, and so forth — are attained through cultivation of deity yoga, itself a means for amassing the collections of merit and wisdom quickly, and their use for the benefit of others amasses even more merit. Through this speedy and profound process the merit necessary for the achievement of Buddhahood is accumulated in less than the three periods of countless great aeons required in the Sutra Vehicle, whereby the path to Buddhahood is shortened.

Na-wang-bel-den's *Presentation of the Grounds and Paths of Mantra*[210] says:

> The attainment of the supreme [state of Buddhahood] by means of the three lower tantra sets depends on prior achievement of worldly feats. . . . Thus, Tsong-ka-pa says, 'Initially, one maintains purely the pledges and vows that are the sources of feats. Then one strives at the yogas with and without signs, and when capacity is attained one effects the achievement of common and uncommon feats whereby progress is made on the path. This mode of procedure should be known for the three lower tantras [Action, Performance, and Yoga]. . . .'
>
> There is a reason why one must first achieve common feats in order to achieve the supreme through the paths of the three lower tantra sets, for as Shantideva's *Engaging in the Bodhisattva Deeds* (*Bodhicharyāvatāra,* IX. 1ab) says:
>
>> All these branches [of giving, ethics, etc.]
>> were spoken
>> By the Subduer for the sake of wisdom.
>
> It is the system of both Mahayanas [Perfection and Mantra Vehicles] that the factors of method enhance

> the wisdom consciousness realising emptiness. In the Perfection Vehicle this wisdom consciousness is caused to possess the capacity to abandon the obstructions to omniscience through training for a limitless time in limitless varieties of giving and so forth. . . . However, the three lower tantras do not say that one trains for a limitless time in limitless varieties of giving and so forth as in the Perfection Vehicle, nor do they set forth a means of generating a special subject [that is, a subtler consciousness] that realises emptiness, as is done in Highest Mantra [Highest Yoga Tantra]. Therefore, the realisation of emptiness must be enhanced through skill in means, such as many common feats and being blessed under the direct care of Buddhas and higher Bodhisattvas. . . .
>
> The mere rough corpus of the path — altruistic mind generation which is the basis of the [Bodhisattva] deeds and training in the six perfections which are the deeds — is common [to the Perfection and Mantra Vehicles] but the training in limitless varieties of giving and so forth is not shared with Mantra.

In Highest Yoga Tantra techniques are used to generate special minds — called the minds of radiant white appearance, radiant red increase, radiant black attainment, and clear light,[211] respectively more and more subtle — which are used to cognise emptiness. The techniques revolve around using in the path the bliss arising from the desire for male-female union. Thus in Highest Yoga Tantra the usage of desire in the path is for the sake of enhancing the wisdom consciousness realising emptiness by way of actually generating subtler consciousnesses that realise it.

In the lower tantras, although desire is used in the path to enhance the wisdom consciousness so that it can gain the capacity to overcome the obstructions to omniscience, it is not used to manifest subtler consciousnesses. Nevertheless, the bliss consciousness that — in the practice of Action Tantra — arises upon the mutual gazing of the meditated god and goddess is used to realise emptiness. However, it is not a subtler consciousness, as in Highest Yoga. Due to this difference between Highest Yoga Tantra and the three lower ones, the feature of the latter's path being faster than the Perfection Vehicle is not described as arising from using desire in the path but from the attainment of common feats. In Highest Yoga Tantra, on the other hand, the feature of achieving Buddhahood in one short lifetime of this degenerate era is through using desire in the path to generate subtler wisdom consciousnesses.

Tsong-ka-pa explains that, therefore, the attainment of Buddhahood in one short lifetime is a distinguishing feature of Highest Yoga and that it is mistaken to hold that such can be done through the paths of the three lower tantras alone without eventually using those of Highest Yoga.

Na-wang-bel-den's *Presentation of the Grounds and Paths of Mantra*[212] says:

> The three lower tantras do involve using in the path the bliss that arises upon looking at, smiling at, and holding hands or embracing a meditated Knowledge Woman [consort]; however, this is not done for the sake of generating a special subject [that is, subtle consciousness] realising emptiness, for such is a distinguishing feature only of Highest Yoga Tantra. Nonetheless, most of [Tsong-ka-pa's] followers explain that this does not mean that the bliss [consciousness] that arises upon looking, smiling, and so forth does not realise emptiness . . . . [Still] Tsong-ka-pa says that the faster speed of the path [in the lower three tantras] comes by way of common feats and so forth. He does not say

> anywhere that it comes from a more powerful mind realising emptiness by way of using desire in the path . . .
>
> [Although the three lower tantras present a path that is faster than the Perfection Vehicle] Tsong-ka-pa's *Great Exposition of Secret Mantra* says, 'The feature of speed in which complete enlightenment [is attained] without depending on the passage of countless aeons is a distinguishing trait of Highest Yoga. Therefore, the attainment of such by the trainees of the lower tantra sets is in dependence on their entering the two stages of Highest Yoga; their own paths alone are not sufficient. Hence, do not hold that all features of speed in Mantra are only to become fully enlightened in one lifetime of this era of disputation or without depending on countless aeons [of practice].'

In Action Tantra the special techniques involved in the four-branched repetition and the concentrations of abiding in fire, of abiding in sound, and on the end of sound make it possible to pass from the path of accumulation to the path of seeing — which usually takes one period of countless great aeons — in as little as several years.

The General Meditation

Action Tantras are of two types, general and specific. General ones present the path and surrounding activities in a manner that is suitable for all three Action Tantra lineages — Tathagata, lotus, and vajra. Specific tantras, on the other hand, present these within the framework of a particular deity and lineage.

It is from the four general Action Tantras — *General Secret Tantra, Questions of Subahu, Susiddhi Tantra,* and *Concentration Continuation* — that Tsong-ka-pa draws his explanation of the general meditation of the Action class. He briefly cites the *General Secret Tantra* in connection with initiation, the main topic of that tantra, and cites the *Questions of Subahu* only a few times — with regard to how to repeat mantra, the qualities of calm abiding, and achieving feats. His presentation is structured around copious reference to the *Concentration Continuation* and the *Susiddhi Tantra.* The former, together with Buddhaguhya's commentary, presents very clearly the actual meditations but does not detail the preliminary rites, pledges, and so forth, which Tsong-ka-pa takes from the *Susiddhi* and Varabodhi's formulation of it into a *Means of Achievement (Sādhana).*

Thus, the presentation of Action Tantra in the *Great Exposition of Secret Mantra* is a general one, in the sense of supplying a mode of procedure applicable to all deities in that class. It is laid out in the order of practice, to be used as a framework for practising a particular deity.

The body of the path is subsumed under three headings — prior approximation, effecting the achievement of feats, and activities (*bsnyen sgrub las gsum*):

Prior Approximation

I Concentration with repetition

A Preliminaries of the four-branched repetition

1 What to do initially in the place of dwelling
  a Making the seal and reciting the mantra of the general lineage
  b Homage to the Buddhas and Bodhisattvas
  c Offering oneself
  d Refuge and altruistic mind generation
  e Protection through mantra and seal
  f Reflection on purity
2 How to bathe outside and enter the place of practice
  a Bathing
    picking up earth
    self-protection
    expelling obstructors in the body
    creating vajra armour
    dispelling obstructors
    casting mantra into the water
    mantrafying the earth
    ablution
    protecting and tying up the hair
    mantrafying, circling, and rubbing earth on the body
    stirring the water
    offering to the Three Jewels
    pouring water on the head
    inviting the deity and bathing his body
  b Entering the temple
3 Blessing the offerings
    removing contamination
    putting on the circlet, *kusha* grass sprinkler, head binder, and image of the crown protrusion
    holding the vajra

dispelling obstructors
generating magnificence

4 Protecting oneself and the place
  a Self-protection
  b Place-protection
    circle of protection
    creating the ritual dagger
    fumigation
    binding obstructors
    creating a fence
    creating a latticework
    closing off the area

B Actual concentration of the four-branched repetition

1 Concentration of the four branches of repetition
  a Other-base: generating a deity in front
  (1) Generation of the residence
  (2) Inviting the deity and asking him to sit
    preparing an oblation
    inviting the deity
    offering a seat
  (3) Displaying seals
  (4) Offering and praising
    offering oblation, foot-bath, bath, clothing, adornments, music, perfume, flowers, incense, food, and lamps
    making praise
  (5) Confession, refuge, admiration, entreaty, supplication, and prayer-wishes
  (6) Cultivating the four immeasurables

  b Self-base: generating oneself as a deity
  ultimate deity: meditation on oneself and the deity as the same in terms of being empty of inherent existence

sound deity: the appearance of the wisdom consciousness as the sounds of the mantra reverberating in space

letter deity: the appearance of the forms of the mantra letters around the edge of the moon

form deity: the transformation of the moon and letters into the body of the deity

seal deity: blessing important places in the divine body with hand gestures

sign deity: meditation on the divine body with clear appearance and divine pride

c Mind: the appearance of the wisdom consciousness as a moon at the heart of the deity in front

d Sound: the forms of the mantra letters set around the edge of the moon in the heart of the deity in front

2 Repetition in dependence on the four branches (oneself as a deity, deity in front, moon, and letters)

a Repetition observing the form of letters

(1) Repetition observing the form of letters in the heart of the deity in front

(a) Observing mainly the deity in front with moon and letters

(b) Repeating mantra first by whisper and then, binding breath and distraction, mentally

(c) When exhaling, observing one's own divine body

(d) Resting

moving from observing the forms of the letters to the moon, to the deity in front, to one's own divine body, to the letter deity, to the sound deity, to the moon disc, to the pride of sameness, to the suchness of self, remaining in meditative equipoise on emptiness

rising as a deity like an illusion

(2) Repetition observing the form of letters in one's own heart

(a) Inhaling, the moon and letters in front move to one's own heart and repetition is done by whisper and then, binding breath and distraction, mentally

(b) Exhaling, the moon and letters are emitted and contemplated in the heart of the deity in front

b Repetition observing the sound of letters

(1) Observing mainly the sounds of the mantra

(2) Repeating first by whisper and then, binding breath and distraction, mentally

C Concluding the concentration of the four-branched repetition

1 Offering the virtue for the sake of the feat
2 Asking forbearance and so forth
3 Requesting departure

II Concentration without repetition

A Concentration of abiding in fire
1 Absorption in suchness
2 Wisdom consciousness appearing in the aspect of the mantra sounds as if recited by someone else, continuous, and within a tongue of flame in the heart of one's own divine body (the flame and sounds are the main objects of observation but one's own divine body with moon at the heart does not disappear)

B Concentration of abiding in sound

1 Placing a small divine body in the flame on the moon disc at the heart of one's own divine body
2 Binding breath and distraction, leaving that (without letting it disappear) and concentrating mainly on only the mantra sounds as if another is reciting them
3 When exhaling, observing one's own divine body
4 Calm abiding is achieved

C Concentration bestowing liberation at the end of sound

1 Cultivating special insight observing the emptiness of inherent existence through alternating analytical and stabilising meditation
2 A union of calm abiding and special insight is attained

Effecting the Achievement of Feats

I Analysing dreams
II Doing the prescribed burnt offerings or repetition, etc.

Activities: the usage of feats and activities of pacification, increase, control, and ferocity for one's own and other's temporary and final aims.

Concentration With Repetition

Approximation occurs before effecting the achievement of feats and thus is said to be *prior*. It is accomplished through concentration (*dhyāna*), which is divided into two types, with and without repetition, structured around a progression from the coarse to the subtle:

meditative stabilisation observing a divine body
meditative stabilisation observing a divine speech mantra

- observing the form or sound of letters and performing whispered repetition
- observing the form or the sound of letters and performing mental repetition
- one's own mind realising the suchness of self appears in the aspect of blazing fire and mantra sounds
- one's own mind appears in the aspect of the mantra sounds

meditative stabilisation observing a divine mind, that is, observing suchness.

Concentration with repetition refers to meditation that eventually involves repetition but does not necessarily do so at all times. Repetition is done in two ways: the coarser is to whisper, and the subtler to repeat the mantra mentally. Repetition is performed within continuous and intense concentration on oneself as a deity and a similar deity in front of oneself. It is called the four-branched repetition because it requires maintenance of four factors: imagination of (1) oneself as a deity, (2) a deity in front, (3) a moon disc either at the heart of the deity in front or one's own heart, and (4) the written letters of the mantra, which are set around the edge of the moon disc.

Whereas the generation of oneself as a deity is done from within meditation on emptiness, the generation in front is a matter of inviting a deity to come. Therefore, the preliminaries of the four-branched repetition involve extensive preparation for the visit of a deity, who is treated like a guest. As Tsong-ka-pa says (p. 113), it is more convenient to generate the deity in front first and oneself as a deity second because the latter involves a one-pointed observation of one's own divine body within stoppage of the breath and thus it would be distracting to do the many activities related with inviting the deity in front.

The generation or imagination of oneself as a deity begins with meditation on emptiness, or the suchness of self; this is called the ultimate deity even though it does not have the face, arms, and so forth of a deity. In brief, after one has identified well the sense of a solidly existent I, reasoning is used to refute its inherent or concrete existence. The contemporary Ge-luk-ba scholar and yogi, Geshe Rabten, said that often a yogi will spend months in merely the first steps of identifying the concrete sense of I that is to be refuted by the view of selflessness. With that sense of I as the target, one applies the reasoning that reveals the falseness of this vivid, seemingly true appearance. Rather than deciding that reasoning is unsuitable to reveal reality because it cannot substantiate the mode of appearance of phenomena, reasoning is used as the tool that reveals the falsity of this concrete mode of appearance, thereby establishing non-inherent existence as the actual mode of being of persons and other phenomena. The vacuity which is the absence or negative of inherent existence appearing to such an analytical consciousness is an emptiness, and, since an actual wisdom consciousness is undifferentiably fused with it, even if a yogi has not achieved such a profound state he imagines that he has, pretending or believing that his mind has become of the entity of emptiness in non-conceptual meditative equipoise. This emptiness is understood as being the ultimate nature both of oneself and of the deity being meditated and thus is called the ultimate deity.

In the next steps this wisdom consciousness is used as the basis of emanation, first appearing as a moon over which the sounds of the mantra of the deity resound, then as the forms of mantra letters on the moon, and then as the form of the deity itself. These steps are part of concentration with repetition, but as they do not involve any whispered or mental repetition the appearance of the wisdom consciousness as the sounds of the mantra above the moon does not constitute repetition. During this phase of meditation the mind is mainly held to one's own body imagined as a deity, occasionally putting more emphasis on the deity in front but without losing the appearance of one's own divine body.

Until a meditative stabilisation observing the divine body becomes firm, the function of repetition is merely that of resting or revivifying the mind. However, when it has become firm, one passes to a subtler cultivation of meditative stabilisation observing a divine speech mantra. This is of four varieties (see p. 219); the first involves performing whispered repetition within observing the form of the letters either in the heart of the deity in front or in one's own heart and then observing the sound of the letters.

When whispered or mental repetition is performed within observing the deity in front with a moon at the heart on which the mantra letters stand, one is as if reading the letters — repeating the mantra neither swiftly nor slowly, such that only oneself can hear it. This meditation is said to have three objects of observation: (1) the deity in front, (2) the moon at his heart, and (3) the letters of the mantra that stand along the rim of the moon disc. Still, during this period one does not lose the appearance of one's own body as a divine body. This is possible because of the previous cultivation of self-generation.

Gradually, as the mind stays more and more on its object, one desists from whispered repetition and, holding the breath, repeats the mantra mentally. During exhalation one views one's own divine body but without losing the appearance of the deity in front.

When it is necessary to leave the session, one proceeds as if backwards through the process of observation, passing from the sound to the form of the letters, to the moon in the heart of the deity in front, to the deity in front, to one's own divine body, to the letters on the moon at one's own heart, to the sounds above the moon, to the moon disc, to the pride of the sameness of the nature of oneself and the deity, and finally to the suchness of self. One remains in equipoise on the emptiness of inherent existence and then rises in a divine body like an illusion. Within such divine pride, one goes about daily activities, maintaining a lesser form of deity yoga so that the periods between sessions and the actual meditative sessions will be mutually supportive.

The next phase of the concentration with repetition involves inhaling into one's own heart the moon disc together with the letters that are in the heart of the deity in front. Whispered repetition is performed, but when the mind becomes steady one holds the breath and recites the mantra mentally, as if one's mind is in the centre of the disc and is reading the letters of the mantra that are on it. With exhalation the moon and letters move to the deity's heart, and then with inhalation return to one's own.

In the next phase the sounds of the mantra become the object of observation, but this does not mean that the deity in front, one's own divine body, the moon, or the form of the letters disappear. Rather, one is focusing on the sounds of the letters which, initially, are being whispered. Then, one stops the breath, whereupon it is impossible to engage in whispered repetition, and mental repetition is done.

When this meditative stabilisation becomes firm, the concentration of the four-branched repetition is complete, after which one offers the virtue of the repetition to the Blessed One for the sake of achieving whatever feat is being sought. One asks the deity to put up with omissions in the conduct of the rite and then requests the guest to depart, asking him to come again.

Concentration Without Repetition

When one has attained capacity in concentration with repetition, one passes on to the subtler concentration of abiding in fire. This also is a meditation observing a divine speech mantra, but repetition is not involved because in this case one's own mind appears in the aspect of the sounds of the mantra, not as if oneself is reciting, but as if hearing another's repetition. This concentration is called an abiding in fire because the sounds are imagined as dwelling in a tongue of fire at the heart of one's divine body. The internal sign of success is that the mantra sounds reverberate continuously, the former sounds not ceasing during the latter.

When this concentration of abiding in fire becomes firm, one is not affected by hunger or thirst and has developed a meditative stabilisation, but still has not generated actual calm abiding. To do this, one passes to cultivation of the concentration of abiding in sound. A small divine body is imagined within the flame that is on the moon disc at the heart of one's divine body. Then, one stops the breath and ceases distraction, 'leaving off' concentration on the small divine body and so forth and concentrating on only the mantra sounds. As in the concentration of abiding in fire, the sounds do not appear as if recited by oneself but by another.

Though one is said to leave the observation of the small divine body and so forth, it does not disappear. The steadiness of mind is such that within appearance of the small divine body, flame, moon, and so forth, one can take as the main object of observation just the mantra sounds in the sense of focusing on them. Then, when exhaling, one's own divine body is observed, loosening the concentration slightly. Because the mantra sounds in the concentrations of abiding in fire and in sound are free of the aspect of one's own recitation, these concentrations are said to be without repetition.

When the concentration of abiding in sound becomes firm, a fully qualified calm abiding is attained; within mental and physical pliancy and bliss, one is able to remain on whatever object one chooses as long as one likes. (For a description of the states leading to calm abiding and the signs of having attained it, see *Meditation on Emptiness*, Part One, Chapter 8.) With the attainment of calm abiding, the cultivation of meditative stabilisation observing a divine speech mantra is complete.

Then one passes to an even subtler cultivation of a meditative stabilisation observing a divine mind, that is to say, observing suchness — the emptiness of inherent existence. This is the concentration bestowing liberation at the end of sound. Realisation of emptiness was cultivated earlier at the point of the ultimate deity in self-generation and is involved in all subsequent steps in that the mind realising emptiness is believingly used as the basis of emanation of the various divine appearances. Also, since Mantrikas — those who have attained the path of accumulation of the Vajra Vehicle — are the sharpest among Bodhisattvas, they have conceptually realised emptiness prior to entering the Mantra path. However, they have not yet realised emptiness with a mind of calm abiding and special insight. Since the four-branched repetition and the concentrations of abiding in fire and in sound are for the sake of achieving calm abiding, during that process one does not engage in analytical meditation with respect to emptiness; rather, one mainly engages in stabilising meditation with respect to a divine body or speech mantra, for analysis would cause the mind to become unstable. Now, however, with the completion of the concentration of abiding in sound, calm abiding has been attained and analytical and stabilising meditation can be alternated — the object of observation now being the emptiness of inherent existence.

Despite the many statements in the text that all other objects are abandoned, the mantra sounds, divine body, and so forth — as Tsong-ka-pa points out — do not necessarily disappear in the concentration bestowing liberation at the end of sound. In terms of ascertainment, just emptiness is being ascertained, but the mantra sounds, divine body, and so forth may *appear* to that consciousness. It is a feature of the Mantra Vehicle (and some say of the Sutra Vehicle also) that the phenomenon being understood to be empty can also appear to a conceptual consciousness realising that emptiness. Na-wang-bel-den's *Presentation of the Grounds and Paths of Mantra*[213] says:

> If the mind realising emptiness is powerful, then the yoga with signs (that is, with appearance of a deity and so forth) which follows it will be conjoined with it. Tsong-ka-pa's *Small Exposition of the Stages of the Path* says, 'If the wisdom realising emptiness is strong, then when one gives gifts, makes obeisance, circumambulates, and so forth, the mind that observes those, though not realising emptiness, will be in possession of the power of that mind [realising emptiness]. There is no contradiction in this. For instance, if at the beginning of a session one initially establishes a firm altruistic aspiration for enlightenment, then, when set in meditative stabilisation on emptiness, it will be conjoined with the force of that altruistic aspiration, which nevertheless is not actually present.' That is the mode of non-separation of method and wisdom in the Sutra system, but in the Mantra system it is not merely that. The non-separation of method and wisdom in the Mantra system is taken as an undifferentiability of

> method and wisdom which are a simultaneous composite, in the entity of one consciousness, of the two — vast deity yoga and the profound wisdom realising non-inherent existence.

Thus, the difference between the concentration bestowing liberation at the end of sound and all those preceeding is that the earlier deity yoga was merely conjoined with the *force* of realising emptiness whereas here in the concentration on the end of sound, the one consciousness that appears as the mantra sounds, divine body, and so forth, also actually realises emptiness.

When through alternating analytical and stabilising meditation the capacity of the mind increases to the point where analysis itself induces calm abiding, a union of calm abiding and special insight with emptiness as the object is attained. This marks the beginning of the Action Tantra path of preparation. It leads to direct realisation of emptiness at the beginning of the path of seeing, at which time merely emptiness appears, a divine body no longer does, for only a Buddha can *directly* cognise emptiness and conventional phenomena at the same time.

Through the power of the special techniques involved in the concentrations with and without repetition, a Bodhisattva is able to pass from the path of accumulation to the path of seeing much faster than in the Perfection Vehicle, where it takes one period of countless aeons. This is enhanced by the feats attained upon successful completion of the concentration on the end of sound. At that point one can come under the direct care of Buddhas and high Bodhisattvas and utilise special talents such as knowing all treatises immediately upon reading them, clairvoyance, and long life, thereby hastening direct realisation of emptiness.

The deity yoga of Action Tantra, found in the concentrations with and without repetition, incorporates these special techniques for the generation of meditative stabilisation which is a union of calm abiding and special insight. The manifestation of a wisdom consciousness as a divine body, divine speech mantra, and divine mind provides means for speedily accumulating the collections of merit and wisdom in order to actualise quickly the Form and Truth Bodies of a Buddha — all in order to help others.

Correlation With the Paths

The five paths — accumulation, preparation, seeing, meditation and no more learning — are presented for the Mantra Vehicle just as they are for the Perfection Vehicle. In Action Tantra a person who has trained in the three principal aspects of the path — the thought definitely to leave cyclic existence, the altruistic mind of enlightenment induced by love and compassion, and the correct view of emptiness — first enters into a mandala of any of the three lineages and receives initiation. Then, when he has cultivated the aspiration to enlightenment for the sake of others such that it manifests spontaneously and non-artificially outside of meditation as it would in intense meditation, he has attained the Action Tantra path of accumulation. It marks his becoming a tantric Bodhisattva and is specifically the thought to attain Buddhahood by way of the Action Tantra path for the sake of others' welfare.

During the path of accumulation the Bodhisattva achieves calm abiding by way of the four-branched repetition and the concentrations of abiding in fire and abiding in sound. He also trains in the concentration bestowing liberation at the end of sound through alternating analytical and stabilising meditation with respect to the emptiness of inherent existence. Then when he generates a consciousness of special insight realising emptiness, he has passed to the Action Tantra path of preparation.

On the four levels of that path — heat, peak, forbearance, and supreme mundane quality — the sense of duality between the wisdom consciousness and its object, emptiness, gradually diminishes. The path of seeing occurs with the initial, direct, totally non-dualistic realisation of emptiness, gained through cultivating the concentration bestowing liberation at the end of sound. It acts as the antidote to the artificial afflictive obstructions, that is to say, the conception of inherent existence and its attendant afflictions as fortified by false teachings and scriptures.

The path of meditation begins with that form of the concentration on the end of sound which is able to act as an antidote to the big of the big innate afflictions and ranges until just before achieving full enlightenment. During this period the yogi passes through nine of the ten Bodhisattva grounds, gradually purifying the mind of the nine degrees of innate afflictions and the four degrees of the obstructions to omniscience:

First ground —	the path of seeing.
Second ground —	from attaining the antidote to the big of the big innate afflictions.
Third ground —	from attaining the antidote to the middling of the big innate afflictions.
Fourth ground —	from attaining the antidote to the small of the big innate afflictions.
Fifth, sixth, and seventh grounds —	from attaining the antidote respectively to the big of the middling, middling of the middling, and small of the middling innate afflictions.
Eighth ground —	from attaining simultaneously the antidotes to the big of the small, middling of the small, and small of the small innate afflictions. The big obstructions to omniscience are also abandoned during a second phase of the eighth ground.
Ninth ground —	from attaining the antidote to the middling obstructions to omniscience.

Tenth ground — from attaining the antidote to the coarse of the small obstructions to omniscience. During a second phase of the tenth ground the antidote to the subtle of the small obstructions to omniscience is attained, at which point one has the exalted wisdom the end of the continuum as a sentient being with obstructions yet to be removed. Immediately after this one becomes a Buddha.

The afflictive obstructions — comprised of the ignorance conceiving inherent existence and the other afflictions such as desire, hatred, enmity, and jealousy which it induces — prevent liberation from cyclic existence. These obstructions are removed gradually by means of the concentration bestowing liberation at the end of sound over the first seven Bodhisattva grounds. Then, on the eighth, ninth and tenth grounds, that same concentration, enhanced by the factors of method, eliminates the obstructions to omniscience — not the conception but the *appearance* of inherent existence. The final path, that of no more learning, is comprised of the states of one who has become a Buddha through the Action Tantra path.

About these, Na-wang-bel-den's *Presentation of the Grounds and Paths of Mantra*[214] says:

> With regard to the way of positing the Action Tantra paths as the five paths and ten grounds, the Action Tantra path of accumulation is comprised of the paths — once pure initiation has been attained — ranging from the point at which non-artificial experience is developed with respect to a mind promising 'I will attain Buddhahood by way of the Action Tantra path' through to but not including the attainment of the

special insight realising emptiness through the force of having cultivated the concentration bestowing liberation at the end of sound. The Action Tantra path of preparation is comprised of the paths ranging from that special insight through to but not including direct realisation of emptiness through the force of having cultivated the concentration on the end of sound. The Action Tantra path of seeing is comprised of the paths ranging from direct realisation of emptiness by that concentration through to but not including generation of the actual antidote to the big of the big afflictions to be abandoned by the path of meditation. The Action Tantra path of meditation is comprised of the paths ranging from the concentration on the end of sound that has become the actual antidote to the big of the big afflictions to be abandoned by the path of meditation through to the point of being about to become fully enlightened by the paths of Action Tantra. The Action Tantra path of no more learning is comprised of the paths of one who has become a Buddha through the paths of this tantra.

From among those the path of seeing is the first ground. The second ground begins with attaining the actual antidote to the big of the big afflictions to be abandoned by the path of meditation. The third ground begins with attaining the actual antidote to the middling of the big afflictions, and the fourth ground with the actual antidote to the small of the big. The fifth, sixth, and seventh grounds are posited from attaining the antidotes respectively to the big, middling, and small of the middling afflictions. The eighth ground is from the simultaneous attainment of the actual antidote to the triple cycle of small afflictions. Also, on the eighth ground the big obstructions to omniscience are abandoned, and then the ninth ground begins with attaining the actual antidote to the middling obstruc-

> tions to omniscience. The tenth ground is from attaining the actual antidote to the coarse of the small obstructions to omniscience. Then the actual antidote to the subtle of the small obstructions to omniscience is posited as the exalted wisdom the end of the continuum.
>
> These and other such topics must be asserted in accordance with the way of the Sutra system Prasangikas. For a mode of abandoning the two obstructions in the three lower tantra sets which is different from the Perfection Vehicle is not explained in any reliable text. Also, such is not established by reasoning.

Thus, although the four-branched repetition and the concentrations are used as means for attaining common feats that enhance the path, these also comprise the very body of the path leading to Buddhahood, for the concentration on the end of sound itself, as it progresses in capacity, removes the obstructions to liberation and to omniscience. The feats gained through the concentration on the end of sound — which is the culmination of deity yoga — bestow powers through which vast merit is achieved. That merit, in turn, further empowers the concentration on the end of sound so that it can overcome the obstructions to omniscience, whereupon the welfare of others is furthered as it could not be otherwise.

Since a Bodhisattva's aim is to help others, he seeks to enhance the wisdom consciousness realising emptiness so that it can remove the subtlest of obstructions to omniscience. This enhancement is done through deity yoga itself as well as the special feats and activities that are at a practitioner's disposal upon completing the concentrations of deity yoga, that is to say upon attaining the concentration bestowing liberation at the end of sound. In this context the objective of deity yoga and of the powers gained through it is the removal of obstructions, thereby allowing progression over the grounds and paths and issuing forth the ability to manifest in form in accordance with the needs of trainees.

Appendices, Glossary, Bibliography, and Notes

Appendix 1: Lineages in Action and Performance Tantra

A translation from Pan-chen Sö-nam-drak-ba's *General Presentation of the Tantra Sets, Captivating the Minds of the Fortunate*[215]

Inner Divisions of Action Tantra

This section has two parts: the divisions of the individual lineages and the general division of the three lineages.

Divisions of the Individual Lineages in Action Tantra

This section has three parts: the Tathagata, lotus, and vajra lineages.

Divisions of the Tathagata Lineage

[The tantras of] the Tathagata lineage have eight [divisions]:

1 tantras of the principal of the Tathagata lineage,
2 tantras of the lord of the Tathagata lineage,
3 tantras of the mothers of the Tathagata lineage,
4 tantras of the crown protrusion of the Tathagata lineage,
5 tantras of the group of fierce males and females of the Tathagata lineage,
6 tantras of the group of messengers of the Tathagata lineage,
7 tantras of the group of Bodhisattvas of the Tathagata lineage,
8 tantras of the groups of serpents and harm-bestowers (*yakṣha*) of the Tathagata lineage.

Tantras of the Principal of the Tathagata Lineage

The principal of the Tathagata lineage is the Teacher Shakyamuni. Without being requested by his retinue, he set forth [the rite of][216] the hundred letters, as well as its benefits.

Requested, he set forth the *Royal Tantra Stating the Three Pledges (Trisamayavyūharāja,* P134) which teaches the mandala in which the Teacher himself acts as the principal. The *[Sutra of] Excellent Golden Light (Suvar-*

ṇaprabhāsottamasūtrendrarāja) in three versions — great, middling, and small (P174-6) — the subject matter of which accords in part [with the above tantras], is included in the set of [tantras of the principal of the Tathagata lineage]. The assertions by one that these are in the sutra class and by another that they are common to sutra and tantra arc not right because these set forth means of achieving Shrimahadevi and the four great kings as well as how to draw their mandalas.

Tantras of the Lord of the Tathagata Lineage

The lord of the Tathagata lineage is Manjushri. There is an extensive *Manjushri Root Tantra (Mañjushrīmūla-tantra*, P162) of thirty-six chapters which teaches the modes of the twelve deeds and so forth. Also, there is a more condensed *Achievement of Manjushri as a Sole Hero (Siddhaikavīramahātantrarāja*, P163) of four chapters. The first chapter teaches how — through Buddhas and Bodhisattvas — to analyse dreams, how to apply the activity of protecting from lightning, and the means of achieving the Jambhala deities. The fourth chapter teaches a compendium of initiations depending on Tara Kurukulle, the mode of the circle of protection of the male and female circles of harm-bestowers facing [each other], and so forth.

Others [mistakenly make reference to] the *Means of Achievement of the Essence of the Perfection of Wisdom Sutra (Prajñāpāramitāhṛdayasādhana)* [which describes] generation of oneself as the Teacher Shakyamuni from within the emptiness of having gathered the environments and beings into clear light. Also there is a *Means of Achievement* (P3464) [which is a commentary on the above][217] said to be by Nagarjuna in which the Great Mother is surrounded by the sons — the Buddhas of the ten directions. There is also the *Permission Rite of the*

Eight Clear Realisations said to be by Pa-dam-ba *(Pha-dam-pa)* [Bodhidharma?]. However, these are just cases of name-borrowing [by spurious authors].

Although some include the two rites of the Medicine Guru — longer and shorter — in the sutra class, these are feasible as Action Tantras. For, Ratnakirti [in his *Sarva-dhāraṇīmaṇḍalavidhi*, P3957][218] proves them to be Action Tantras 'due to their involving assumption [of a day] of purification and renewal, etc.' and since they speak of four-sided, four-doored mandalas, etc.

Tantras of Mothers of the Tathagata Lineage

The mothers of the Tathagata lineage are Marichi and the five guards *(rakṣha)*. [The tantras] are the *Retention of Marichi (Mārīchināmadhāraṇī*, P182) as well as its rite [the *Imagination of Marichi (Māyāmārīchijātatantrād uddhitaṃ kalparāja*, P183) and so forth].

In the *Illusory Imagination of Marichi (Māyāmārīchi-maṇḍalavidhi mārīchijātadvādashasahasra-uddhitaṃ kal-pahṛdayasaptashata)* there are manifest presentations of the [stages of] generation and completion as well as channels, winds, and drops [which are topics found exclusively in Highest Yoga Tantra]. Therefore, it is said that [this text] seems to be a corruption in which Highest Yoga and Action Tantra are confused.

The five guards are Pratisara, Mahamayuri, Shitavati, Mantranudharini, and Sahasrapramardani.[219] Ratnakara-shanti (P3947) presents the rites of their mandalas and their activities in detail. There also are *Means of Achievement* [of the five] individually and in common by Jetari.[220]

Tantras of the Crown Protrusions of the Tathagata Lineage

These are Vijaya Ushnisha, Sitatapatra Ushnisha, Vimala Ushnisha, and Jvala Ushnisha (Victorious, White

Umbrella, Stainless, and Blazing Crown Protrusions). With respect to the first, there is the *Retention of Ushnisha Vijaya Purifying All Bad Migrations (Sarvadurgatiparishodhanī-uṣhṇīshavijayanāmadhāraṇī,* P198) together with [the rite] of applying its activities. This was requested of Vijaya by Shakra, the King of Gods, for the sake of the Devaputra Very Steady [who had foreseen rebirth in bad migrations].[221] There is also an *Imagination of Vijaya (Sarvatathāgatoṣhṇīṣhavijayanāmadhāraṇīkalpa,* P200), which teaches how to make a reliquary of Vijaya, how to make imprinted holy objects *(sāchchha)* to put inside it, and so forth.[222]

Sitatapatra Ushnisha has four [tantras], the *Unconquerable by Others (Sarvatathāgatoṣhṇīṣhasitātapatrā-nāma-aparājitāpratyaṃgiramahāvidyārajñī,* P202), the *Paramasiddhi (Tathāgatoṣhṇīṣhasitātapatre aparājitā-mahāpratyamgirāparamasiddhināmadhāraṇī,* P203), and the two *Lessers* without introduction which appeared in lands of gods [*Tathāgatoṣhṇīhasitātapatre aparājitānāmadhāraṇi,* P204, 205].[223] Among these, the first two, except for being different translations, are the same, the *Paramasiddhi* being the better translation. Its commentary by Shuramgamavarma has explanations of secret mandala, knowledge mantra, essence mantra, and quintessential mantra.

There are about fourteen miscellaneous texts by Chandragomin, which include a *Mandala Rite, Rite of Food Offering* (P3904), *Rite of the Circle of Protection* (P3906), *Rite of Burnt Offering* (P3922), and so forth. There are also rites of mandala by Vajrasana (P3929), Tikshnavajra (P3926), and Vajrankusha.[224] Although there are mandala rites by Padmankusha (P3932) and Varmavajra (P3927), they are not correct because the maintaining of the vows of the five lineages [which occurs only in Yoga and Highest Yoga Tantra] and so forth appear frequently in them. Also, there are a rite written by a Tibetan who borrowed Chandragomin's name, a [work on] the creation of food-offering figures for practice which is said to be from India, and a rite by Po-rok Gön-bo-dor-jay *(Pho-rog mGon-po-rdo-rje)* which is the system of explanation initially in Tibet.

With respect to Vimala Ushnisha, there are [tantras] teaching how to create a mandala of perfumed water and the creation of the one hundred and eight reliquaries. Regarding these, there are a general compendium and individual compendia by the master Sahajalalita.

With respect to Blazing Ushnisha, there is, for instance, the first chapter of the *Manjushri Root Tantra* treated separately.

The 'Black Ushnisha' is unquestionably made up by a non-human of Tibet.

Tantras of the Group of Fierce Males and Females of the Tathagata Lineage

These are the two, the *Secret Imagination Conquering the Three Worlds (Krodhavijayakalpaguhyatantra*, P291) and the *Retention of the Goddess Chundi (Chundidevīdhāraṇī*, P188).

Tantras of the Group of Messengers of the Tathagata Lineage

These are the *Retention of Parnashavari (Parṇashavarināmadhāraṇī*, P186), the *Imagination of Parnashavari* and so forth.

Tantras of the Group of Bodhisattvas of the Tathagata Lineage

These are, for instance, the *One Hundred and Eight Names of Avalokiteshvara (Avalokiteshvarāṣhṭottarashatakanāmadhāraṇīmantrasahita*, P320) set out separately.

Tantras of the Groups of Serpents and Harm-Bestowers of the Tathagata Lineage

These are, for instance, the *Tantra Giving Rise to Wealth* and the *Tantra Issuing Forth Ambrosia (Amṛtabhavanā-madhāraṇī*, P354) which teaches a water-offering.

Divisions of the Lotus Lineage

The lotus lineage has five divisions [comprised of the tantras of]:

1 the principal of the lotus lineage,
2 the lord of the lotus lineage,
3 the mother of the lotus lineage,
4 the fierce males and females of the lotus lineage,
5 the group of messengers.

Tantras of the Principal of the Lotus Lineage

The principal of the lotus lineage is Amitayus. With respect to his tantras, there are the two which arose in lands of gods and which are corrupt[225] and the *Deathless Drum Sound Tantra* which is not corrupt.

Tantras of the Lord of the Lotus Lineage

The lord of the lotus lineage is Avalokiteshvara. The three [texts] of the *Tantra of the Lotus-Netted Avalokiteshvara (Avalokiteshvarapadmajalamūlatantrarāja)* in twelve thousand stanzas was not translated into Tibetan, but the shorter one (P364) in one thousand stanzas teaches two mandalas of 1,227 deities among whom Avalokiteshvara acts as the main [figure]. There are also the beginning of a translation of the *Imagination of the Eleven-Faced [Avalokiteshvara]* and longer and shorter *Lion's Roar Retentions (Avalokiteshvarasiṃhanādanāma-dhāraṇī*, P386, and *Siṃhanādatantra*, P385).

Tantras of the Mother of the Lotus Lineage

The mother of the lotus lineage is Arya Tara. With respect to her tantras, the third chapter of the thirty-five chapters [of the *Tantra of the Various Arisings from Tara, the Mother of all Tathagatas (Sarvatathāgatamātanitā-ārevishvakarmabhavatantra,* P390)] which teaches one hundred and eight mandalas and the currently [popular] *Twenty-One Homages (Ekaviṃshatistotra,* P77) are the same.

Objection: Those are not the same because the third chapter of that [text] must be taken as an Action Tantra whereas Chandragomin[226] interpreted it as Highest Yoga.

Answer: That reason is indefinite, for the *Expression of the Names of Manjushri (Mañjushrījñānasattvasya paramārthanāmasaṃgīti,* P2), for instance, is interpreted (1) in accordance with Kalachakra in Rik-den-padma-garbo's great commentary [*Stainless Light (Vimālaprabhā,* P2064)]; (2) in accordance with Guhyasamaja in Aryadeva's *Lamp Compendium of Practice (Charyāmelakapradīpa,* P2668); and (3) in accordance with Yoga [Tantra] by the masters Lilavajra and Manjushrikirti[227] (P3357).

Tantras of the Fierce Males and Females of the Lotus Lineage

The Fierce One of the lotus lineage is Hayagriva. The extensive tantra of Hayagriva was not translated into Tibetan. The abbreviated is the *Hayagriva Tantra* ([?] *Avalokiteshvarahayagrīvadhāraṇī,* P379, 531).

Tantras of the Group of Messengers of the Lotus Lineage

These are the *Mahalakshmi Sutra (Mahāshrīyasūtra,* P399) and so forth.

Divisions of the Vajra Lineage

The vajra lineage has the same five divisions [as the lotus lineage].

Tantras of the Principal of the Vajra Lineage

The principal of the vajra lineage is the Tathagata Akshobhya. There is a *Vajra Akshobhya Tantra (Sarvakarmāvaraṇavishodhanīnāmadhāraṇī*, P401) which teaches the mandala purifying bad migrations.

Tantras of the Lord of the Vajra Lineage

The lord is Vajrapani. There are the three tantras of Vajrapani — root, explanatory, and continuation. Also, there are the *Vajrapani Taming of Elementals Tantra (Bhūtaḍāmara*, P404) and the *Vajravidarana Tantra (Vajravidāraṇānāmadhāraṇī*, P406). With respect to the *Vajravidarana* the translators made it into twenty-one stanzas and said it was spoken on the vajra seat [at Bodh Gaya]. The system of the pandita Buddhaguhya [however] is that the vajra seat is the place [where Buddha] tamed the demons and became enlightened and is not a place where he turned the wheel of doctrine. Thus, he does not assert that the *Vajravidarana Tantra* was spoken there.

Question: Then, where was it spoken?

Answer: It was spoken in a cave in the Vajra Mountain to the south-east of Meru, an area of Knowledge Mantra Bearers. With respect to the manner in which it was spoken, King Ajatashatru had killed his father King Bimbisara and was being called by the name 'Perverse Heart'. At that time, since the non-virtues were being widely committed in the world, great famine arose, whereupon four great kings made a request [to Buddha]. The Blessed One spoke to Vajrapani, who emanated the body of Vidarana and spoke. The Blessed One, having said 'Good', spoke [this tantra] which has one hundred and eight chapters together with this [section by Vajrapani].

Tantras of the Mother of the Vajra Lineage

There is the *Tantra of Blazing Flames (Vajrājitānala-pramohaṇīnāmadhāraṇī*, P408).

Tantras of the Fierce Ones of the Vajra Lineage

There is the *Amritakundali Tantra (Kuṇḍalyamṛtahrda-yachaturthanāmadhāraṇī*, P755).

Tantras of the Groups of Messengers of the Vajra Lineage

There are the *Great Power Tantra (Mahābalanāmamahāyā-nasūtra*, P416) and the *Vajratunda Tantra (Vajratundanā-manāgasamaya*, P411). It should be known that the *Vajra Hook* ([?] *Lohatuṇḍanāmadhāraṇī*, P413, 414) and the *Vajra Garuda Wing Tantra* are fakes.

General Division of the Three Lineages

[The Action Tantras of the three lineages in general] are the *General Secret Tantra*, *Susiddhi*, *Questions of Subahu*, and *Concentration Continuation*. The first of these teaches the mandala rites of Action Tantra in general, ranging from the rite for the place [where initiation will be conferred] through the bestowal of initiation. It also sets forth the three thousand five hundred mandalas related with the three lineages.

The *Susiddhi* teaches the approximation and achievement related with the fierce Susiddhi, the detail of his activities, and those topics in the presentation of initiation in the *General Secret Tantra* which needed supplement. The *Questions of Subahu* teaches the measure of [having completed] approximation of the deities indicated in the *General Secret Tantra* and the *Susiddhi* as well as how to achieve the limitless activities.

The Action Tantra [called] the *Concentration Continuation* teaches the mode of progressing on the paths in Action Tantra in general — the concentrations of the four branches of repetition, abiding in fire, abiding in sound, and bestowing liberation at the end of sound as well as what to do before and after those, rites for [achieving] feats, rites of burnt offering, how to practise, in what sort of place, and so forth.

Inner Divisions of Performance Tantra

A Performance Tantra of the Tathagata lineage is, for instance, the *Vairochanabhisambodhi*. One of the lotus lineage is, for instance, the *Extensive Tantra of Hayagriva,* but it was not translated into Tibetan. Tantras of the vajra lineage are the *Vajrapani Initiation Tantra* and so forth.

Appendix 2: Structure of the Presentation

An illustration in tabular form of the structure of Tsong-ka-pa's *Great Exposition of Secret Mantra,* continued from *Tantra in Tibet*.

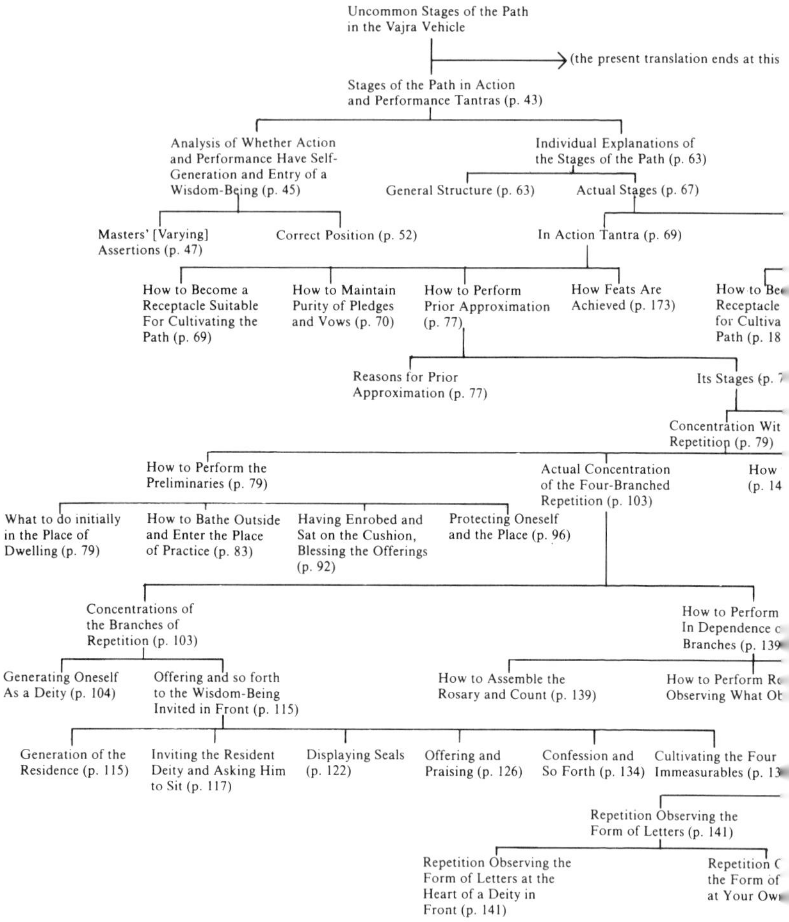
Uncommon Stages of the Path in the Vajra Vehicle
(the present translation ends at this
Stages of the Path in Action and Performance Tantras (p. 43)
Analysis of Whether Action and Performance Have Self-Generation and Entry of a Wisdom-Being (p. 45)
Individual Explanations of the Stages of the Path (p. 63)
General Structure (p. 63)
Actual Stages (p. 67)
Masters' [Varying] Assertions (p. 47)
Correct Position (p. 52)
In Action Tantra (p. 69)
How to Become a Receptacle Suitable For Cultivating the Path (p. 69)
How to Maintain Purity of Pledges and Vows (p. 70)
How to Perform Prior Approximation (p. 77)
How Feats Are Achieved (p. 173)
How to Be
Receptacle
for Cultiva
Path (p. 18
Reasons for Prior Approximation (p. 77)
Its Stages
Concentration Wit
Repetition (p. 79)
How to Perform the Preliminaries (p. 79)
Actual Concentration of the Four-Branched Repetition (p. 103)
How
What to do initially in the Place of Dwelling (p. 79)
How to Bathe Outside and Enter the Place of Practice (p. 83)
Having Enrobed and Sat on the Cushion, Blessing the Offerings (p. 92)
Protecting Oneself and the Place (p. 96)
Concentrations of the Branches of Repetition (p. 103)
How to Perform
In Dependence
Branches
Generating Oneself As a Deity (p. 104)
Offering and so forth to the Wisdom-Being Invited in Front (p. 115)
How to Assemble the Rosary and Count (p. 139)
How to Perform
Observing What
Generation of the Residence (p. 115)
Inviting the Resident Deity and Asking Him to Sit (p. 117)
Displaying Seals (p. 122)
Offering and Praising (p. 126)
Confession and So Forth (p. 134)
Cultivating the Four
Repetition Observing the Form of Letters (p. 141)
Repetition Observing the Form of Letters at the Heart of a Deity in Front (p. 141)
Repetition
the Form of
at Your

e Tantra (p. 183)

- Maintain of Pledges ws (p. 184)
- How to Perform Prior Approximation (p. 185)
- How to Achieve Feats (p. 202)

visions of the Yoga . 185)

Meaning of the Divisions (p. 189)

- Yoga with Signs (p. 189)
  - External Four-Branched Repetition (p. 189)
  - Internal Four-Branched Repetition (p. 194)
- Yoga without Signs (p. 197)

oncentration Without epetition (p. 155)

- trations of Abiding and in Sound (p. 155)
- Concentration on the End of Sound (p. 160)
  - Stages of Leaving the State of Sound (p. 160)
  - The Actual Concentration (p. 167)

w to Reinstate the Repetition nfavorable Conditions Arise (p. 148)

etition Observing the nd of Letters (p. 145)

Glossary

English	*Tibetan*
accumulation of merit	bsod nams kyi tshogs
accumulation of wisdom	ye shes kyi tshogs
Action Tantra	bya rgyud
activities	las
altruistic mind of enlightenment	byang chub kyi sems
analytical meditation	dpyad sgom
bliss of physical and mental pliancy	lus sems shin sbyangs kyi bde ba
burnt offering	sbyin sregs
calm abiding	zhi gnas
channels	rtsa
clear light	'od gsal
Complete Enjoyment Body	longs sku
concentration	bsam gtan
concentration bestowing liberation at the end of sound	sgra mthar thar pa ster ba'i bsam gtan
concentration of abiding in fire	me gnas kyi bsam gtan
concentration of abiding in sound	sgra gnas kyi bsam gtan
concentration with repetition	bzlas brjod dang bcas pa'i bsam gtan
concentration without repetition	bzlas brjod la ma bltos pa'i bsam gtan
concentrations of the three principles	de nyid gsum gyi bsam gtan
deity yoga	lha'i rnal byor
divine approximation	lha'i bsnyen pa
divine pride	lha'i ngar rgyal
dualistic elaborations	gnyis snang gi spros pa
Emanation Body	sprul sku
emptiness	stong pa nyid
emptiness yoga	stong pa'i rnal byor
entry of a wisdom being	ye shes pa gzhug pa
excitement	rgod pa
exertion	rtsol ba
feat	dngos grub
ferocity	drag shul
fierce activities	drag po'i las
Form Body	gzugs sku

English	*Tibetan*
form deity	gzugs kyi lha
four-branched repetition	bzlas brjod yan lag bzhi ldan
generation in front	mdun bskyed
Highest Yoga Tantra	rnal 'byor bla med
illusory body	sgyu lus
imputedly existent person	btags yod kyi gang zag
increase	rgyas pa
initiation	dbang
introspection	shes bzhin
knowledge bearers	rig 'dzin
knowledge mantra	rig sngags
laxity	bying ba
lethargy	rmugs pa
letter deity	yi ge'i lha
mandala	dkyil 'khor
mantra	sngags
meditative stabilisation	ting nge 'dzin
mindfulness	dran pa
other-base	gzhan gyi gzhi
pacifying activities	zhi ba'i las
path of accumulation	tshogs lam
path of meditation	sgom lam
path of no more learning	mi slob lam
path of preparation	sbyor lam
path of seeing	mthong lam
Perfection Vehicle	phar phyin gyi theg pa
Performance Tantra	spyod rgyud
pledge	dam tshig
pledge-being	dam tshig pa
pliancy	shin sbyangs
pride of ordinariness	tha mal pa'i ngar rgyal
prior approximation	sngon du bsnyen pa byed pa
repetition	bzlas brjod
scattering	'phro ba
seal	phyag rgya

English	*Tibetan*
seal deity	phyag rgya'i lha
secret mantra	gsang sngags
self-base	bdag gi gzhi
self-generation	bdag bskyed
sign deity	mtshan ma'i lha
sound deity	sgra'i lha
special insight	lhag mthong
stabilising meditation	'jog sgom
stage of completion	rdzogs rim
stage of generation	bskyed rim
suchness	de kho na nyid
tantra	rgyud
Truth Body	chos sku
ultimate deity	don dam pa'i lha
vitality	srog
vow	sdom pa
wind	rlung
wind yoga	rlung gi rnal 'byor
wisdom-being	ye shes pa
withdrawal	slar sdud pa
yoga of signlessness	mtshan med kyi rnal byor
Yoga Tantra	rnal 'byor rgyud
yoga with signs	mtshan bcas kyi rnal byor
yoga without signs	mtshan med kyi rnal 'byor

Bibliography

In the first section the titles are arranged alphabetically according to the English, followed by the Sanskrit and Tibetan; in the second section, by author. Here and in the notes, for works found in the Tibetan canon 'P' refers to the *Tibetan Tripitaka* (Tokyo-Kyoto, Suzuki Research Foundation, 1955), which is a reprint of the Peking edition. The English titles are usually abbreviated.

I *Sutras and Tantras*

Cloud of Jewels Sutra
Ratnameghasūtra
dKon mchog sprin gyi mdo
P897, vol. 35

Compendium of Principles/Compendium of the Principles of All Tathagatas
Sarvatathāgatatattvasaṃgrahanāmamahāyānasūtra
De bzhin gshegs pa thams cad kyi de kho na nyid bsdus pa zhes bya ba theg pa chen po'i mdo
P112, vol. 4

Concentration Continuation Tantra
Dhyānottarapaṭalakrama
bSam gtan gyi phyi ma rim par phye ba
P430, vol. 9

Extensive Tantra of Vajravidarana/Extensive Vidarana Tantra
[not translated into Tibetan]

General Secret Tantra/General Tantra
Sarvamaṇḍalasāmānyavidhiguhyatantra
dKyil 'khor thams cad kyi spyi'i cho ga gsang ba'i rgyud
P429, vol. 9

Guhyasamaja Tantra
Sarvatathāgatakāyavākchittarahasyaguhyasamājanāmamahākalparāja
De bzhin gshegs pa thams cad kyi sku gsung thugs kyi gsang chen gsang ba 'dus pa zhes bya ba brtag pa'i rgyal po chen po
P81, vol. 3

Hevajra Tantra
Hevajratantrarāja
Kye'i rdo rje zhes bya ba rgyud kyi rgyal po
P10, vol. 1

Kalachakra Tantra
Paramādibuddhoddhṛtashrīkālachakranāmatantrarāja
mChog gi dang po'i sang rgyas las byung ba rgyud kyi rgyal po dpal dus kyi 'khor lo
P4, vol. 1
Manjushri Root Tantra
Mañjushrīmūlatantra
Jam dpal gyi rtsa ba'i rgyud
P162, vol. 6
Questions of Subahu Tantra
Subāhuparipṛchchhānāmatantra
dPung bzang gis zhus pa zhes bya ba'i rgyud
P428, vol. 9
Samputa Tantra
Saṃpuṭanāmamahātantra
Yang dag par sbyor ba zhes bya ba'i rgyud
P26, vol. 2
Scriptural Division of the Knowledge Bearers
Rig 'dzin gyi sde snod
[?]
Susiddhi Tantra
Susiddhikaramahātantrasādhanopāyikapaṭala
Legs par grub par byed pa'i rgyud chen po las sgrub pa'i thabs rim par phye ba
P431, vol. 9
Sutra on Skill in Means
Upāyakaushalyanāmamahāyānasūtra
Thabs mkhas pa zhes bya ba theg pa chen po'i mdo
P927, vol. 36
Ten Principles/Introduction to the Ten Principles
De kho na nyid bcu pa
[?]
Vairochanabhisambodhi Tantra
Mahāvairochanābhisambodhivikurvatī-adhiṣhṭhānavaipulyasūtra-indrarājanāmadharmaparyāya
rNam par snang mdzad chen po mngon par rdzogs par byang chub pa rnam par sprul ba byin gyis rlob pa shin tu rgyas pa mdo sde'i dbang po rgyal po zhes bya ba'i chos kyi rnam grangs
P126, vol. 5
Vajrapani Initiation Tantra
Vajrapāṇyabhiṣhekamahātantra
Lag na rdo rje dbang bskur ba'i rgyud chen mo
P130, vol. 6
Vajroshnisha Tantra
rDo rje gtsug tor gyi rgyud
[not translated into Tibetan]

Wisdom Vajra Compendium
Jñānavajrasamuchchayanāmatantra
Ye shes rdo rje kun las btus pa
P84, vol. 3

II *Other Works*

Ānandagarbha (Kun dga' snying-po)
Illumination of the 'Compendium of Principles'
Sarvatathāgatatattvasaṃgrahamahāyānābhisamayanāmatantravyākhyā-tattvālokakarī
De bzhin gshegs pa thams cad kyi de kho na nyid bsdus pa theg pa chen po mngon par rtogs pa zhes bya ba'i rgyud kyi bshad pa de kho na nyid snang bar byed pa
P3333, vols. 71-2
Āryadeva ('Phags-pa-lha)
Lamp Compendium of Practice
Charyāmelāpakapradīpa
sPyod pa bsdus pa'i sgron ma
P2668, vol. 61
Asaṅga (Thogs-med)
Bodhisattva Levels
Yogacharyābhūmau bodhisattvabhūmi
rNal 'byor spyod pa'i sa las byang chub sems dpa'i sa
P5538, vol. 110
Atīsha (982-1054)
Means of Achievement of Vimaloshnisha
Dri med gtsug tor gyi sgrub thabs
[?]
Buddhaguhya (Sangs-rgyas-gsang-ba)
Commentary on the 'Concentration Continuation'
Dhyānottarapaṭalaṭīkā
bSam gtan phyi ma rim par phye ba rgya cher bshad pa
P3495, vol. 78
Commentary on the 'Vajravidarana Tantra'
Vajravidāraṇī[or vidāraṇā]nāmadhāraṇīṭīkāratnābhāsvarā
rDo rje rnam par 'joms pa zhes bya ba'i bzungs kyi rgya cher 'grel pa rin po che gsal ba zhes bya ba
P3504, vol. 78
Condensation of the 'Vairochanabhisambodhi Tantra'
Vairochanābhisambodhitantrapiṇḍārtha
rNam par snang mdzad mngon par rdzogs par byang chub pa'i rgyud kyi bsdus pa'i don
P3486, vol. 77
Bu-dön (Bu-ston, 1290-1364)

Extensive General Presentation of the Tantra Sets, Jewelled Adornment of the Tantra Sets
rGuyd sde spyi'i rnam par gzhag pa rgyud sde rin po che'i mdzes rgyan
Collected Works, Part 15 ba (New Delhi, International Academy of Indian Culture, 1969)
Chandrakīrti (Zla-ba-grags-pa)
Brilliant Lamp, Extensive Commentary [on the 'Guhyasamaja Tantra']
Pradīpoddyotananāmaṭīkā
sGron ma gsal bar byed pa zhes bya ba'i rgya cher bshad pa
P2650, vol. 60
Dharmakīrti (Chos-kyi-grags-pa)
Commentary on (Dignaga's) 'Compendium of Prime Cognition'
Pramāṇavarttikakārikā
Tshad ma rnam 'grel gyi tshig le'ur byas pa
P5709, vol. 130
Dul-dzin-drak-ba-gyel-tsen ('Dul-'dzin-grags-pa-rgyal-mtshan)
Presentation of the General Rites of Action and Performance Tantra and Their Application to the Three Lineages, Set Down by Dul-dzin According to the Foremost [Tsong-ka-pa's] Practice
Bya spyod kyi spyi'i cho ga'i rnam par bzhag pa rigs gsum la sbyor tshul rje'i phyag bzhes bzhin 'dul ba 'dzin pas bkod pa
Collected Works of Tsong-ka-pa [from the library of His Holiness the Dalai Lama, no other data]
Hopkins, Jeffrey
Meditation on Emptiness
Valois, N.Y., Snow Lion, 1981
Hundred Means of Achievement
Translated by Tsul-trim-gyel-tsen (Tshul-khrim-rgyal-mtshan)
P3964-4126, vol. 80 [?]
Indrabhuti'/'Indrabodhi'
Explanation of the 'Condensation of the Samvara Tantra'
Chakrasaṃvaratantrarājashambarasamuchchayanāmavṛtti
Khor lo sdom pa'i rgyud kyi rgyal po bde mchog bsdus pa zhes bya ba'i rnam par bshad pa
P2129, vol. 49
Jetāri (sGra-las-rnam-rgyal)
Means of Achievement of the Five Guards
Pañcharakṣhāvidhi
bSrung ba lnga'i cho ga
P3940-4, vol. 166
Jinadatta (rGyal-bas-byin)
Commentary on the Difficult Points of the 'Guhyasamaja Tantra'
Guhyasamājatantrapañjikā
dPal gsang ba 'dus pa'i rgyud kyi dka' 'grel
P2710, vol. 63
Kamalashīla

Stages of Meditation
Bhāvanākrama
sGom pa'i rim pa
P5310-12, vol. 102
Kay-drup (mKhas-grub, 1385-1438)
Mkhas-Grub Rje's Fundamentals of the Buddhist Tantras
Translated by F.D. Lessing and Alex Wayman
The Hague, Mouton, 1968
Lakṣhmi (dPal-mo)
Means of Achievement of the Eleven-Faced Avalokiteshvara
Bhaṭṭārakāryaikādashamukhāvalokiteshvarasādhana
rJe btsun 'phags pa spyan ras gzigs dbang phyug zhal bcu gcig pa'i sgrub thabs
P3557, vol. 79
Lo-sang-chö-gi-gyel-tsen (bLo-bzang-chos-kyi-rgyal-mtshan, 1567(?)-1662)
Presentation of the General Teaching and the Four Tantra Sets
bsTan pa spyi dang rgyud sde bzhi'i rnam par gzhag pa'i zin bris
Collected Works, vol. 4 (New Delhi, Gurudeva, 1973)
Nāgārjuna (kLu-sgrub)
Means of Achievement of the Retention of the Thousand-Armed and Thousand-Eyed Avalokiteshvara
Sahasrabhujāvalokiteshvarasādhana
sPyan ras gzigs dbang phyug phyag stong sgrub thabs
P3555, vol. 79
Na-wang-bel-den (Ngag-dbang-dpal-ldan, 1797-?)
Presentation of the Grounds and Paths of Mantra/Illumination of the Texts of Tantra, Presentation of the Grounds and Paths of the Four Great Secret Tantra Sets
gSang chen rgyud sde bzhi'i sa lam gyi rnam bzhag rgyud gzhung gsal byed
Rgyud smad par khang edition: no other data
Ocean of Means of Achievement
Sādhanasāgara
sGrub thabs rgya mtsho
Translated by Drak-ba-gyel-tsen (Grags-pa-rgyal-mtshan)
P4221-466, vols. 80-1
One Hundred and Fifty Means of Achievement
[Identified in Kay-drup as Toh. 3645-704]
Pa-bong-ka (Pha-bong-kha-pa, 1878-1941)
Miscellaneous Notes from Jo-nay-Pandita's Explanation of the 'Great Exposition of Secret Mantra'
rJe btsun bla ma co ne paṇḍi ta rin po che'i zhal snga nas sngags rim chen mo'i bshad lung nos skabs kyi gsung bshad zin bris thor tsam du bkod pa
Collected Works, vol. 2 (New Delhi, Chophel Legdan, 1972)
Padmasaṃbhava (Padma-'byung-gnas)
Means of Achievement of Mahakarunika
Thugs rje chen po'i sgrub thabs
[?]

Pan-chen Sö-nam-drak-pa (Paṇ-chen bSod-nams-grags-pa, 1478-1554)
General Presentation of the Tantra Sets, Captivating the Minds of the Fortunate
rGyud sde spyi'i rnam par bzhag pa skal bzang gi yid 'phrog
Dharamsala, Library of Tibetan Works and Archives, 1975
Ratnākarashānti (Shāntipa or Rin-chen-'byung-gnas-zhi-ba)
Means of Achievement of the Five Guards
Pañcharakṣhāvidhi
bSrung ba lnga'i cho ga
P3947, vol. 80
Precious Lamp, Commentary on the Difficult Points of the 'Krishnayamari Tantra'
Kṛṣhṇayamārimahātantrarājapañjikāratnapradīpa
gShin rje'i dgra nag po'i rgyud kyi rgyal po chen po'i dka' 'grel rin po che'i sgron ma
P2782, vol. 66
Shāntideva (Zhi-ba-lha)
Engaging in the Bodhisattva Deeds
Bodhisattvacharyāvatāra
Byang chub sems dpa'i spyod pa la 'jug pa
P5272, vol. 99
Shrīdhara (dPal-'dzin)
Innate Illumination, Commentary on the Difficult Points of the 'Yamari Tantra'
Yamāritantrapañjikāsahajāloka
gShin rje gshed kyi rgyud kyi dka' 'grel lhan cig skyes pa'i snang ba
P2781, vol. 66
Subhagavajra (sKal-pa-bzang-po'i-rdo-rje)
Stages of the Mahayana Path
Mahāyānapathakrama
Theg pa chen po'i lam gyi rim pa
P4540, vol. 81
Tsong-ka-pa (Tsong-kha-pa, 1357-1419)
Explanation of the Ethics Chapter
Byang chub sems dpa'i sdom pa byung nas tshul khrims kyi phung po yongs su dag par bya ba'i tshul rnam par bshad pa byang chub gzhung lam zhes bya ba
P6145, vol. 154
Explanation of the Root Infractions
gSang sngags kyi tshul khrims kyi rnam bshad dngos grub kyi snye ma (rTsa ltung gi rnam bshad)
P6188, vol. 160
Great Exposition of Secret Mantra/The Stages of the Path to a Conqueror and Pervasive Master, a Great Vajradhara: Revealing All Secret Topics
rGyal ba khyab bdag rdo rje 'chang chen po'i lam gyi rim pa gsang ba kun gyi gnad rnam par phye ba
P6210, vol. 161
Basic edition for the translation: Dharamsala, Shes rig par khang, 1969
Also Collected Works, vol. 4, (New Delhi, Ngawang Gelek, 1975)

Great Exposition of the Stages of the Path Common to the Vehicles
Lam rim chen mo
P6001, vol. 152
Small Exposition of the Stages of the Path
Lam rim chung ba/Lam rim 'bring
P6002, vol. 152
Varabodhi (Byang-chub-mchog) also Ye-shes-mchog)
Clear Realisation of Susiddhi
Susiddhikarasādhanasaṃgraha
Legs par grub par byed pa'i sgrub pa'i thabs bsdus pa
P3890, vol. 79
Ye-shay-gyel-tsen (Ye-shes-rgyal-mtshan, 1713-93)
Illumination of the Meaning of Action Tantra
Bya rgyud don gsal
Collected Works, vol. 9 (New Delhi, Tibet House, 1976)

Notes

For full Sanskrit and Tibetan titles see the bibliography. Abbreviations used are:

Dul-dzin: Dul-dzin-drak-ba-gyel-tsen's *Presentation of the General Rites of Action and Performance Tantra and Their Application to the Three Lineages, Set Down by Dul-dzin According to the Foremost [Tsong-ka-pa's] Practice,* Collected Works of Tsong-ka-pa [from the library of His Holiness the Dalai Lama, no other data]

Kay-drup: *Mkhas Grub Rje's Fundamentals of the Buddhist Tantras,* translated by F.D. Lessing and Alex Wayman (The Hague, Mouton, 1968)

Pa-bong-ka: Pa-bong-ka-pa's *Miscellaneous Notes from Jo-nay Pandita's Explanation of the 'Great Exposition of Secret Mantra,'* Collected Works, Volume 2 (New Delhi, Chophel Legdan, 1972)

Pan-chen: Pan-chen Sö-nam-drak-pa's *General Presentation of the Tantra Sets, Captivating the Minds of the Fortunate* (Dharmsala, Library of Tibetan Works and Archives, 1975)

Ye-shay-gyel-tsen: Ye-shay-gyel-tsen's *Illumination of the Meaning of Action Tantra,* Collected Works, Volume 9 (New Delhi, Tibet House, 1976)

1 For the most part Tsong-ka-pa is reworking Bu-dön's (*Bu-ston*) encyclopedic presentation of this issue in his *Extensive General Presentation of the Tantra Sets,* Collected Works, Part 15 ba, (New Delhi, International Academy of Indian Culture, 1969), 86.6-88.7. Bu-dön here sides with those who say that Action Tantra does not involve generation of oneself as a deity, but earlier, when presenting the path of Action Tantra (54.5-61.7), he follows Buddhaguhya's assertion of the opposite, repeatedly and explicitly describing self-generation in Action Tantra. Tsong-ka-pa takes apart Bu-dön's later argument against self-generation in Action Tantra step by step. Then in the later sections Tsong-ka-pa uses Buddhaguhya's commentary on the *Concentration Continuation Tantra,* as Bu-dön did, to present the path of self-generation in Action Tantra, though in much greater detail than his predecessor. Thus Tsong-ka-pa's presentation is both in dependence on and in contradistinction to that of Bu-dön, whose seeming contradiction is explained only in the encyclopedic nature of his work.

2 Bu-dön's *Extensive General Presentation of the Tantra Sets* mentions this text (86.7).

3 P430, vol. 9, 53.2.8.

4 P3495, vol. 78, 69.5.7-70.1.2.

5 P3495, vol. 78, 70.5.1-4.

6 P431, vol. 9, 64.1.2. This is cited in Varabodhi's *Clear Realisation of Susiddhi* (P3890, vol. 79, 272.1.7). For Tsong-ka-pa's commentary see p. 147. Instead of *ma gtang ba* the Peking edition reads *ma gtogs pa* as does Ye-shay-gyel-tsen (504.2).
7 P3495, vol. 78, 70.5.8-71.1.3.
8 An ichneumon is a small squirrel-like animal called a 'jewel-bag' because it spits forth jewels; it is held in the hand of this deity as a hand-symbol. At the end of the stanza there is a gap in the quoted text. The latter part of the quote is found in Bu-dön's *Extensive General Presentation of the Tantra Sets*, 86.7.
9 Tsong-ka-pa's own opinion, as given on pp. 52-3, is that the *Vairochanabhisambodhi* is clearly a Performance Tantra.
10 P3890, vol. 79, 270. 1.4-6. This is cited in Bu-dön's *Extensive General Presentation of the Tantra Sets* (87.4) which confirms *bstan to* rather than *bstan te*. The Sanskrit of '*Clear Realisation of Susiddhi*' has been constructed in order to accord with the Tibetan, using *abhisamaya (mngon rtogs)* rather than *sādhana;* in the Peking catalogue it is *Susiddhikarasādhana-samgraha*. Bu-dön refers to the *Dashatattva* as the *Dashatattvāvatāra*, 87.5.
11 See *Tantra in Tibet*, pp.156-9.
12 See note 1.
13 P430, vol. 9, 55.3.4. The commentary is P3495, vol. 78, 73.2.7.
14 Kay-drup, 136.18. It is also said that it is entitled *Dhyānottara* because of presenting the latter concentrations — those following the initial practices explained earlier in the *Vajroshnisha*. See Buddhaguhya (P3495, vol. 78, 73.2.5).
15 P3495, vol. 78, 73.3.3. Tsong-ka-pa also quotes this in the Performance Tantra section (68b.5), using a different translation; see p. 192 for that and six omitted lines.
16 P3504, vol. 78, 140.3.6. Bu-dön's *Extensive General Presentation of the Tantra Sets* quotes this (56.2) and mentions it again (87.3).
17 P3333, vol. 71, 135.5.1.
18 The bracketed material is a contextual conjecture. Both Pan-chen Sönam-drak-ba (22b.2-4) and Kay-drup (166.18-28) cite texts mentioned in the first hypothesis as reasons why there is self-generation in Action Tantra whereas Tsong-ka-pa indicates that at least some of them cannot serve as *bona fide* Action Tantra sources.
19 The reading has been amended from *skyod* to *spyod*.
20 To have lineage means to have the lot of being a suitable vessel for the teaching.
21 P430, vol. 9, 55.5.2.
22 P3495, vol. 78, 80.5.7-81.1.8.
23 Tsong-ka-pa literally says 'the three, knowledge mantra and so forth' to stand for these three, curiously putting the middle term of the reference at the head.
24 *'jug* to *mjug*.
25 This material is taken from Kay-drup, 144.21ff, 148.8, and 140.7; the last

sentence is also found in Na-wang-bel-den's *Presentation of the Grounds and Paths of Mantra, (rGyud smad par khang* edition), 2b.2.

26 Kay-drup, 154.7.

27 P431, vol. 9, 56.1.1-3.4. This is quoted in Ratnakarashanti's *Precious Lamp, Commentary on the Difficult Points of the 'Krshnayamari Tantra'*, P2782, vol. 66, 259.2.8-5.7.

28 *Tirthika,* non-Buddhist practitioners who are called Forders because of having a ford to liberation.

29 This is specifically a pastry cooked in sesame oil (*snum 'khur*) according to Pa-bong-ka (650.3).

30 Pa-bong-ka (650.3) says *'cung peng ni skyur rtsis snyal ba phyis sman zhes grags pa de yin.'*

31 This is most likely the meat, blood, fat, and so forth which demons eat.

32 The Delhi edition, (103.2) has *byi byad,* whereas the *Susiddhi* itself (P431, vol. 9, 56.2.5) and Bu-dön have *bya byed*, which is unlikely. The translation is uncertain.

33 *Lo ma,* as confirmed by the Delhi edition (103.3) and the *Susiddhi* (P431, vol. 9, 56.2.5).

34 Food that increases desire.

35 *'Jol nyog,* which has the same meaning, in the *Susiddhi* (P431, vol. 9, 56.2.8).

36 *Sad* means *nyams sad pa.*

37 P431, vol. 9, 56.5.1.

38 The first fifteen days of the first month in the lunar year.

39 P431, vol. 9, 57.2.2-5.

40 Probably the vows of individual emancipation and the ethics of abandoning the ten non-virtues.

41 *Nyid* to *nyin.*

42 Probably self-entry.

43 P2782, vol. 66, 260.3.2-6.

44 'And so forth' includes having a special purpose or taking into account the customs of one's area.

45 P430, vol. 9, 53.2.8. Buddhaguhya's commentary is P3495, vol. 78, 69.1.1-70.1.7. 'Sages' (*rshi*), according to Pa-bong-ka (650.4), are those whose body, speech, and mind have been straightened or, according to Buddhaguhya (70.1.5), restrained.

46 The five clairvoyances are those of the divine eye, divine ear, memory of former lifetimes, knowing others' minds, and magical emanation.

47 'Secret mantra' here refers to a deity.

48 *Rig* to *rigs.*

49 *'Jug* to *mjug.*

50 This section follows Varabodhi's *Clear Realisation of Susiddhi,* P3890, vol. 79, 268.1.1ff. With respect to the mantras that text reads *tathāgatodbhavāya, padmodbhavāya,* and *vajrodbhavāya;* it repeats *kāya-vāk-chitta* after the second *sarva-tathāgata.* In general, the mantras have been left unedited, with only occasional variants cited in the notes. The smaller section headings are added from Varabodhi.

51 Pa-bong-ka (650.5) identifies *mNol-ba-med-pa* as *sMe-ba-brtsegs-pa, Bhurkumkūta.*

52 The text reads *shuddha* and *dharmā*, which were changed to accord with Dul-dzin (5b.6).

53 Dul-dzin, 2a.6.

54 Dul-dzin (2a.6) inserts here the pledge seal and secret mantra of the lineage which Tsong-ka-pa mentions on the next page as preceding picking up earth.

55 This section follows Varabodhi's *Clear Realisation*, P3890, vol. 79, 268.2.6ff.

56 Dul-dzin has *vasudhe*, and Varabodhi *vaisudhe*.

57 Varabodhi reads *om hūm khakīli*.

58 Varabodhi reads *oṃ hana dhuna matha vidh[v]aṃsaya udsaraya phaṭ*.

59 Dul-dzin, 3a.3.

60 Dul-dzin (3b.3) describes how to do an actual ablution: 'Squat, stop talking, and put your two hands between your knees. Bend a little the middle and ring fingers of the right hand with the palm turned upwards, and hold this towards your mouth. Wipe the mouth many times with water [in which] anthers [have been soaked], and having touched the two ear-holes, two eyes, nose, mouth, hands, navel, and head two or three times, drink three gulps of the water, wiping the lips twice.'

61 Dul-dzin, 3a.5.

62 Dul-dzin (3b.2) refers to the group of deities.

63 Dul-dzin (3b.3) specifies the mantra, e.g., *oṃ sarva-tathāgata-ushṇīsha-sitātāpatre hūṃ phaṭ svāhā*.

64 See note 60.

65 Dul-dzin makes this clear (3b.5).

66 This section is from Varabodhi, P3890, vol. 79, 269.3.2.

67 Dul-dzin, 4a.1.

68 The lucky posture is like that of Maitreya, sitting on a 'chair'. The lotus posture is with the soles of the feet touching; the vajra cross-legged is the one usually called the lotus posture in the West.

69 This is a conjecture based on Dul-dzin's (4a.5) not mentioning 'image'; the identifications of the reference and the mantra are his (4a.5).

70 Dul-dzin, 4a.3.

71 In both the Delhi edition and Varabodhi the mantra reads this way; the Dharmsala edition was obviously miscopied.

72 This sentence has been moved in translation for the sake of clarity since it refers to the circlet; it appears in the text after the second *Susiddhi* quotation.

73 The long *ā* is from Dul-dzin. These are the essence mantras of the three lineages, the appropriate one of which is to be repeated.

74 This sentence is omitted in Dul-dzin.

75 According to Lati Rinbochay obstructors range from the external, such as war and plague, to the internal such as sleep and sickness, and the secret, such as unserviceability of the mind in the direction of virtue.

76 *Bab* to *bab pas*.

77 This section follows Varabodhi's *Clear Realisation*, P3890, vol. 79, 268.5.7-269.1.3.
78 *Las* to *lus*.
79 This section follows Varabodhi, P3890, vol. 79, 269.1.8ff.
80 According to Lati Rinbochay this means to cause them to dissolve into the Truth Body.
81 Dul-dzin refers to the upper demonic gods (*steng gi lha'i gdon rnams*, 5a.1).
82 *De nas* to *de ni*, as confirmed by Dul-dzin's (5a.2) *zhes pa rigs gsum gyi rig pa'i rgyal po'i sngags brjod pas*, identifying the above as the secret mantra of the knowledge kings rather than referring to something else.
83 The fence is made of big vajras standing on end, filled in between with small ones.
84 Dul-dzin (5a.5) mentions only the dagger seal (seal 15); he identifies the Kilikila mantra as that on p. 97, not the one on p. 88.
85 *Kara kara* has been added from the Delhi edition and Varabodhi.
86 P430, vol. 9, 53.2.3. Buddhaguhya's commentary is P3495, vol. 78, 71.3.3-4.6. In the citation of the commentary Tsong-ka-pa is paraphrasing 71.3.3-5.
87 *La* to *las* in accord with P3495, vol. 78, 71.3.4.
88 This and the next paragraph paraphrase Buddhaguhya's commentary, P3495, vol. 79, 269.4.7-5.3.
89 P430, vol. 9, 53.3.2. Buddhaguhya's commentary, from which the bracketed paragraph following the quote is taken, is P3495, vol. 78, 71.4.6-72.2.5. Tsong-ka-pa is now primarily following Buddhaguhya's commentary, the section on the six deities being 71.4.6-72.4.3.
90 P3890, vol. 79, 269.5.3-8.
91 See p. 83.
92 One rises not in the sense of getting up from the meditation but of ceasing to use the suchness of self as the *main* object of meditation. At this point Tsong-ka-pa does not mention imagining the sounds of the mantra as reverberating above a moon disc; neither do Buddhaguhya (P3495, vol. 78, 72.3.7), Dul-dzin (5b.3), or Kay-drup (160.3). However, later when explaining how to rest (p. 143) Tsong-ka-pa, in going through the reverse process, puts the dissolution of the moon disc after the sound deity, suggesting that it appears prior to or at least simultaneous with the mantra sounds. In cases where the text is not clear on procedure lamas often advise a practitioner to do whatever is more appealing. In the introduction the Dalai Lama describes manifestation of a moon disc at this point, but on another occasion he explained the sound deity as the mere reverberation of the mantra sounds in the sphere of emptiness.
93 For the example see Ye-shay-gyel-tsen's *Illumination of the Meaning of Action Tantra*, 487.3.
94 P3890, vol. 79, 270.1.1.
95 P3890, vol. 79, 270.1.1-4.
96 Kay-drup, 160.22.
97 P3890, vol. 79, 270.1.7.

98 P3495, vol. 78, 71.1.1 (the first and second sides on this page have been transposed) and 72.4.3. Based on Bo-dong's *General Presentation of Action Tantra,* Collected Works, vol. 24 (New Delhi, Tibet House, 1971), 320.5, it can be conjectured that the sign deity is so called because of being like the arising of a sign upon being impressed with a seal.

99 P3495, vol. 78, 72.2.5ff. The citation from Buddhaguhya's *Commentary on the 'Vidarana Tantra'* is P3504, vol. 78, 140.3.6.

100 The text has letter before sound, which is usually interpreted as merely for the sake of euphony; however, Pan-chen Sö-nam-drak-ba takes it literally in his commentary (23b.1).

101 P3495, vol. 78, 72.4.3. The Delhi edition correctly reads *re shig spyi'i gsang sngags;* the Dharmsala edition has omitted *spyi'i*

102 This section follows Buddhaguhya, P3495, vol. 78, 72.4.8ff.

103 P430, vol. 9, 53.3.3. The commentary is P3495, vol. 78, 72.2.8.

104 This most likely means to meditate *at least* through to the form deity since normally one would proceed through to the sign deity.

105 About this Pan-chen Sö-nam-drak-ba (23b.6-24a.5) says, 'The *prāṇāyāma* explained here [in Action Tantra] and in Highest Yoga are similar in name but not in meaning, time, purpose, or mode. They differ in meaning, for in the *Guhyasamaja* of Highest Yoga *prāna* is explained as wind and *āyāma* as lengthening, whereby it refers to a life-lengthening wind. In the *Kalachakra* [also Highest Yoga] *prāna* is explained as wind and *āyāma* as stopping the movement of winds in the right and left channels as well as causing them to enter the central channel. Here [in Action Tantra] *prāna* is explained as wind, *āyāma* as conceptuality, and binding as stopping the passing outwards of wind and conceptuality and binding them inside.

'[Highest Yoga and Action Tantra] differ with respect to the time [of practising *prāṇāyāma*] because in Highest Yoga it is only during the stage of completion whereas here it is only during [the yoga] with signs. The purpose differs because in Highest Yoga it is for the sake of gathering the winds in the central channel whereas here it is for the sake of generating clear appearance of a deity through the force of eliminating the movement of conceptuality to objects by stopping the movement of wind to the outside. The mode [of practice] differs because in Highest Yoga the mind is held on an object of observation such as the upper or lower points of the central channel whereas here the mind is held on the clear appearance of a deity without letting conceptuality operate on objects through the force of stopping the movement of wind outside and binding it inside.'

106 This section follows Varabodhi, P3890, vol. 79, 270.1.7ff.

107 Dul-dzin has *sarvathā kham udgate.*

108 P3890, vol. 79, 272.2.7.

109 This section for the most part follows Varabodhi, P3890, vol. 79, 270.2.8ff.

110 Dul-dzin (8b.1) reads *ehyehi* throughout.

111 P431, vol. 9, 61.5.5. The next sentence refers to the same, 61.4.2.

112 P430, vol. 9, 53.5.2.
113 P3495, vol. 78, 80.5.4.
114 The two stanzas are found in Dul-dzin, 9b.5.
115 This section follows Varabodhi, P3890, vol. 79, 270.4.8-271.1.1.
116 This section follows Varabodhi, P3890, vol. 79, 271.1.2-4.4.
117 The recitation as well as the offering of the foot-bath do not appear in Varabodhi, but are in the *Susiddhi Tantra* itself (P431, vol. 9, 62.1.3).
118 According to Dul-dzin (10a.6), for Sitatapatra the mantra to be put at the head of each offering mantra is *oṃ sarva-tathāgata uṣhṇīsha-sitātapatre saparivāra.* For the foot-bath Dul-dzin reads *oṃ pravara-sadkāraṃ padyaṃ pratīchchha svāhā.*
119 Dul-dzin, 10b.2.
120 Dul-dzin (10b.3) describes how to do these.
121 Dul-dzin (11a.6) has *vidhyādhara* and continues with an offering of pleasant sounds.
122 Varabodhi (P3890, vol. 79, 271.4.4) mentions praising and gives the mantra found at the end of this section but not the actual offering verses which are found in the *Susiddhi Tantra* (P431, vol. 9, 62.5.7).
123 *Gzhi* to *zhing* in accordance with the *Susiddhi* (P431, vol. 9, 62.5.7) and Ye-shay-gyel-tsen (469.1).
124 See note 127.
125 The titles of the sub-sections are taken from Varabodhi (P3890, vol. 79, 271.4.5) and Kay-drup (184.26). Tsong-ka-pa has taken the text from the Susiddhi (P431, vol. 9, 63.1.3-3.2).
126 Not being omniscient, one does not know all one's sins, but the Buddhas do, and thus one confesses sins in accordance with what they know.
127 This and the next stanza are not in the Peking *Susiddhi.*
128 In this section the introductory prose is from Varabodhi (P3890, vol. 79, 271.4.7-8) and the stanzas from the *Susiddhi* (P431, vol. 9, 63.2.2-7).
129 *Sems cad* to *sems can.*
130 *Rten du bab* to *rten du bdag.*
131 *Bsags pa'i* to *bsags pa.*
132 This section, except for the first two sentences, is a compilation of the *Susiddhi,* P431, vol. 9, 63.3.3-7) and Varabodhi (P3890, vol. 79, 271.5.2-272.1.1).
133 P431, vol. 9, 63.3.7.
134 *Adbhate* to *adbhute* in accordance with the Delhi edition and Varabodhi.
135 According to Dul-dzin (13b.4) one does this by reciting *oṃ guru-sarva- tathāgata-kāya-vāk-chitta-praṇamena sarva-tathāgata-vajra-pāda-vandanaṃ karomi.*
136 The Delhi edition has *jatanajeya* whereas the *Susiddhi* reads *jatanajaya.*
137 P430, vol. 9, 53.3.4; the commentary is P3495, vol. 78, 73.4.1.
138 The bracketed material in this paragraph is drawn from Kay-drup, 188.2.
139 This section follows Buddhaguhya's commentary, P3495, vol. 78, 74.1.4-8.
140 P430, vol. 9, 53.3.4; the explanation is drawn from Buddhaguhya's commentary, P3495, vol. 78, 74.2.6ff.
141 *Dang* to *rang.* The switching need not be done with each inhalation and

exhalation but with *an* inhalation and *an* exhalation.

142 P430, vol. 9, 53.3.5. Buddhaguhya's commentary is P3495, vol. 78, 74.4.7-75.2.6.

143 The rite of observing the sounds of a mantra.

144 Buddhaguhya (P3495, vol. 78, 75.1.2) indicates the importance of mental repetition: 'Since mental repetition is a cause of subtle meditative stabilisation, one should always perform it; however, if one wants to perform whispered repetition, then one should do it with this application [observing the sounds of the mantra].'

145 P3495, vol. 78, 75.2.3.

146 P3890, vol. 79, 272.1.1.

147 The remainder of this section is drawn from the *Susiddhi* (P431, vol. 9, 63.4.4-64.1.5).

148 P431, vol. 9, 63.4.6.

149 The first two paragraphs of this section are drawn from the *Susiddhi* (P431, vol. 9, 64.1.4-4.8); the remainder is drawn from Varabodhi (P3890, vol. 79, 272.4.7-5.4).

150 P3890, vol. 79, 272.5.2.

151 P3890, vol. 79, 272.5.4.

152 This section is mainly from Varabodhi (P3890, 272.2.4-4.2).

153 In the *Susiddhi* this is found at P431, vol. 9, 64.1.8-2.2.

154 Preferably a virgin.

155 P3890, vol. 79, 272.4.2. Dul-dzin (16b.6) identifies this as a purification of the faults of yawning, sneezing, and so forth.

156 P430, vol. 9, 53.3.8; Buddhaguhya's commentary is P3495, vol. 78, 75.5.1ff.

157 P430, vol. 9, 53.3.8; Buddhaguhya's commentary is P3495, vol. 78, 75.5.8ff, from which the bracketed material is taken.

158 Pa-bong-ka, 63.5.

159 P3495, vol. 78, 77.1.7.

160 Ibid.

161 P430, vol. 9, 53.4.2; Buddhaguhya's commentary is P3495, vol. 78, 77.2.1-5.4.

162 P430, vol. 9, 53.4.4; Buddhaguhya's commentary is P3495, vol. 78, 78.1.3-5.8.

163 P3495, vol. 78, 78.1.6.

164 P3495, vol. 78, 78.5.4.

165 *Dmigs pa'i* to *dmigs pas*.

166 P3495, vol. 78, 78.5.2.

167 *Bskyed* to *bskyod*.

168 For a discussion of these see Hopkins's *Meditation on Emptiness* (Valois, N.Y., Snow Lion, 1981). Part One, Chapters eight and nine.

169 Often the term 'view' refers to emptiness, the objective view, but here it refers to the consciousness realising emptiness, the subjective view (*yul can gyi lta ba*).

170 P3495, vol. 78, 72.1.5.

171 P3495, vol. 78, 72.1.7.

172 P3495, vol. 78, 72.2.1. With respect to the word 'observation' in the first sentence the Peking edition reads *yan lag med pa dmigs pa* but the Cone edition has *dmigs pa med pa*, which is being followed here.
173 Kay-drup, 200.13.
174 The feats described in this chapter are the common ones, not the uncommon temporary feats of the paths or the final feat of Buddhahood (which are described in the Supplement at the end of this book). In the three lower tantras Buddhahood must be achieved through enhancement of the path by way of common feats; thus, these are explained.
175 P431, vol. 9, 63.4.8.
176 P430, vol. 9, 53.3.6.
177 This section is from the *Susiddhi*, P431, vol. 9, 60.3.3-61.2.5.
178 P431, vol. 9, 69.3.3.
179 P431, vol. 9, 59.5.5-60.3.5 and 69.2.6; however, the *Susiddhi* has the times for pacifying and increasing activities reversed.
180 P431, vol. 9, 55.4.4-56.1.1.
181 P431, vol. 9, 59.5.7-60.3.8. The lotus cross-legged posture may be the lotus posture in which the soles of the two feet are together in front of oneself. The lucky posture is said to be that of Maitreya, sitting on a throne with the feet flat on the floor.
182 The first half of this sentence is in the *Susiddhi*, P431, vol. 9, 61.3.3.
183 P431, vol. 9, 61.1.6-3.2.
184 P431, vol. 9, 65.2.1-4.1.
185 P431, vol. 9, 64.3.4.
186 P430, vol. 9, 53.5.3-6.
187 *Zin* to *zil* in accordance with the Delhi edition.
188 These are his *Condensation* (P3486, vol. 77) and *Explanation*(P3487, vol. 77) or *Commentary* (P3490, vol. 77), the last two appearing to be different translations of the same text.
189 This is quoted in part in Buddhaguhya's *Condensation*, P3486, vol. 77, 103.3.6.
190 This is quoted in Buddhaguhya's *Condensation* (P3486, vol. 77, 104.5.4 and 106.3.5); the text itself is P126, vol. 5, 255.5.7-256.1.3.
191 The reference is to the section in Action Tantra on the ultimate deity (pp. 104-6).
192 P126, vol. 5, 256.2.7-3.1. The part on supramundane yoga is cited in Buddhaguhya's *Condensation*, P3486, vol. 77, 106.4.6.
193 P4540, vol. 81, 193.5.7-194.1.1.
194 See p. 83.
195 P126, vol. 5, 252.1.5; this is cited in Buddhaguhya's *Condensation*, P3486, vol. 77, 105.5.1.
196 P126, vol. 5, 252.1.7; *Condensation*, P3486, vol. 77, 107.2.4.
197 P126, vol. 5, 256.2.7.
198 P3486, vol. 77, 106.1.6.
199 Lo-sang-chö-gi-gyel-tsen, *Presentation of the General Teaching and the Four Tantra Sets*, Collected Works, vol. 4 (New Delhi, Gurudeva, 1973), 30b.6.

200 Ibid. 31a.1.
201 P126, vol. 5, 252.1.8; *Condensation*, P3486, vol. 77, 107.2.4.
202 P126, vol. 5, 256.2.1; *Condensation*, P3486, vol. 77, 109.5.7.
203 P126, vol. 5, 253.1.5; *Condensation*, P3486, vol. 77, 103.5.4.
204 P3486, vol. 77, 106.2.4.
205 P126, vol. 5, 256.1.4; *Condensation*, P3486, vol. 77, 104.1.8-2.6.
206 P126, vol. 5, 256.2.1; *Condensation*, P3486, vol. 77, 104.2.6-3.2.
207 P3486, vol. 77, 106.4.3-6. The text here differs slightly from that on p. 197 probably due to being a different translation.
208 The Dharmsala edition reads *rims*, but the explanation has *rigs*, as does the Delhi edition in both places.
209 The source for this is Kensur Lekden's oral teachings.
210 Na-wang-bel-den, *Illumination of the Texts of Tantra, Presentation of the Grounds and Paths of the Four Great Secret Tantra Sets* (rGyud smad par khang edition, no other data), 6b.7-7b.3. The three supplements mostly revolve around this work.
211 For an extended description of these in relation to the process of death see Lati Rinbochay and Jeffrey Hopkins's *Death, Intermediate State, and Rebirth in Tibetan Buddhism* (London, Rider and Co., 1980). The translation of the selections from Na-wang-bel-den avoids the author's rendering of these points in argumentative form.
212 op. cit., 7b.4-8b.1.
213 ibid., 4b.4-5a.1. The citation begins in mid-sentence.
214 ibid., 8b.3-9a.4.
215 The selections are from 16b.1-20a.2 and 25a.6-b.1 (Dharmsala, Library of Tibetan Works and Archives, 1975). A longer presentation of this topic is given in Lessing and Wayman's translation of *Mkhas Grub Rje's Fundamentals of the Buddhist Tantras*, pp.100-39; a debt to their translation and bibliographic work is acknowledged.
216 Kay-drup, 104.6.
217 Kay-drup, 108.22.
218 Kay-drup, 108.18.
219 See Kay-drup, p. 113, for their tantras.
220 See Kay-drup, p. 113.
221 Kay-drup, p. 115.
222 This is most likely number four in Kay-drup, p. 115.
223 Kay-drup, notes 16 and 17, p. 116.
224 See Kay-drup, p. 119.
225 See Kay-drup, pp. 125-6.
226 Kay-drup (p. 127) identifies the author's name as Suryagupta.
227 The Sanskrit name is taken from Wayman (Kay-drup, p. 127).

Index